VIOLENCE

IN THE BLACK PATCH

OF KENTUCKY AND TENNESSEE

VIOLENCE

IN THE BLACK PATCH

OF KENTUCKY AND TENNESSEE

SUZANNE MARSHALL

University of Missouri Press

Columbia and London

Copyright © 1994 by
The Curators of the University of Missouri
University of Missouri Press, Columbia, Missouri 65201
Printed and bound in the United States of America
All rights reserved
5 4 3 2 1   98 97 96 95 94

Library of Congress Cataloging-in-Publication Data

Marshall, Suzanne, 1958–
  Violence in the Black Patch of Kentucky and Tennessee / Suzanne
Marshall.
    p. cm.
  Includes bibliographical references and index.
  ISBN 0-8262-0971-8 (alk. paper)
  1. Black Patch War, 1906–1909. 2. Violence—
Kentucky—History. 3. Kentucky—Rural conditions. 4. Violence—
Tennessee—History. 5. Tennessee—Rural conditions. I. Title.
F456.M37 1994
976.8'051—dc20   94-30773
                                                                          CIP

∞™ This paper meets the requirements of the American National Standard
for Permanence of Paper for Printed Library Materials, Z39.48, 1984.

Text Design: Rhonda Miller
Jacket Design: Stephanie Foley
Typesetter: Connell-Zeko Type & Graphics
Printer and Binder: Thomson-Shore, Inc.
Typefaces: Gill Sans, New Century Schoolbook, and Billboard-Plain

To Grandmother
In memory of Granddaddy

CONTENTS

PREFACE

A weathered placard hung slightly askew on the dingy wall of the old western Kentucky schoolhouse. Faded block letters spelled out "Dark-fired Tobacco" above an advertisement for a tobacco warehouse. Those words, *dark-fired*, sounded mysterious, ominous, even dangerous, and piqued the imagination of the child reading them. She knew about tobacco. It was the tall, leafy plant her grandfather grew on his Lyon County farm. He still plowed the tobacco patch with a glossy, blackish-brown mule. Sometimes the girl sat upon the warm back of the slow-moving animal as it made its way across the field to the sound of her grandfather's calls of "gee" and "haw."

She knew that in the late summer sweating men and boys cut the tobacco and hung it in the towering tobacco barn that stood beyond the stables. The building's plank exterior covered an old hand-hewn, narrow structure, the original barn of years ago. Its massive logs had been blackened by smoke, and the dirt floor was hard as stone with shallow sunken trenches where the fires had once burned every fall. An ancient aroma of hickory wood smoke, dust, tobacco, men, and mules permeated the air within and lingered in the child's mind for years.

Because she visited only at Christmas or during summers, the child never witnessed the curing of the tobacco for market, but one winter holiday, she accompanied her grandfather to the dilapidated one-room Fungo School, where her mother and other kin had re-

ceived their educations in the 1930s. The building no longer sheltered barefoot country scholars. Now it served as a storage shed and
stripping room. Grandfather and granddaughter entered one of the two
front doors to join neighbors and relatives in the dimly lit, kerosene-
heated room. There everyone was busy stripping the cured leaves
and tying them into "hands," or bundles.

People talked and laughed as the youngster tried to tie her first
hand. It was an awkward attempt. Stripping leaves was easier to
master, so she turned to that and listened to the talk around her. The
camaraderie, the warmth from the glowing heater, and the pungent
odors of the shadowy room set the mood for the tales the workers
told. During the afternoon, talk of other children's first attempts at
learning the skills and customs of tobacco cultivation gave way to
jokes and ghost stories, which led to sketchy tales of angry farmers
who rode during the darkest hours of winter nights long ago to burn
tobacco barns. The tone of voice people used to tell the night rider
stories warned the child against asking questions. And so, not knowing more, she connected the old placard's words, "Dark-fired," with
the angry farmers who rode out into the night to set barns aflame.
An image formed in her mind of the hell the Baptist preacher roared
about on Sunday mornings in the pristine clapboard church where
these same people filled the pews.

I later learned that dark-fired merely designated a specific type of
dark green, "black," heavy-leafed tobacco that thrived in the region
of western Kentucky and middle Tennessee where my grandparents
lived and farmed. But the mobs of night riding farmers proved more
difficult to understand. I kept asking myself, what threatened residents of the region so that they resorted to such violence as a solution; and why was this violence a culturally acceptable course for the
family-loving, God-fearing people of the Black Patch? Those questions would not go away. This study seeks to answer them.

Of the characteristics that define the South, violence may be the
most important. The tradition of violence in the South has certainly
been thoroughly studied. Scholars attribute the pervasive violence
to a broad spectrum of factors: frontier conditions, white male individualism and honor, whites' Indian-killing, the oppressive system
of black slavery, Old Testament–based religion, alcohol abuse, political divisions, and class, gender, and race antagonisms. Southern

violence grows from a complex root made up of all of these components operating in specific cultural regions, such as the Kentucky and Tennessee Black Patch.[1]

Culture, most broadly defined, means a way of life. T. S. Eliot described the term as "all the characteristic activities and interests of a people." The South, it can be argued, has a distinctive culture, as do the various regions that make it up. As W. J. Cash recognized, many Souths exist where "a fairly definite mental pattern, associated with a fairly definite social pattern—a complex of established relationships and habits of thought, sentiments, prejudices, standards, and values and associations of ideas" function to make a place unique. The Black Patch is such a place.[2]

This book is concerned with violence in the culture, the "world of violence" about which Robert Penn Warren wrote. The Black Patch culture of violence was primarily created by white men in order to maintain their power over their families, blacks, and the community. The culture they created was the heritage of later generations, who also took up violence as a tool. Although some were perpetrators of violence while others were victims, no one, male or female, black or white, escaped the effects. All suffered damage, but paradoxically, few considered violence inherently damaging. Justifiable violence, the kind that established and maintained white male power, they would argue, created a society that they proudly defended. This book is simply one historian's interpretation of the Black Patch culture of violence.

---

1. W. J. Cash, *The Mind of the South;* Bertram Wyatt-Brown, *Southern Honor: Ethics and Behavior in the Old South;* Edward L. Ayers, *Vengeance and Justice: Crime and Punishment in the Nineteenth-Century American South.*

2. Charles Reagan Wilson and William Ferris, eds., *Encyclopedia of Southern Culture,* xv–xvii. T. S. Eliot was cited in the above, xvi. Cash, *Mind of the South,* viii; Kai Erikson, *Everything in Its Path: Destruction of Community in the Buffalo Creek Flood,* 79–84.

ACKNOWLEDGMENTS

This book could never have been written without the interest, enthusiasm, and contributions of the Black Patch people whom I have been fortunate to meet during my years of research. Their voices, expressing memories, thoughts, and ideas, called my attention to this region for study and compelled me to finish the story. To each one who talked to me or granted me an oral interview, I offer a sincere thank-you. Some of the Black Patch people, kinfolks of mine and friends, assisted me in my journeys to the region in ways that I can never repay. Rick and Patti Gregory welcomed me into their Robertson County, Tennessee, home for meals, rest, and long discussions of Black Patch history. Rick, the premier Black Patch scholar, gave me my first tour of the Tennessee Black Patch, shared every piece of evidence from his own research, and influenced my thinking greatly. My grandmother, Eunice McCarty, shared her home and her years of knowledge with me when I worked from her house. Kaye Warner provided weeks of free bed and board while I searched the archives in Murray, Kentucky. Oral history projects she had done with her middle school students ten years before proved to be invaluable sources for my work. My parents, Fred and Wilma Marshall, welcomed me home again when I went to research in Louisville, Frankfort and Lexington, Kentucky.

I would never have begun this study without the initial direction and continual encouragement I received from Dan Carter, Allen Tullos, and James Roark, advisers and friends at Emory University. I thank them for their dedication as teachers and their patience while I worked on this seemingly endless project.

Friends and colleagues have taken an interest in my work over the years and have lent their support, assistance, and good cheer. Rebecca Sharpless, a staunch friend from graduate school days, remains a constant source of encouragement and intellectual stimulation. Joy Mobley Herring spent hours proofreading text and notes while listening to me fret and worry. Harvey H. Jackson, chair of the Jacksonville State University history department, has gone far beyond the call of duty in supporting this project. He has commented on portions of the manuscript, provided teaching schedules to allow me time to finish, and always remained excited about the book. Audrey Smelley, our departmental secretary, saved my sanity by typing the manuscript onto disks for my new computer. No words are adequate thanks for all the things she did to make this project happen. Ed Hill, our university photographer, expertly copied old photos for use in the book. Mentors at Kennesaw State College—Ann Ellis, Fred Roach, Tom Keene, Howard Shealy, Gird Romer, Eugene Huck, Linda Papageorge, J. B. Tate, and Tom Scott—followed my academic career through the years and helped me become a historian. Kelly Gregg, geographer and colleague at Jacksonville State University, willingly agreed to prepare the maps in a short time for no charge. He was ably assisted by Michael J. Marvinny, who also tirelessly removed all the hard returns and other mistakes I made while preparing the electronic manuscript.

Finally, the many archivists, librarians, and scholars who have assisted my research deserve great praise and gratitude. I thank the staffs of the Filson Club, the Kentucky Historical Society, the Kentucky Museum and Library at Western Kentucky University, the Pogue Library at Murray State University, the Kentucky Oral History Commission, the Kentucky State Library and Archives, the Tennessee State Library and Archives, M. I. King Library, University of Kentucky, and the University of Louisville Photographic Archives. I also want to thank the people at the Lyon County clerk's office, and at the Trigg, Caldwell, and Christian County courthouses for their assistance with the dusty old records in their offices. Thanks also to William Turner, historian at Hopkinsville Community College, who shared his valuable collection of Night Rider documents and hosted my visit during the Hopkinsville Raid reenactment. Bill Cunningham, lawyer and writer in Lyon County, took time out of his schedule to discuss the issue, introduced me to Joe Scott, and shared his own research with me. Nancy Gher, director of the Handmade Harvest exhibit at the Kentucky Museum in Bowling Green, shared her knowledge of tobacco culture and her oral interview tapes with me. I thank the editors of the *Register of the Kentucky Historical Society* for permission to use materials previously published in that journal.

Without the help of all these fine people, this book would still be a dream. They've contributed to my insights about the region; however, I take full responsibility for whatever flaws remain.

VIOLENCE

IN THE BLACK PATCH

OF KENTUCKY AND TENNESSEE

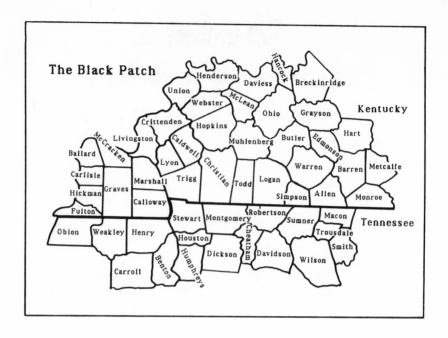

The Black Patch

Kentucky

Tennessee

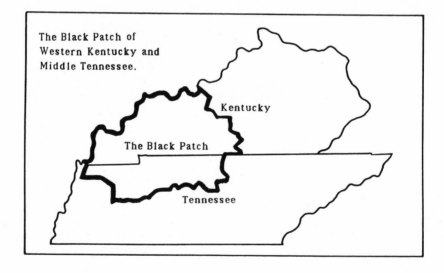

The Black Patch of
Western Kentucky and
Middle Tennessee.

Kentucky

The Black Patch

Tennessee

I

SOWERS OF THE SEEDS

I t was almost an unbroken wilderness from Virginia to Kentucky and this wilderness was filled with thousands of hostile Indians, and many thousands of the emigrants to Kentucky lost their lives by these savages," wrote Peter Cartwright about his journey to the Black Patch in the late 1780s. Two hundred families, including the Cartwrights, traveled west guarded by a hundred young men. Once on the way, Cartwright recalled, "We rarely traveled a day but we passed some white persons, murdered and scalped by the Indians." Anxious, worried, and watchful, the party continued through the threatening wilderness.[1]

On the evening of "a dark, cloudy day, misty with rain," the pioneers halted to rest at Camp Defeat, where a group of settlers had been killed not long before. Animals were tended, families fed, guards were posted, and the weary immigrants settled down for the night. Later, as Cartwright's father stood watch, he heard a suspicious noise—something "grunting like a swine." Taking no chances, he fired at a dark object in the distance. The crack of the gun caused "an awful screaming throughout the encampment by women and children." Immediately, some of the men ran to the spot where the elder Cartwright had shot "and there they found an Indian, with a rifle in one hand and a tomahawk in the other, dead," shot through the head.[2]

Immigrants to western Kentucky and middle Tennessee feared the unknown territory and its inhabitants, but they expected to settle the land and came armed to take and defend it. Violence cleared the way for all the settlers.

Few whites questioned the destruction. Most thought it a dan-

1. Peter Cartwright, *Autobiography of Peter Cartwright*, with an introduction by Charles Wallis, 25.
2. Ibid., 26.

gerous, but critical, part of settlement. By the 1820s, whites had forced out the Indians who lived and hunted in the region, and settlers were able to live, according to William B. Allen, "under our own vine and fig tree, allowed to worship the God and father of our spirits, according to the dictates of our own consciences, and no one to molest or make us afraid." From the white settlers' perspective, ousting the Indians constituted a great achievement. The Black Patch was theirs to exploit.[3]

When the Cartwright family reached Kentucky, after their harrowing journey through hostile territory, they rented a farm in Lincoln County, where they stayed for two years. In the autumn of 1793 they moved to the Green River country in Logan County, south of Russelville, the county seat. Peter grew up in the region and later became a Methodist preacher; he helped spark the early 1800s Great Revival camp meetings on Red River, where his powerful oratory prompted hundreds to convert.[4]

"We left Cumberland County, Virginia, September 1, 1804 in two six horse wagons," recalled Jane Henry Thomas, a pioneer woman, of her three-month journey to the West. Like many settlers, Thomas's group traveled on the road that passed through Cumberland Gap and the Sequatchie Valley, leading to the frontier town of Nashville "opposite where Lick Branch empties into the river. There we crossed on a ferry."[5]

Settlers came from Virginia, North Carolina, South Carolina, Tennessee, and from other Kentucky counties. Some of the earliest arrived to claim Revolutionary War land grants or to take up soldiers' grants they had purchased. Early migrants into Christian County "squatted in the north part of the county, among the hills and springs and the timber." They noticed the soil "was light and fresh, and, while not so rich as in the barrens" of southern Christian, which

3. Rick Gregory, "Origins of Black Patch Violence," 1986 (photocopy), 15; William B. Allen, *A History of Kentucky,* 147; Gary B. Nash, *Red, White, and Black: The Peoples of Early America,* 54–67.

4. Cartwright, *Autobiography,* 25, 29–31.

5. Jane Henry Thomas, *Old Days in Nashville* (Nashville, Tenn.: Nashville Publishing House, Methodist Episcopal Church, Barbee and Smith, Agents, 1897), 22; N. S. Shaler, *Kentucky: A Pioneer Commonwealth,* 49–50. Also see, Harriet Arnow, *Seedtime on the Cumberland.*

they thought less attractive because of the lack of trees, "once they cleared the undergrowth of the forests . . . and the large trees [were] deadened," they found cultivation of the soil easy.[6]

Settlers eventually discovered that the unfertile appearance of the land was an illusion. Beneath the surface of the gently rolling landscape was a rich "sub-soil of red or chocolate colored clay." Upon these "cavernous limestone or 'barren' lands" developed the "far-famed 'Hopkinsville Shipping Tobacco,'" which made western Kentucky and middle Tennessee famous for the production of black, or dark-fired, tobacco, source of the region's name, the Black Patch.[7]

The Virginians and Carolinians of the Piedmont had produced tobacco since the early colonial period. Planters developed the distinctive fire-curing of the dark green, heavy-leafed tobacco, which involved curing with open fires and smoke. Farmers who had grown tobacco in the East used their skills on the frontier. They believed the best soil for tobacco was found "in the poplar timbered lands, where it is a deep, ash colored mould, rich, durable." After 1812, the European market, primary consumer of most fire-cured tobacco, began to demand the dark-fired type grown in Kentucky and Tennessee. In 1816, a traveler passing through the Cumberland Valley reported that he "scarcely passed a plantation which had not a tobacco field." He noted that the "country merchants were offering from twelve to fifteen dollars a hundred in advance" for the plant.[8]

As migrants moved into the Black Patch, the population increased steadily until the 1820s. A second period of growth occurred between 1840 and 1860, when farmers increased tobacco cultivation in the fertile limestone soil of southern Logan, Todd, and Christian Counties in Kentucky and the northern portions of Robertson and Montgomery Counties in Tennessee. Many new arrivals during this period were slaves who had been purchased by planters to labor in the

6. Hughie Lawson, "Geographical Origins of White Migrants to Trigg and Calloway Counties in the Antebellum Period," 286–304; Carl O. Sauer, *The Geography of the Pennyroyal*, 138; William Henry Perrin, *Counties of Christian and Trigg, Kentucky, Historical and Biographical*, 45; Shaler, *Kentucky*, 28–30.

7. Sauer, *Geography*, 139; Lewis Collins, ed., *Collins' History of Kentucky*, 375–76; Perrin, *Counties*, 25–26; Shaler, *Kentucky*, 32.

8. J. R. Brown, *Gazeteer*, 84, quoted in Sauer, *Geography*, 138–39; Lawson, "Geographical Origins," 298–301; Shaler, *Kentucky*, 32.

tobacco fields. Consequently, Christian County became the largest slaveholding county in the Kentucky Black Patch. Robertson County became the greatest producer of dark tobacco in the Black Patch and the home of the largest slaveholding family in the region, the Washingtons.[9]

As the population grew, local leaders in the region called for the formation of new counties. By the middle of the nineteenth century, the Black Patch comprised twenty-eight counties in southern and western Kentucky and eighteen in middle Tennessee. New counties were carved out of larger, older ones as populations rose. For instance, two Kentucky counties gave up land to form Trigg County in 1820. The initial population was 3,874. By 1850, the population had grown to 10,129; and in 1910, it peaked at 14,539.[10]

Typical of the whites who settled the Black Patch were several Tennessee and Kentucky families: the Killebrews, the Ligons, the Thomases, the Cunninghams, the Martins, and the McCartys. Buckner Killebrew, born in Edgecomb County, North Carolina, in 1753, headed west across the mountains into Tennessee in 1795 or 1796, and settled on Spring Creek in Montgomery County. He cleared a site of its black jack oaks and scrub hickories and began to farm. He later met and married Mary Whitefield, and together they had several children, including a son, Bryan Whitefield Killebrew. Bryan married Elizabeth Smith Ligon of Halifax County, Virginia, in the spring of 1829. The Ligons had left the East, wrote son Joseph Killebrew about his mother's family, "at that period [when] the lands sold very high in Virginia, and the glowing reports" from the West concerning "the goodness of the soil, the amenity of the climate, the cheapness of the lands . . . induced a large emigration." Elizabeth Ligon's father had been a hero of the Revolutionary War. He came to Port Royal, Tennessee, in Montgomery County at the age of fifty-five, rented a farm, and began to buy slaves. By the age of eighty, he

9. Sauer, *Geography*, 132–33.

10. Wendell H. Rone, Sr., *An Historical Atlas of Kentucky and Counties,* 42–43; Lloyd G. Lee, *A Brief History of Kentucky,* 13–26, 208–10, 226–28, 395–402, 534–40; William Turner, "Maps of the Black Patch" (in his possession, Hopkinsville Community College, Hopkinsville, Kentucky); Lawson, "Geographical Origins," 287–99; United States Department of Commerce, Bureau of the Census, *Thirteenth Census of the United States* (1910).

owned over one hundred slaves, who worked several hundred acres of rich tobacco land.[11]

The newly married couple, Bryan and Elizabeth Ligon Killebrew, rented a farm, a common way for young people in the Black Patch to establish a separate household. A son, Joseph Buckner Killebrew, who later became a tobacco expert, author, editor of *Southern Farm Magazine*, proponent of scientific farming, and secretary of the Bureau of Agriculture, was born there. By 1834, Bryan had managed to save twelve hundred dollars to purchase two hundred acres of land in Stewart County, Tennessee, near the homes of a cousin and a friend. The land proved rich, but water had to be hauled from Big Rock, five miles away. Bryan owned four slaves—three men and one woman. He also used the labor of several slaves on loan to him, whom he later inherited. Together, they worked the land. According to Joseph, their "cattle, hogs, sheep, and young horses were turned out on the commons and fared luxuriously upon the highway pasturage."[12]

The people and the animals, Joseph recalled, fed upon the "blackberries, black haws, hazel nuts, hickorynuts, walnuts, chestnuts, and wild grapes [that] grew" in the Black Patch's forests and fields. While there was an abundance of food, water was scarce, and Bryan decided to dig a cistern "plastered and covered with cedar logs," to collect rainwater. In the 1830s, the white family lived in two fifteen-feet-square rooms "built of logs and adjoining each other without any passage between," Joseph wrote. The house was typical of those used by middling prosperous Black Patch farmers. However, Joseph added, "the tobacco barns were much better built than the dwelling." He did not mention what structures sheltered the slaves.[13]

A second white family destined to be prominent in the Black Patch came from North Carolina. Soon after the Revolution, James Thomas, a soldier and son of James and Sarah Barnes Thomas, returned to his Bertie County home—a run-down four-hundred-acre plantation held by his widowed mother. For eight years Thomas worked to revive the farm. He also courted Mary Standley, marrying her in

11. Joseph B. Killebrew, "Recollections of My Life: An Autobiography," vol. 1, written in 1896–1897, Tennessee State Library and Archives, Manuscripts Division, Nashville, Tennessee, i–iv, vi–ix.

12. Ibid., xii.

13. Ibid., xii, 2–3.

1760 after his mother's death. The couple lived in the walnut log house that James's father had built in 1751 on the banks of the Cashie River. During the next fourteen years the Thomases had six children.

By 1804 James and Sarah Thomas had begun to contemplate a move to Kentucky, perhaps because they had heard of the rich land across the mountains.[14] The hunters and explorers who had seen it had praised it on their return to their eastern homes. One of the first, John Filson, wrote enticingly of "the large trees of many kinds . . . those which are peculiar to Kentucky are the sugar-trees," which could provide "every family with plenty of sugar." Also, the honey locust which "is curiously surrounded with large thorny spikes, bearing broad and long pods in the form of peas," which have a "sweet taste and makes excellent beer" to quench the thirst of hardworking farmers. Other plants, such as sugar cane, flourished in Kentucky, and Filson reported, "Where no cane grows there is abundance of wild-rye, clover, and buffalo grass . . . wild herbage," and lovely herbs that the "Shawnee called wild lettuce, and pepper grass."[15]

The abundance of life on the Kentucky frontier impressed Filson. "The land fowls are turkeys, which are very frequent, pheasants, partridges, and ravens." Fish in the river and streams, Filson claimed, swam in great numbers and included "mullet, rock, perch, gar-fish, and eel." When he visited the region west of the Appalachians, Filson "found many deer, elks, and bears . . . also panthers, wildcats, and wolves. Beavers, otters, minks and muskrats . . . foxes, rabbits, squirrel, racoons [sic], groundhogs, pole-cats and opossums" roamed the land. Large mammals, such as bear, disappeared from the Black Patch soon after settlements encroached on their territory, but other game animals remained. From them came warm skins to wear or sell and savory wild meats. Hunting and trapping continued as a source of extra income for middling successful and poor farmers and as sport for all men into the twentieth century.[16]

14. Edison H. Thomas, *The Thomas and Bridges Story, 1540–1840* (Louisville: T and E Publishers, 1972), 13–15.

15. Willard Rouse Jillson, *Filson's Kentucke: A Facsimile Reproduction of the Original Wilmington Edition of 1784*, 23–24.

16. Ibid., 26; Thomas F. Hamilton, interview by David Sullivan, tape recording, June 28, 1976, Western Kentucky History and Culture Collection, Land

A veteran of the Revolution, James Thomas qualified for a land grant in Tennessee provided by the state of Virginia. Surveyors laid off the land in 1782, but Thomas did not take the claim. He was too concerned with working his mother's place and trying to provide for his younger sisters still at home.[17]

After Kentucky became a state in 1792, James Thomas decided to move. In December 1795, the General Assembly of Kentucky passed a land act concerning vacant lands south of the Green River. The lands had been reserved for Virginia veterans, but the act declared that the region would be opened to others in 1797. The area encompassed a broad territory of western Kentucky roughly bound by the Green River, the Cumberland Mountains, and the Tennessee and Ohio Rivers.[18]

The Kentucky Act permitted anyone who was over twenty-one and the head of a household to settle land in the territory. From one hundred to two hundred acres could be acquired if the family resided on the homestead for one year prior to filing for ownership. The Thomas family arrived in the summer of 1806. They took advantage of the act and claimed a two-hundred-acre tract on Donaldson's Creek. The Thomases reared seven children on the homestead. Their sons grew up and bought land nearby, and the family eventually owned nearly four thousand acres.[19]

Blacks immigrated to the region along with whites. Some entered Kentucky and Tennessee as slaves of the earliest settlers. Among those early settlers was Henry Northington. In the last decades of the eighteenth century, Northington brought two slave brothers, William and Jack Northington, to middle Tennessee. The brothers spent their lives hired out to neighboring farmers since Northington had sufficient labor for his needs. Free blacks made the pioneer journey as well. Six-year-old Kitty Carr, born in Virginia in 1815, was given by her mother to a white woman, Mrs. Edmond Winston, who

---

between the Lakes Series, Forrest C. Pogue Oral History Institute, Murray, Kentucky; Mrs. C. W. Bell, interview by Jan Daily, n.d. MSS 1972–5, Folklore and Folklife Collection, Department of Library Special Collections, Folklife Archives, Western Kentucky University, Bowling Green, Kentucky.

17. Thomas, *Thomas and Bridges*, 16.

18. Ibid., 17; Willard Rouse Jillson, *Kentucky Land Grants* (Louisville: Standard Printing Co., 1925), 5, 7, 9.

19. Thomas, *Thomas and Bridges*, 17–20, 82–84.

took the child to Montgomery County, Tennessee. Kitty lived with and worked for the Winstons until she reached adulthood, when she met and married a neighbor's slave named Horace Johnson. Shortly after their union, her husband was sold to James Carr of Port Royal, Tennessee, and Horace changed his last name to Carr. Since Kitty was free, she could live with her husband but not without trouble from local whites, who resented her freeborn status. Rumors said she would be enslaved. However, due to the intercession of a white man, Dick Blount of Fortson's Spring, the county court issued legal papers formally establishing her free status and, thus, ensuring her freedom. Thus, the Carrs gained a measure of security, and despite the precarious position granted them by the whites of the region, they survived and reared a family.[20] Kitty earned an income through spinning, weaving, baking, and midwifery. Her husband arranged to hire himself from his mistress for two hundred dollars a year, which he earned by operating a ferry on the Red River, working as a carpenter, and later, serving as a Baptist preacher.

Slaveholders continued to migrate into the region. Often members of the same family moved together and settled near each other so that they could help one another in the difficult first years. Social networks of kin and neighbors, characteristic of the Appalachian south, formed the Black Patch communities. Personal relationships based on shared labor, loans, bartering, and other social interactions enabled the pioneers to survive in the semi-isolated areas and made possible cooperation across class, gender, and, sometimes, racial lines. A complex network of relationships arose.[21] Edward Mitchusson and his wife, Alsey Hampton, along with their four sons, three daughters, and thirteen slaves lived in 1790 in Lawrence County, South Carolina. After about ten years, Mitchusson received a land grant on the banks of Eddy Creek in western Kentucky.[22] He and his brother William led about sixty settlers to western Kentucky in 1797

20. Harriet Parks Miller, *Pioneer Colored Christians*, 3–18, 41; Marion B. Lucas, *A History of Blacks in Kentucky: From Slavery to Segregation, 1760–1891*, 40–41.
21. Glenn Martin, *History of the Martin-Mitchusson Families*, 14; Ralph Mann, "Mountains, Land and Kin Networks: Burkes Garden, Virginia, in the 1840s and 1850s," 411–13.
22. Martin, *Martin-Mitchusson*, 14–28. Also see Arnow, *Seedtime*, for a detailed description of pioneer settlers.

or 1798. After the required year's residence, the Mitchussons finalized their grants.

Both Mitchusson brothers had been active in politics in South Carolina. William had served as a justice of the peace in South Carolina, in Tennessee, and finally in Christian, Livingston, and Caldwell Counties in Kentucky. He served as Caldwell County sheriff in 1811 and 1812. Edward was his deputy. White men who had been politically and economically successful in the East often became members of a new elite in the Black Patch.[23]

Occasionally outsiders, through a combination of good luck and hard work, managed to break into the ranks of the Black Patch's upper class. A young Virginian, William McCarty, who came to Caldwell County in 1810, met the Mitchusson family, and in 1824 he married Edward Mitchusson's daughter, Sarah. Three years later Edward died. In the years since his arrival in Kentucky, Edward's property holdings had increased from 360 to 460 acres, and he had acquired six slaves, for a total of twelve. At the time of his death on December 22, 1827, Edward owned nine adult slaves—Daphne, Class, Eady, Abigail, Lucy, David, Ben, George, and Anthony—and three girls—Celia, Hagar, and Maxia. The black slave population worked for and with the whites, but it lived in the shadow of the white world. The slaves, too, knew the skills of tobacco production and passed them on. Their descendants in the Black Patch, some of whom became landowners and many of whom became sharecroppers and tenant farmers, continued to raise dark tobacco.[24]

Upon her father's death, Sarah Mitchusson McCarty received the maid, Hagar, plus one hundred dollars since the slave girl was small. Edward Mitchusson had chosen his son-in-law, William McCarty, as executor of his will. In this case, McCarty, who had arrived in the Black Patch alone in 1810 with only three horses, managed to rise in status through marriage as well as through hard work. Stories like his seemed to confirm the white men's belief that on the frontier anyone could achieve wealth and prominence.[25]

23. Martin, *Martin-Mitchusson*, 18.

24. Ibid., 18–19; Waldrep, "Immigration and Opportunity," 392–95; *Slave Narratives: A Folk History of Slavery in the United States from Interviews with Former Slaves*, MSS 45.

25. Martin, *Martin-Mitchusson*, 19.

Sarah Mitchusson McCarty and William McCarty lived in Caldwell County and raised a large family. As did many rural women in the region, Sarah gave birth to a new baby approximately every two years. The McCartys named their children for themselves, their grandparents, and other kin, a practice that increased the bonds among the generations and contributed to the rich folk memory of pioneer forbears. The large number of children proved advantageous, even vital, for farm labor. More children could plant and tend more acres of the money crop, tobacco, and keep the self-reliant family farms operating.[26]

Not everyone who migrated to the Black Patch saw their hopes for success materialize. Nancy Mitchusson, another daughter of Edward and Alsey Mitchusson, married a young man from North Carolina named Lewis Martin. Lewis's father, Martin Martin, was a Revolutionary War veteran from Virginia whose economic status declined. In 1823, when he applied for a pension, his meager holdings included fifty acres, a dozen hogs, a few sheep, and some household items totaling only $82.75. He wrote the pension office that "by occupation, I, a farmer, am unable to support myself by labor" due to infirmities. "My family seven, in number—wife—sixty years of age and subject to rheumatism, a daughter . . . Slina 31 years unsupported, Willis, 21 years old," and two grandchildren. "These are all healthy and as far as their abilities will allow are able to labor for their support."[27]

Many people left their homes on the eastern seaboard to escape difficult circumstances; they hoped to better their lives on the frontier. By the time his father made the petition, Lewis had left home to go West. In 1810 he owned a single residence in Caldwell County and one horse. Perhaps he moved to Kentucky because of favorable reports from the Mitchussons, whom he had known in the Carolinas. He renewed contact with them in Kentucky and married Nancy on July 29, 1813. A year later, Lewis Martin owned fifty acres and two horses. Possibly, Nancy brought him the land at their marriage, or she may have brought a cash dowry that allowed Lewis to purchase the acreage. In

26. Ibid., 18–19; Eunice Stovall McCarty, interview by author, tape recording, Lyon County, Kentucky, March 9, 1987; George McCarty, interview by author, tape recording, Lyon County, Kentucky, March 10, 1987, and April 20, 1987; Luke McCarty, letter, 1972 (photocopy) in author's possession. Bertram Wyatt-Brown, *Honor and Violence in the Old South* (New York: Oxford University Press, 1986), 69.
27. Martin, *Martin-Mitchusson*, 26.

1815, Lewis bought one black servant and entered the ranks of slave-holders. His holdings remained stable until 1826, when he purchased another horse and an additional twenty-five acres of land at four dollars per acre. He bought the tract from the widow of Nancy's cousin Edward Mitchusson. In this way, white families supported their kin socially and economically to ensure family members' status and protect the family's interests. Lewis and Nancy's fortunes continued to rise, and in 1845 they increased their holdings of slaves and stock.[28]

By 1838 Lewis Martin had acquired five hundred acres of land, which he kept until around 1848. Years later, in 1874, he deeded his land to his five children. Each child received different acreage, but the lots were equal in value. At his death, Martin's property consisted of $40 in cash and notes from twenty-six people totaling $3,100. Lewis Martin and all of his children lived in the Rock Springs community of Caldwell County near Eddy Creek on the original tract granted to William Mitchusson, brother of Lewis Martin's father-in-law, Edward. The family members, except for son William, always lived in close proximity of one another.[29]

The Martins became closely tied to other families in the vicinity through marriages. Through such links, Black Patch families forged stronger bonds with others and further strengthened white community social, political, and economic networks. Blood and conjugal ties bound the white community while tempering class distinctions. For example, six of the children of Lewis and Nancy Martin married: Mary Jane and William married a brother and sister, James and Nancy Gray; Lucretia and Elizabeth married brothers, John and Jesse Satterfield. Such double ties of marriage cemented kin ties, neighbor relationships, and community bonds. In the Black Patch, sibling exchange marriages were not uncommon; they served to unite many families in very complex webs of kinship and contributed to the formation of family-kin culture areas.[30]

28. Ibid., 20–33.
29. Ibid., 33–34.
30. Ibid., 34. A family-kin culture area is defined as a distinct area or neighborhood settled by a single family line or kin group in which the families intermarried and eventually established a family-based culture. See Elmora M. Matthews, *Neighbor and Kin: Life in a Tennessee Ridge Community;* Mann, "Mountains, Land, and Kin Networks," 411–13.

A strong, enduring family-kin neighborhood developed in Trigg County among the Cunninghams. The first ancestor, William Cunningham (1765–1823), gathered his family in 1818 and moved them from Albemarle County, Virginia, to the wilds of the area that is now Trigg County, Kentucky, on Green Creek, where he purchased 223 acres of virgin farmland. William was an active citizen in Virginia, a farmer and tailor like his father, and he served in the United States Army from 1792 to 1794 to aid in quelling the Whiskey Rebellion. A small landholder in Virginia with an 163–acre farm wedged between two larger plantations, Cunningham saw little chance of buying more land in the crowded Old Dominion. In early 1818, Cunningham, his sons, and a slave journeyed to Green Creek and built a house and stable on their property. They returned to Virginia to settle affairs and collect the rest of the household.[31]

Once in Kentucky, William and his wife, Nancy Carr Cunningham, worked together to develop a thriving farm, growing tobacco, corn, and the necessary foodstuffs to support their eleven children. Both husband and wife were crucial to the farm economy. Although sex roles defined the work and place of each, the two formed a whole that made family life, culture, and society function. Families helped build the Black Patch into a stable tobacco culture region.[32]

Necessity forced William Cunningham, and other pioneers, to become skilled in several occupations. He worked among the people as a self-taught country doctor and built and operated a grist mill. Cunningham soon rose to prominence in the area, and when Trigg became a county in 1820, he served as an official in the first elections. In 1829 he became a member of the third session of the circuit court, while holding the position of Trigg County road commissioner. William died at the age of fifty-eight, only three years after establishing himself in Kentucky, leaving his wife, eight children still at home, and thirteen slaves valued at $3,750.[33]

After her husband's death, Nancy Carr Cunningham remained on the Trigg County farm. Her adult children assisted her with the

31. Bertie C. Gingles, *History and Genealogy of William Cunningham and Wife Nancy (Carr) Cunningham*, 1–4, 6–7; Bertie C. Gingles, interview by author, tape recording, Calloway County, Kentucky, April 14, 1987.

32. Gingles, *History and Genealogy*, 6–7.

33. Ibid., 6–7, 30; Lee, *Brief History of Kentucky*, 537.

work and the rearing of the younger children. Nancy epitomized the role of the southern white farm woman. She oversaw the running of the household, which included managing slave labor, doing housework, cultivating and preparing food, supervising care and education of children, nursing, making clothing, and in peak seasons, even working in the fields. Like other American white women of the period, Nancy Cunningham encouraged the values of Protestant morality, religion, and the work ethic. She entered the public realm through church work and served as a religious and moral guide for her household and the neighborhood. A preacher baptized her into the faith in April 1823, and in 1842, she helped organize Mount Pleasant Baptist, a neighborhood church five miles from the Cunningham homeplace. Generations of Cunninghams worshipped in this country church, along with Hurricane Baptist, founded in 1845.[34]

Pioneer couples like the Cunninghams represented one piece of the overall pattern that made up the cultural "quilt" of the Black Patch of Kentucky and Tennessee. William and Nancy, small landholders and slaveowners, were forced to head west by the poor soil and tight land situation in Virginia. They planned and carried out a move to Kentucky. There, they claimed land and turned their experience and the labor of their slaves to building a plantation, a mill, and a medical practice. They became respected active citizens. No doubt their status came in part from the wealth accrued in the East and brought to Kentucky in the form of slaves and the land purchased with money from the sale of their Albemarle County lands. At that time, Virginia society was hierarchical. Wealth and slaves meant status. The Cunninghams were squeezed out of an elite social position in Virginia, but with a move to the West they achieved a high social position. Other settlers from the East recognized social status and leadership, because with wealth came political responsibility and leading positions in the community. Cunningham recognized this and thoroughly exploited his talents to achieve leadership. Nancy fulfilled her role as mother of a large, prosperous family, mistress

34. Lee, *Brief History of Kentucky*, 32. Harland D. Hagler, "The Ideal Woman in the Antebellum South: Lady or Farmwife?" 405–18; Elizabeth Fox-Genovese, *Within the Plantation Household: Black and White Women of the Old South*.

and manager of a productive farm household, and upholder of the family and cultural norms of morality and Protestant religion.[35]

Certainly, wealth and property were preserved within families and served to maintain their status. Just as important was a family's perception of its role in society as a leader. Members often refer to a famous or hardworking founding father and mother to explain family success and also to inspire further efforts. Stories of ancestors' exploits and good (or bad) deeds are passed on to children. Grandparents and other ancestors become heroes to be emulated, and it becomes a matter of pride to continue and contribute to the family's reputation.[36]

Every white migrant and black slave had unique backgrounds, beliefs, and traditions brought from their original homes. Attracted by the "hills with level meadows between, virgin timber . . . springs . . . and the Little River" of the Green Creek valley of Trigg County, Kentucky, so similar to Albemarle County in Virginia, they settled and adapted their customs to the new environment. Where possible they conserved traditional ways, and if necessary, they adapted old ways to pioneer conditions. Often entire kin groups settled along the same creek or valley. Intermarriage among white families like the Cunninghams, Mitchussons, and McCartys, which served to create a social network, confused identification, especially for people unacquainted with so many families with the same surname. Inhabitants often solved the problem through nicknames, which were given to different families to distinguish the blood lines and simplify identification among relatives. But some outsiders remained bewildered.[37]

Among the Cunningham clan, one family that lived near Little River was dubbed the "Duck" Cunninghams. Members of the line were called by their given name plus "Duck," such as Bill "Duck" (Cunningham). Another line was nicknamed "Buck," while others

35. Gingles, *History and Genealogy*, 5, 32; Allan Kulikoff, *Tobacco and Slaves: the Development of Southern Cultures in the Chesapeake, 1680–1800*, 3–20.

36. Gingles, interview; Robert Parker, interview by author, tape recording, Caldwell County, Kentucky, July 15, 1987; Thomas, *Thomas and Bridges*, passim.

37. Gingles, *History and Genealogy*, 16–28; Lawson, "Geographical Origins," 295–99.

were known as "Dab," "Tank," or "Rat," Cunningham. The story told by a descendant describes the difficulties these names could cause outside visitors.[38]

One day a stranger rode into the Green Creek neighborhood and paused at one of the Cunningham homesteads to ask the whereabouts of the young Cunningham boy's father. His father had "gone across the river to wash rats," the son replied matter-of-factly. The perplexed stranger repeated his question a few times but was unable to elicit another response. Finally, he gave up and headed off down the dusty road. He soon met another person and queried him on the location of the Cunningham man and wondered aloud, "Why would any man wash rats?" He was informed that what the boy had meant was that his father was at his kinsman Washington "Rat" Cunningham's house across the creek.[39]

This kin-culture nomenclature developed because of the stable location of the families through the generations in the Green Creek vicinity. Families renamed themselves in order to distinguish one another and the different family lines. This re-naming created cohesion among the kin and a heritage of lore about the family. These family narratives, in turn, gave members a sense of history, pride, and purpose in the community. Nicknaming also worked to keep outsiders from joining the community. It distinguished regional and neighborhood residents, who knew the nicknames, from strangers, who did not. The uninitiated often perceived such kin-culture practices as clannish, backward, and at times, incomprehensible or hostile. For insiders it meant close ties, mutual understanding, shared meaning, and memories. Whole families could build and preserve good "names" or reputations in the community in this way. And a good reputation in the Black Patch meant everything because a person's social standing was based on family background first and personal achievements second. As in Virginia, from which the Cunninghams emigrated, one's family and wealth determined social position. People who hoped to re-create a society similar to the hierarchical Virginia tobacco society that they left behind were very

38. Lawson, "Geographical Origins," 295–99.
39. Ibid.

conscious of how important family name, appearances, and reputation were in establishing an elite place for themselves in the community.[40]

Families like these came to western Kentucky and middle Tennessee to build new lives on the frontier. The Killebrews, Ligons, Martins, Mitchussons, McCartys, Cunninghams, and other whites yearned for a place to better their fortunes. Black slaves came with no expectation of betterment. Yet, a free woman, Kitty Carr, and her slave husband, managed to create a meaningful life in the slave-based society. Some whites, like the Cunninghams, hoped to emulate the old hierarchical Virginia society, to become the new elite. If they came with wealth and slaves, they often succeeded. The men became political leaders, church deacons, and paternalistic heads of the hierarchical society. However, like the colonists of Virginia who never attained the heights of the English gentry life they sought, the Black Patch white pioneers seldom achieved the great wealth and material splendor of the tidewater gentry. Nevertheless, they occupied the highest station in the Black Patch society and were proud of the achievement.[41]

Others, such as the lone Virginian, William McCarty, arrived with little but dreams of making a fair living in the promising new land. He did well, and became one of the middling status farmers of the region. He owned over one hundred acres of land, a few slaves, who had belonged to his wife, and passed land and material wealth on to his children. Neither he nor his descendants held high political office; rather they became sheriffs, deputies, and solid landowning farmers.[42]

The wealthy and middling white farmers brought slaves to the Black Patch to help break the land, till the fields, and serve the white household. Bryan Killebrew brought four African American slaves, three men and one woman, to help build his western home. Often slaves worked alongside their white masters in the tobacco patch. Farmers in the hillier, poorer sections owned few slaves, usually less than ten. In southern Christian, Logan, and Todd counties in Kentucky and Robertson and Montgomery counties in Tennessee, where the richest tobacco soils existed, slaveholders might own ten or more slaves. A few became

40. Ibid.; Kulikoff, *Tobacco and Slaves*, 8.
41. Kulikoff, *Tobacco and Slaves*, 6–7, 161, 206–7.
42. Martin, *Martin-Mitchusson*, 17–20; Luke McCarty, letter.

scions of huge plantations. George A. Washington and his 274 slaves of
Robertson County built Wessyngton, which in 1860 contained 13,100
acres and produced 250,000 pounds of dark tobacco each year. Washington was the largest slaveholder in the Black Patch and one of the top
producers of dark-fired tobacco in the world.[43]

Finally, some status-seeking whites arrived, such as Christopher
Hammond, a South Carolinian and a farm tenant for a time in east
Tennessee, who moved to Kentucky and gained wealth in land and
slaves, but not a high position in society. None of Hammond's sons,
who lived in Caldwell County, achieved the wealth of their father.
The hope many pioneers had of bettering each succeeding generation did not always come to fruition, especially after the 1820s, when
the prime land had been claimed. The landowners with smaller claims
(fifty to one hundred fifty acres) made up the lower middling group
of sturdy yeomen in the Black Patch. Those whites who lost all
property became hired laborers, tenants, or left the region for better
opportunities farther west in Missouri, Indiana, Arkansas, or Texas.[44]

The pioneer families who remained, black and white, slave and
free, their children and grandchildren, created by the 1840s and
1850s the Black Patch culture. They centered it upon the growing of
dark-fired tobacco, the basis of the regional agricultural economy,
the family, the neighborhood, and the church. The work they did in
the tobacco patch, the corn fields, the kitchen, and the chicken yard
provided a subsistence living for the white majority of middling farm
families, and a comfortable, even luxurious life, for the wealthy with
rich land and slave labor. Slave and free blacks helped create the
culture although social, political and economic success was denied in
the racist society. Whatever their station in life, Black Patch people
became interconnected through ties of kinship and neighborliness,
shared customs, similar values, religious beliefs, and agricultural
practices. And, at the same time, these people also created a tradition of violence that characterized the region.

43. Joseph B. Killebrew, "Recollections," 2; Waldrep, "Immigration and Opportunity," 407; Rick Gregory, "Robertson County and the Black Patch War, 1904–
1909," 343; Washington Family Papers, Tennessee State Library and Archives,
Manuscripts Division, Nashville, Tennessee.
44. Gregory, "Robertson County," 392–94; Waldrep, "Immigration and Opportunity, 406–7.

2

A DESPERATE STATE
OF SOCIETY

"Many refugees, from almost all parts of the Union," wrote
Methodist preacher Peter Cartwright "fled to escape justice
or punishment." The refugees poured into Logan County, Kentucky, in the 1790s and the early 1800s. "For, although there was law,
yet it could not be executed, and it was a desperate state of society.
Murderers, horse thieves, highway robbers, and counterfeiters fled
here until they combined and formed a majority," claimed Cartwright.
The smaller population of "honest and civil . . . citizens would prosecute these wretched banditto, but they would swear each other
clear." These two groups, each with its own concept of appropriate
civic behavior and justice, struggled over whose form of social and
legal organization would dominate the Black Patch.[1]

"They really put all law at defiance," Cartwright goes on, "and
carried on such desperate violence and outrage that the honest part
of the citizens seemed to be driven to the necessity of uniting and
combining together and taking the law into their own hands under
the name of Regulators." A contest for control arose in the 1790s
between settlers who sought social stability and the "evil" elements
in the county. According to Cartwright, "This was a very desperate
state of things."[2]

People in the county who, like Cartwright's family, valued an orderly community and a system of justice based on Protestant morals,
opposed the large numbers of lawless people living in the region. The
"honest and civil" residents of Logan County, Cartwright said, "formed
themselves into a society, and established their code of by-laws,"
corresponding to their idea of an orderly society. Afterward, "on a
court day at Russellville the two bands met in town." Tempers flared,

1. Cartwright, *Autobiography*, 30.
2. Ibid. Also see Richard Maxwell Brown, *The South Carolina Regulators*.

"soon a quarrel commenced, and a general battle ensued between the rogues and Regulators, and they fought with guns, pistols, dirks, knives, and clubs." The melee ended, lamented Cartwright, after "some were actually killed, [and] many wounded," but "the rogues proved victors, kept the ground, and drove the Regulators out of town."[3]

The Regulators, persistent, hardy men, shortly "rallied again, hunted, killed and lynched many of the rogues, until several of them fled, and left for parts unknown." During these violent days "many lives were lost on both sides, to the great scandal of civilized people." Yet, the "civilized" law-respecting citizens, those who had risen to leading roles through honesty, hard work, and success at farming, with whom Cartwright sympathized, managed through violent vigilante action to wrest control of Logan County from those they considered incorrigible. Significantly, both groups used and condoned violence as a means to an end. In the Black Patch, violence became an acceptable tool to bring change.[4]

Cartwright's "honest and civil" fellow citizens' legal justice, achieved through violence, replaced that of the outlaws in Rogue's Harbor. The new white settlers imposed their own social order, defined by Protestant religious morality, white supremacy, respect for private property, safety, and the rule of law. In their view, they had replaced chaos with peace and stability. The violence and vigilantism of the 1790s set a precedent in the Black Patch. Nine separate uprisings of Regulator violence occurred between 1793 and 1850 in the region. The local elite, "who comprised many of the very best citizens," wrote local historian William Perrin, neither acted "rashly, nor did they punish any man without a trial." The movement leaders, such as those in Christian County in the 1840s, established and maintained their own moral and legal structures, first through the legal system, which was backed up by the threat of force, and then by violence, if necessary. Participating in the vigilante movements bound the middling and elite whites together, reinforcing their concept of a good society and their sense of legitimate leadership.[5]

3. Cartwright, *Autobiography*, 30.
4. Ibid.; Brown, *South Carolina Regulators*, 24–29.
5. Gregory, "Origins of Violence," 16–17; Richard Maxwell Brown, *Strain of*

Establishing order in the Black Patch took time. Discord persisted through the 1840s in Christian County, Kentucky, to the annoyance of law-abiding citizens. The leading men of the county, upset by the questionable activities of one Alonzo Pennington, formed a Regulator movement to reestablish in the county their "conservative values of life, property, and law and order." Pennington was representative of all they deplored.[6]

Alonzo Pennington was the youngest son of Francis Pennington, a Carolina slave owner who settled on the West Fork of Pond River around 1800. By 1829, Francis had prospered and been elected sheriff. The son, however, chose not to emulate the father, and, according to a local writer, Alonzo's behavior did not "reflect on the honor or integrity of the old man."[7]

Alonzo, wrote a local historian, was "a young man of good appearance, had an alert mind and was better educated than most of his neighbors, and soon became noted for his sharp trades that frequently involved him in litigation." He loved to buy and sell racehorses and constructed a racecourse on his property "which became a general headquarters for that kind of sport and of a class of men whose morals were not of the highest order." Pennington's neighbors in Wilson Precinct were not pleased and accused him of cheating them in business deals. In the meantime, the neighborhood suffered a series of horse thefts and slave kidnappings, and several slaves ran away. Many suspected that Pennington and the men who followed him were involved.[8]

Then on May 9, 1845, the murder of an Irish stonemason and farmer, Sam Davis, stunned the community. Until April, Davis and his young wife had lived on a small place that she had inherited. The couple farmed and owned a horse, two cows, and one slave girl.

Violence: Historical Studies of American Violence and Vigilantism, 99–100, 311–12, 316; Perrin, *Counties*, 81.

6. Arthur K. Moore, *The Frontier Mind: A Cultural Analysis of the Kentucky Frontiersman*, 38–39; Richard Maxwell Brown, "The American Vigilante Tradition," in *Violence in America: Historical and Comparative Perspectives*, 154–58; Perrin, *Counties*, 72; Charles Mayfield Meacham, *A History of Christian County, Kentucky: From Oxcart to Airplane*, 73.

7. Meacham, *History*, 73–74; Perrin, *Counties*, 303.

8. Perrin, *Counties*, 73; Meacham, *History*, 73–74.

Davis's wife had died in April, and it seemed that the acreage would revert back to her kin. He and his in-laws were contending over the farm land when Davis decided to sell and leave the county. During a muster at Pleasant Hill Church in the Fruit Hill Precinct, Davis met Pennington, who offered to buy the farm. They left together, and Davis was not seen again.[9]

Pennington soon moved to the Davis place and told neighbors that the former owner had left. Suspicion arose when Pennington told conflicting stories concerning Davis's whereabouts. Then, someone saw Davis's sorrel mare in Todd County in the possession of B. F. Cisney, a man who had also been at the muster field the day Davis vanished. Rumors started and accusations flew. Soon a group of self-described gentlemen led by Col. James Robinson of Fruit Hill met at Antioch Church to organize a committee to look into the matter. Robinson had served in the War of 1812 at the Battle of New Orleans, and he retained his title as a badge of honor. He was known for his fighting prowess and for having "had a memorable first encounter with one Wilkins, who [was] said to have been worsted by his antagonist." Colonel Robinson enjoyed the honor and respect of the community.[10]

In July of 1845, with Robinson leading them, the group set up the Safety Society, later called "Regulators" like other groups that expelled undesirables in nearby counties. Society members each paid one dollar to join. Now the community elite, with the assistance and backing of the middling farmers, ventured forth to bring the society back to order.[11]

They brought B. F. Cisney before the Safety Committee, but he admitted nothing. So members of the group took Cisney to a wooded area and threatened him with switches and a hangman's rope. With that he decided to confess, and he led them to the body of Sam Davis, which was hidden on the rocky ledge of a limestone cave. Cisney claimed he had only held the horses while Alonzo Pennington bludgeoned Davis to death.[12]

9. Meacham, *History*, 75.
10. Ibid.; Perrin, *Counties*, 302.
11. Meacham, *History*, 76–77; Brown, "American Vigilante Tradition," 156–58.
12. Meacham, *History*, 76–77.

With Cisney's confession as evidence, the grand jury indicted "Alonzo Pennington, laborer," on July 26, 1845, for the murder of Sam Davis. Pennington, hearing of this, fled to Lamar County, Texas, where he remained a fugitive for a year before being arrested and returned to Kentucky for trial. The jury consisted mainly of south Christian farmers, men from the wealthiest areas of the county. John McLarning served as Commonwealth's Attorney; Col. J. F. Buckner took Pennington's case; and Judge John Shackleford presided. The jury returned a guilty verdict and recommended a death sentence, which the good people of the region accepted as appropriate. At the first attempt to hang him the rope broke. While repairs were being made, Pennington cried that Cisney had killed Sam Davis, but it was too late. The Commonwealth succeeded on its second attempt to execute Pennington.[13]

Alonzo's mother witnessed the gruesome events at the hanging tree and provided a scene for the gossips to discuss for days afterward. According to Newton Allen, the jailer, who passed the story down to his granddaughter, Mrs. Pennington arrived at the pin oak hanging tree in an old wagon. She was seated in back, atop her son's coffin knitting, and to the horror of onlookers, she continued her work during the execution. This only confirmed, if the spectators needed confirmation, that the Penningtons were a strange family who deserved to be outcasts.[14]

In the Pennington affair, the elite had moved to reestablish an orderly community. Pennington, laborer, slick horse trader, and associate of incorrigibles, represented the county's unruly, outsider element; he was someone not even a mother could mourn. His death was an example to other deviants. Local historian Perrin reflected the elite's values in his account of the movement, explaining that "the Regulators, though not a lawful organization, did the county good, and succeeded in doing what the law had failed to accomplish— the breaking up of a desperate band of outlaws, and banishing them from the country." The Regulators protected their interests through organized violence, and Perrin maintained, "There are cases where it may be exercised with beneficial results to a community." Perrin's

13. Ibid., 76–77, 87, 90, 99.
14. Ibid., 77; Perrin, *Counties*, 322.

pragmatic attitude about Regulators and vigilante movements was common among the Black Patch's better citizens, who saw the violence as necessary to control disorderly groups in society.[15]

Yeomen farmers and townspeople agreed with Regulator action as long as the vigilantes acted within unspoken bounds, by which they meant an orderly manner and a trial even "though it may have been but a drum head court-martial," Perrin reported. Regulators could whip a man and warn him out of the country without the bother of a trial. Such acts ridded the community of people deemed undesirable by those in power. When Alonzo Pennington's brother, Morton—who had fled the county after the hanging—returned to see his sister-in-law, the Regulators set a time limit on his visit. When he tarried too long and Alonzo's widow complained, the Regulators whipped him and sternly warned him to leave the neighborhood.[16]

The widow had maintained a good reputation despite her unfortunate marriage. She realized, though, that her good name was a precious commodity in the community and that to preserve it she could never consort with Pennington's family. Her plea to the Regulators to punish her brother-in-law proved her to be a loyal, decent citizen. She also ensured her children's security in a culture in which one's good name and the perception that one came from an upright moral background were essential to success.[17]

The regulators, who were themselves white, used violence against other whites to establish social control, enforce morality, and maintain order as they and their supporters defined it. A separate system of control and discipline existed in the region, devised by slaveholders to preserve the hegemony of the slave-based society. Whites and blacks learned the value of violence as a means of force, control, and punishment. In the South and the Black Patch, daily subjugation of black slaves became a way of life. Even non-slaveholders served as patrollers who enforced the slave code. Control of slaves always involved the threat of violence. The whip was considered an indispensable tool of the master.[18]

15. Perrin, *Counties*, 81.
16. Ibid., 81–82.
17. Ibid., 82.
18. Joseph B. Killebrew, "Recollections," 32, 55.

Joseph Killebrew, the son of a slaveholder, grew up on a Tennessee Black Patch tobacco plantation where overseers managed the laborers. Some of these supervisors, Killebrew acknowledged, could be very cruel; however, he claimed that "it was to the master's interest to treat his slaves humanely." Even in the Killebrew house, the paternalistic ideal of slave management did not always hold sway. Killebrew claimed that his stepmother was "so prejudiced . . . that she would apparently seek excuses to have these slaves punished, and they were sometimes punished for the most trivial offenses."[19]

Slaves responded to violence in kind. They committed violent acts against other slaves and sometimes against whites, although the latter was a dangerous undertaking. In August of 1837, George Hampton Trigg, an uncle of Mary Catherine Killebrew, "was killed by the negroes or one negro on August 3rd 1837." The fear of slaves taking revenge tormented many white southerners. To prevent uprisings, force and threats of force were vital in the slaveholders' view. Whites' violence against slaves contributed to the cultural pattern of violent behavior. The potential for extremes of violence between whites and blacks in the antebellum period blazed high in 1856.[20]

White fear of potential slave violence was ever-present in the Old South. Rumors of black insurrection could provoke hysterical reactions. Whites believed that large concentrations of slaves provided fertile ground for conspiracy. Some sections of the Black Patch held large black populations, including southern Logan, Todd, and Christian Counties in Kentucky and Robertson and Montgomery Counties in Tennessee. Also in Tennessee, in the land between the Cumberland and Tennessee Rivers, was an iron industry that by 1856 employed nearly three thousand slaves. These bondsmen posed a potent danger in the estimation of whites. In 1856, an insurrection scare began there and swept through the Black Patch.[21]

19. Ibid., 32, 55.
20. Mary Catherine Killebrew, "Recollections of a Lifetime," Tennessee State Library and Archives, Manuscripts Division, Nashville, Tennessee; Lucas, *History of Blacks in Kentucky*, 59–61; Charles B. Dew, "Black Ironworkers and the Slave Insurrection Panic of 1856," 321–39; Harvey Wish, "The Slave Insurrection Panic of 1856," 206–22.
21. Lucas, *History of Blacks in Kentucky*, 59–61; Wish, "Slave Insurrection Panic," 206–9; Dew, "Black Ironworkers," 325.

The election of 1856 aroused southern whites from Texas to the Carolinas. The Buchanan-Fremont presidential campaign, the stories of bloodshed in Kansas, the Dred Scott decision, the beating of Charles Sumner by Preston Brooks, and the rise of the Republican party raised tensions between the sections. The southern press vividly described and hotly debated these political events, increasing the anxiety among southerners. The tension was released in waves of white panic in the wake of alleged slave revolt conspiracies. First in Texas, and later in other southern states, papers began reporting suspected slave plots. These reports spawned wild rumors, creating intense excitement throughout the South and in the Black Patch, where panic struck hardest in the white communities of Stewart and Montgomery Counties, Tennessee. The nineteen thousand white residents outnumbered the twelve thousand slaves living in the two counties, but in some neighborhoods, blacks formed a majority. In the iron industry villages, slaves worked under the oversight of only a few whites. Black Patch papers published conflicting accounts and unsubstantiated details of a slave conspiracy planned for Christmas Day, 1856.[22]

As a result, neighborhoods in the counties quickly organized vigilance patrols. Whites in Clarksville formed a guard to police the county each night. The Clarksville town council restricted slave activity during the holiday season. In Dover, Stewart County, Tennessee, a slave who ran away from the Cumberland Ironworks to avoid joining the plot provided information that allowed the police to arrest eighty slaves along with three men associated with the Free Soil Party. Local officials drove the three whites out of the state, extracted confessions from many of the black men, and finally hanged nineteen slave ironworkers.[23]

The rumors and panic spread into other parts of the Black Patch. In Lafayette, Christian County, whites formed a vigilance committee and asked for military assistance from Hopkinsville, the county seat. Whites in Cadiz, Trigg County, claimed that they had discovered another rebel conspiracy, allegedly led by a free black preacher, Solomon Young. They hanged Young on December 19 and arrested

22. Wish, "Slave Insurrection Panic," 205–11; Dew, "Black Ironworkers," 321–25.
23. Dew, "Black Ironworkers," 210–12.

many others, all of whom were released after the hysteria died. In Logan County, to the east of the ironworks, whites whipped to death a black Tennessee ironworker who happened to be in the county.[24]

During the two months of panic, no slave uprising happened. No whites died. Yet the panic spread to Memphis and across the borders to Arkansas and Missouri. Other states experienced panics during 1856 and 1857 that were not directly connected to the Black Patch, but which indicated the tense emotions of the time. Characteristically, whites vented their political frustrations by acting upon rumors of black revenge with violence.[25]

The insurrection panic of 1856–1857 became part of the folklore of the Black Patch and reinforced the regional acceptance of violence as a solution to problems. For the slaves, the memories of hysterical white violence served to remind them of their place in society and their powerlessness in halting the rampage. For whites, the hysteria confirmed their belief that slave plots and revolts could be controlled by lethal force. Violent heroes and villains figured prominently in the folklore and memories of Black Patch people. Among whites, violent heroes won wars, subdued slaves, and conquered rivals. Blacks created a folklore that included ghost stories and tales warning of white violence. Folklore entertained, educated, and socialized Black Patch people in the ways of the culture, including the violence.[26]

Robert Parker of Caldwell County, Kentucky, always begins his family narrative with a male forbear who "was one of the trouble makers in Lexington" before migrating to Kentucky. Parker described his ancestor as a troublemaker, rather than as a revolutionary patriot. The American rebellion is secondary in a tale in which migration west to Kentucky is paramount. This "troublemaker" claimed a four-hundred-acre war-service land grant, purchased additional acres, and later relished the prestige of having the settlement, Parkersville, named in his honor. The ruffian turned landowner is an honored theme of family histories in the Black Patch. Whether the story is true is irrelevant; the perception of a rough, law-flouting ancestor is

24. Ibid., 212–15.
25. Ibid., 213–19.
26. For information on folklore see Gladys-Marie Fry, *Night Riders in Black Folk History;* Richard M. Dorson, *Handbook of Folklore.*

a matter of pride. People tell the stories to children and outsiders to show the courage, ingenuity, and success of the family.[27]

County histories are replete with tales of courageous violent men. Lyon County traces its founder, Matthew Lyon, to Wicklow County, Ireland, where his father was executed for resisting British landlords. Following his father's death, in 1765, fifteen-year-old Lyon indentured himself to a sea captain and sailed for America. Due to his exemplary service on board the vessel, Lyon's term of service was shortened. Once freed, he worked two years for Ethan Allen at the Allen Iron Works in Salisbury, Connecticut. In 1771, he married Allen's niece and moved to Vermont, where he joined the Green Mountain Boys.[28]

After his first wife died in 1782, Lyon married Beulah Chittenden Galusha, the eldest daughter of Colonel Thomas Chittenden, first governor of Vermont. Lyon helped construct the town of Fair Haven, Vermont, and in 1796 he established a newspaper, the *Fair Haven Gazette*. He turned to politics in 1797 and was elected to Congress. There Lyon had the misfortune to come into conflict with the Federalist party and was indicted and convicted under the sedition laws. He spent four months in prison and was fined one thousand dollars for his crime.[29]

Following his incarceration, Lyon traveled to Tennessee, where he met Andrew Jackson, who suggested he might be happier in a new location in the West. Lyon moved to the busy Cumberland River town of Eddyville in 1801. Once established in the state, he returned to politics and entered the Kentucky state legislature. His Lyon Ship Yards built the first steamboats in the West and made Eddyville a thriving port.[30]

Lyon Countians revere the "Old Fighting Lyon from Vermont," as founding father, wise leader, and brave gentleman. His rise from indentured servitude to fighting Green Mountain Boy, town founder, and national statesman made him a model of success. Matthew Lyon's

27. Robert Parker, interview by author, tape recording, Caldwell County, Kentucky, July 15, 1987; Wyatt-Brown, *Honor and Violence*, 68.

28. Lyon County High School Seniors, *One Century of Lyon County History*, 99–100.

29. Ibid., 100–102.

30. Ibid.

sedition conviction gave him an aura of martyrdom, but one in which he overcame his defeat through individual skill and hard work. His courage and bold action were traits revered in the Black Patch.[31]

John Montgomery, another hero, a Scotch-Irish Revolutionary War veteran who came to the region in the 1780s, founded Clarksville, Tennessee. This settlement grew to be the primary dark-fired tobacco market of the Black Patch. Montgomery also served with George Rogers Clark's Illinois campaign. In 1794, Indians killed him at the mouth of the Cumberland River. His skill as a soldier, frontiersman, hunter, and Indian fighter made him a popular legend and hero. The folklore extolling such characteristics serve as heroic models in the culture and instill respect and fear in outsiders.[32]

Black Patch people still tell of a famous bout that occurred at dawn on May 30, 1806, when two Tennesseans, Maj. Gen. Andrew Jackson—war hero, Indian fighter, and future president—and Charles Dickinson, chose to settle an argument with a duel in a poplar grove on the Red River at Harrison's Mills in Logan County. In Jackson, the Black Patch has its quintessential violent white folk hero.[33]

The affair began over a forfeited horse race between Jackson's horse, Truxton, and Plowboy, a stallion owned by Dickson's father-in-law, Capt. Joseph Ervin. Plowboy went lame, and the race was canceled with Erwin promising to pay eight hundred dollars to Jackson. The affair appeared settled when Jackson heard that Dickinson, during a drinking bout, had insulted his wife, Rachel, by taking her "sacred" name into his "polluted mouth." An incensed Jackson confronted Dickinson and angrily demanded an apology. Dickinson complied, citing drunkenness as the cause.[34]

New problems then arose over the eight hundred dollars Ervin was to pay Jackson for the forfeited race. Gossipers said the notes Ervin offered were not the same as Jackson had chosen. Thomas Swann repeated the tales to Charles Dickinson and began to relay messages between Dickinson and Jackson. At one point, Dickinson told Swann that Jackson had called him a liar, which prompted

31. Ibid., 99–104.

32. Arnow, *Seedtime*, 168.

33. Robert V. Remini, *Andrew Jackson and the Course of American Empire, 1767–1821*, 125–43.

34. Ibid., 136; Wyatt-Brown, *Honor and Violence*, 131–33, 146–53.

Swann to write an indignant letter to Jackson. Jackson replied, calling Dickinson a "base poltroon and a cowardly tale-bearer." Swann then demanded satisfaction as a gentleman in a duel, but Jackson caned him in a tavern, which was considered suitable punishment for a meddler of lesser status. When Dickinson heard of the caning, he wrote Jackson, calling him a coward and revealing his distaste for being called a "tale-bearer." The affair heated up when Swann made it public in the Nashville newspaper. Jackson followed the teaching of his mother, who had long ago told him, "Never tell a lie, nor take what is not your own, nor sue anybody for slander or assault and battery. *Always settle them cases yourself!*" In a published statement, he claimed Swann had been "the puppet and lying valet for a worthless drunken blackguard scoundrel."[35]

Jackson verbally assaulted Nathaniel A. McNairy, a friend and supporter of Swann's and Dickinson's. McNairy challenged Jackson in the paper to "risk yourself for once on equal terms, at least at ten yards." He also insulted Jackson's supporter John Coffee, who challenged McNairy to a duel across the border in Kentucky.[36]

Dickinson was in New Orleans when this exchange occurred. He returned and began attacking Jackson in the newspaper. Jackson, fed up with the insults, challenged him to a duel for bringing dishonor on his name. He chose to meet Dickinson because neither Swann nor McNairy were of equal social station or skill. At the appointed site, the two duelists met; both were aware that Dickinson was the better shot. When the second ordered the call to fire, Dickinson aimed and hit Jackson in the chest. To the surprise of the spectators, he did not fall. Instead, he carefully, deliberately aimed and pulled the trigger. The gun misfired. He recocked and blasted a hole in Dickinson's chest, inflicting a fatal wound. Some in Nashville criticized Jackson for killing when he could have fired in the air or only wounded Dickinson. However, Jackson believed that he deserved satisfaction and that Dickinson meant to kill him. In any case, the duel gave him "a reputation as a fearful, violent vengeful man."[37]

35. Wyatt-Brown, *Honor and Violence*, 137; Charles S. Sydnor, "The Southerner and the Laws," 12.
36. Remini, *Jackson*, 138–39.
37. Ibid., 141–43.

Black Patch people, who admired the heroic, soldierly image of Andrew Jackson, did not worry over the details of the duel. Rather they respected a man who protected his wife's and his own family name in the honorable way, a duel. Families passed along stories of famous violent men, and also, of violent kinsmen, friends, or local toughs. The stories glorified violence and contributed to an acceptance of violent behavior.[38]

In the Black Patch such legends about a man's meanness and fighting prowess preceded him. His tough reputation in the community defined his identity and his place. Aggression became a virtue on the frontier, where the hazards posed by everyday life were constant. In addition, the patriarchal family, strenuous farm labor, the vagaries of agriculture in the wilderness, diseases, sudden death, oppression of slaves, and religious beliefs contributed to a milieu conducive to violent acts and acceptance of violence.[39]

Entertainment for southern white men was also violent. Life was hard on the frontier, but often very dull. Exciting entertainment could relieve the tedium. A rousing brawl could be a vivid, painful experience in which being alive challenged a man and gave daily existence a brutal sense of reality. Even after the fight was over, a story remained to be told and embellished for the benefit of one's family, friends, and enemies. The winner gained prestige, and the loser suffered embarrassment over his diminished status. Both combatants shared in the fact that they had met as equals in a fair, manly contest. These affrays were also vital social happenings that people discussed on court day, at the market, after church, or around the table.[40]

Once the backwoods began to develop into an organized patriarchal, white-dominated, lawful society, a process completed by the 1850s in the Black Patch, the use of violence in some people's lives changed. Black Patch tobacco producers made their livings through semi-subsistence agriculture combined with timbering and herding in the poor hilly areas and by plantation farming in the richer flat

38. For an analysis of Southern dueling see Wyatt-Brown, *Southern Honor;* on duels in Kentucky see J. Winston Coleman, Jr., "The Code Duello in Antebellum Kentucky," 54–62; Elliot J. Gorn, "Gouge, Bite, Pull Hair and Scratch: The Social Significance of Fighting in the Southern Backcountry," 18–43.

39. Gorn, "Gouge, Bite, Pull Hair," 22–24.

40. Ibid., 30–32; Wyatt-Brown, *Honor and Violence,* 131.

lands of the region's southern reaches. Farming in either area was attuned to the rhythms of tobacco cultivation and subject to the natural violence of calamitous crop failures, devastating weather, and harsh living conditions. In the local kin-based society, both communal activities and fierce individualism coexisted.[41]

Some laborers, tenants, middling farmers, and wealthy planters channeled their propensity for violence into competitiveness. Work itself became a contest. Men bragged about their superior skills in tobacco cutting, hanging, and housing. Farmers boasted about their work skills in a way similar to the tall tales told by the frontiersmen of their exploits fighting Indians and wild beasts. "I was always an expert tobacco cutter and I was considered the fastest man in the barn there was in this part of the [Black Patch]," Bob Parker recalled. "I usually worked at the bottom [of the barn while housing the weed] and they usually put two men on the wagon when I was working." In this way, men revealed their physical abilities, skills, and perseverance and also upheld the virtues of the Protestant work ethic in a positive way. The sober farmers took pride in possessing the best-built tobacco barns, the neatest fields and fence rows, the most vigorous tobacco plants, the fattest stock animals, and the best horseflesh. Hunters told wild tales about the abilities of hound dogs during the hunting season, and fishermen found glory at the fish pond where huge catfish awaited their fate.[42]

White women, too, competed on a more subtle level by cooking the finest meals, dressing their children in the prettiest hand sewn clothes, keeping a clean house, a snow white bedspread, and neatly painted white outbuildings, and converting their husbands to religion. The women defined their lives by such achievements because attaining the high standards brought respect and status to a woman and her entire household. Any slips could ruin the reputation of the family for good. Women and children—black and white—were also the victims of violence in the patriarchal families, where authoritarian men ruled their families based on the Old Testament model.[43]

41. Ibid., 34–35.
42. Parker, interview; Gayle McCarty, interview by author, tape recording, Union County, Kentucky, August 25, 1987.
43. Martyne Parker, interview by author, tape recording, Caldwell County,

Women could influence the society, exert powerful control through gossip—the communication of personal information usually through face-to-face contact. Women (and men) gossiped at social events, shared work gatherings, church, the general store, and any place else people came together. Gossip can be negative or positive information, but it is characterized by its judgmental flavor. Black Patch people cared very much about their families' and their own reputations. Negative gossip could destroy reputations, thus it was a powerful tool used by a subordinate group, women, to influence the social order. Among men, negative talk, often called insults rather than gossip, spurred men to fight or duel. Both sexes and races used talk to control the behavior of kin and community.[44]

Long before the 1840s Regulator movements, other means had been used to bring order and morality to the backwoods society in the Black Patch. Although some of the settlers had participated in religious gatherings and established churches prior to emigrating, the western wilderness hardly benefited from church discipline in the frontier days. The Great Awakening swept across the Black Patch in the early 1800s bringing some change, but paradoxically reinforcing the violent culture. Western Kentucky and middle Tennessee remained an unruly place despite the work of regulators, lawmen, and evangelists.

Kentucky, July 15, 1987; Elizabeth Freeman, interview by author, tape recording, Lyon County, Kentucky, July 16, 1987; Mellie McGowan, interview by author, pen and pad, Caldwell County, Kentucky, July 16, 1987; John Bennett, "Food and Social Status in Rural Society," 561–69.

44. Patricia Meyer Spacks, *Gossip* (Chicago: University Press of Chicago, 1985), 34, quoted in Karen V. Hanson, "The Power of Talk in Antebellum New England" (paper presented at the Symposium on Rural Farm Women in Historical Perspective, University of California, Davis, 1992), 1–3, 23–25.

3

AS MEN SLAIN IN BATTLE

I was naturally, a wild, wicked boy, and delighted in horse-racing, card-playing, and dancing," wrote Peter Cartwright about his boyhood. Transgressions like these filled the lives of boys in the Black Patch and proved disturbing to their parents and the community. "My father restrained me but little, though my mother often talked to me, wept over me, and prayed for me, and often drew tears from my eyes." Although he "often wept under preaching, and resolved to do better and seek religion," failure plagued him. "I broke my vows, went into young company, rode races, played cards and danced." Some boys added drinking and fighting to their list of sins and flouted authority by brawling during public gatherings, even church services.[1]

Peter Cartwright grew up with the region. He overcame his wild boyish behavior, became a Methodist minister, and spent his life preaching the gospel and organizing churches in the wake of a powerful spiritual transformation that began in the Black Patch. Logan County proved difficult to tame, but it was there, on the banks of the Red River, that the mighty Second Great Awakening exploded soon after the turn of the nineteenth century; it was to influence southerners' views on and practice of religion for years to come.[2]

Itinerant ministers of various sects ventured into the Black Patch with the first settlers. Cartwright's father allowed a Methodist Episcopal preacher, Jacob Lurton, use of his cabin in 1793 to hold a meeting. Peter notified the neighbors, and they filled the home to overflowing. The Methodist minister "was a real man of thunder. He preached with tremendous power, and the congregation were almost melted to tears," Cartwright recalled years later. "Some cried aloud for mercy, and my mother shouted aloud for joy."[3]

1. Cartwright, *Autobiography*, 31.
2. Moore, *The Frontier Mind*, 38–41.
3. Cartwright, *Autobiography*, 29.

Following this successful assembly, a group of neighbors organized a small class, which Peter's mother joined. Similar classes met in cabins all across the region. Cartwright's met every Sunday and included thirteen members plus a preacher, an exhorter, and a class leader. It survived until 1799 when local revivals increased the number of new converts, enabling the group to build Ebenezer Church in the Cumberland Circuit of the Kentucky District, Western Conference.[4]

Prior to the Great Awakening, the frontier was a disorderly, lawless, violent place. Rowdy communities, like Cartwright's Rogue's Harbor, existed throughout the Black Patch. Since first settlement, the population had grown, and those settlers who had been church members in the East yearned for a spiritual community. The swift transition from frontier towns to settled agricultural society prompted middling and elite whites to long for the coherence, orderliness, and stability that the organized church offered. Settlers were deprived of excitement and the company of others for extended periods of time, and the revivals appealed to people of all races and classes. Congregants camped at the revival site, gathered around glowing fires after the preaching and singing ended, and enjoyed the company. Everyone sang rousing hymns, which drew together the illiterate and the educated. From these simple hymns, worshipers learned the meaning of their religion and passed it on to the next generation. "The old timey songs," said Henry Baggett, "there's more sermons in these religious songs than anybody getting up preaching."[5]

Southern upcountry Protestant religion's formation began during the frontier awakenings of the early nineteenth century. A revival of spirit first flamed in June 1800 at Red River in Logan County. Another flared up at the first camp meeting site at Gasper River in the hot days of July. A witness to these outpourings of the spirit, Barton W. Stone, carried the zeal to Bourbon County, Kentucky, where he sparked a revival at Cane Ridge Church in the late summer of 1801 that drew thousands of sinners, men and women, black and white.

4. Ibid., 30.

5. Bruce, *And They All Sang Hallelujah,* 13–15, 90–95, 96–122; Henry Baggett, interview by author, tape recording, Robertson County, Tennessee, July 14, 1987.

"Hundreds," recalled Cartwright, "fell prostrate under the mighty power of God, as men slain in battle."[6]

From this camp meeting, claimed Cartwright, "the news spread through all the Churches, and through all the land, and it excited great wonder." Moreover, the Great Revival "kindled a religious flame that spread all over Kentucky and through many other states." It brought a huge increase in church membership among the Baptists, Methodists, and the Cumberland Presbyterians. In 1800 the six Baptist associations had just 4,766 members; two years later the rolls had swelled to 13,569 brothers and sisters. The Western Conference of the Methodist Church of Kentucky and Tennessee claimed 3,030 souls in 1800, but by 1805 the sect possessed 10,158 converts.[7]

Congregations built churches to hold the worshipers as the Black Patch expanded, adding to the network already in place. "Even in Rogue's Harbor," wrote Cartwright, "there was a Baptist Church, a few miles west of my father's and a Presbyterian congregation a few miles north and Methodist Ebenezer, a few miles south." They were all a part of the neighborhood geography so characteristic of the Black Patch. Eventually, there were at least three or four congregations within walking or mule-riding distance from each family's homestead. Christian County converts formed Little River Baptist Church in 1804 during the height of the Great Revival. Yeomen farmers organized Lyon County's New Bethel Baptist Church in April of 1812 at the home of John Cammuch. Often a new congregation arose from a defunct group or split off from a viable one as the result of a dispute or simply in order to build a church closer to members. At New Bethel, members constructed a building, and whites and blacks worshiped together there until the Civil War. However, slaves recognized that there was no equality among congregants. They sat in the back or in the balcony and received communion last. They understood that white preachers taught slaves subservience and obedience. Religion in the hands of white ministers was a form of social control. As often as possible, slaves sought to worship independently by meet-

6. John B. Boles, *Religion in Antebellum Kentucky*, 23–27; Bruce, *And They All Sang Hallelujah*, 51–58; Cartwright, *Autobiography*, 34; Albert J. Raboteau, *Slave Religion: The "Invisible Institution" of the Antebellum South*, 59–60.

7. Cartwright, *Autobiography*, 29; Boles, *Religion in Kentucky*, 29.

ing late at night protected by an upside-down kettle placed nearby, which caught the noise of the faithful. In Bowling Green, Kentucky, the First Baptist Church's black members used the whites' sanctuary for separate services until 1845, when they built their own place of worship.[8]

The Great Awakening arose and flourished, allowing the white lower and middling groups to assert power and build a community in their image. For blacks, religion provided a haven and release from the agonies of slavery; the church was a place of respect, liberty, and equality among black congregants. In the Black Patch, the Awakening powerfully reinforced the whites' view of a strict, vengeful God who would condemn them to a fiery hell if they failed to repent their sins and accept Jesus Christ. Revivalists like Cartwright and Samuel McGready preached that unless one repented "he [was] lost and damned forever." Violence, now condoned by an Old Testament–based religion, became more deeply rooted in the Black Patch culture.[9]

Many of the people who attended the revivals respected preachers like Peter Cartwright because they had been raised in the backwoods. These men possessed a deep understanding and empathy for the lives of their neighbors and converts. They had the advantage of knowing the people well and could intuitively sense how best to appeal to the sinners among them and bring their souls to God through songs, emotional orations, and prayers. Cartwright "melted" one congregation to tears after he "gave out a hymn, sang, and prayed" then preached on "the text of Isaiah xxvi, 4: 'Trust ye in the Lord forever: for in the Lord Jehovah is everlasting strength.'" The God, Jehovah, gave the believer the power to withstand temptation and trouble. Jehovah was also the powerful, warriorlike manifestation of God, the violent deity. Cartwright and the other revivalists

8. Cartwright, *Autobiography,* 30–33; John R. Stilgoe, *Common Landscapes of America: 1580–1845,* 72–74, 81–83, 240–45. Perrin, *Counties,* 146; Meacham, *History,* 306; "Fiftieth Anniversary Edition—Organization of Churches," Lyon County *Herald-Ledger,* supplement, September 19, 1974; Marion Williams, *The Story of Todd County, Kentucky, 1820–1970,* 278–79; Lucas, *History of Blacks in Kentucky,* 118–20; Raboteau, *Slave Religion,* 59–60.

9. Donald G. Mathews, *Religion in the Old South,* xiv–xv; Gregory, "Origins of Violence," (12) contains McGready's quote, which is from Cleveland, *The Great Revival in the West,* 45–57; Eunice McCarty, interview; Bailey, *Southern White Protestantism,* 3.

were familiar with the local belief in the Old Testament God and the rough, violent customs of the backcountry. They did not shrink from violence if it was necessary to save a soul from the devil.[10]

Peter Cartwright feared no one and even employed physical force to convert the unruly masses at the camp meetings. After being assigned to the Scioto Circuit of the Ohio District in 1805, Cartwright preached at a camp meeting where a "collection of rabble and rowdies," like those he had seen in Kentucky, harassed him during the service. Two young men entered the tent and stood in the congregation talking and laughing. Cartwright asked them to be seated and listen, but they did not heed his warning. Two magistrates were afraid to arrest the men, so Cartwright told the officers "as I left the stand, to command me to take them, and I would do it at the risk of my life."[11]

He moved toward the men, and "one of them made a pass at my head with his whip, but I closed in with him, and jerked him off the seat. A regular scuffle ensued." He threw his opponent down and threatened to "pound his chest well." To Cartwright, "it seemed at the moment that I had not power to resist temptation, and I struck a sudden blow in the burr of the ear and dropped him to the earth." The violent scene ruined the night's preaching and disturbed the worshipers, but Cartwright believed he had acted correctly in attacking the disorderly men. He went on to preach the next day that "the gates of hell will not prevail."[12]

Incidents similar to this occurred in Black Patch country churches of all denominations throughout the nineteenth and twentieth centuries. Eunice McCarty recalled a time in the 1920s "when a protracted meeting was going on at Pleasant Hill [Baptist], our home church." During the sermon "a bunch of boys were sitting on the back seat acting up." The preacher, "Brother Rhodes . . . [who] had such a loud voice he waked [sic] up every sleeping baby" grew upset at the boys' behavior. He interrupted his sermon and said, "You fellows back there, especially the one slinging his head of hair like a slobbering horse, straighten up and respect the House of God!"[13]

10. Cartwright, *Autobiography*, 54; Boles, *Religion in Kentucky*, 14; Gregory, "Origins of Violence," 10; Bruce, *Violence and Culture*, 17, 112.

11. Cartwright, *Autobiography*, 70–73.

12. Ibid.

13. Eunice McCarty, letter to the author, October 29, 1988.

The excitement of the camp meetings stood in sharp contrast to the dull routine of the daily round of farm life. People of all denominations traveled to the meetings seeking both spiritual renewal and the opportunity to socialize. The large crowds of young folks found in the revivals not just social opportunities, but perhaps, a way to traverse the rocky path from childhood to adulthood and to find a source of identity and community in the evangelical religion.[14]

Religion was a potent force in the minds of individuals in the Black Patch, and partly as a result of the frontier revivals, a religious folk culture arose and spread across the South. Although the religion emphasized saving individual souls, the churches, besides filling an evangelistic goal, also functioned to impose order on society, to create a community based on middling class values such as sobriety, the work ethic, and Protestant morality. Church trials in the Baptist Saturday business sessions brought sinning members before the congregation to confront them with their lapses in behavior and urge them to repent and return to the church. Members welcomed backsliders, who had committed sins of drinking, dancing, fighting, even adultery, back into the congregation and the community if they confessed their guilt, apologized, and asked to be reinstated. There were powerful incentives for sinners to do so. For many, exclusion from the church also meant ostracism by the community. In neighborhoods where ties were established over generations, such condemnation by kin and friends could be painful and persuasive.[15]

Evangelical Old Testament teachings guided parents in the discipline of their children. Preachers exhorted about the God Jehovah, who meted out harsh punishment to his recalcitrant children among the Christian flock. The earthly father, in the role of Christian patriarch, applied discipline with varying degrees of severity when children (or slaves) disobeyed. The woman, mother of the family, subordinate to Jehovah and man, obeyed both and oversaw the rearing of

14. Boles, *Religion in Kentucky*, 21; Bruce, *And They All Sang Hallelujah*, 54.

15. Boles, *Religion in Kentucky*, 30–31; Macedonia Baptist Church Records, Department of Library Special Collections, Western Kentucky University, Bowling Green, Kentucky; Eunice McCarty, interview.

the children on a daily basis. "Spare the rod and spoil the child" was a saying repeated often by Black Patch parents. In the early nineteenth century, parents sought to break the will of their young children. By the late nineteenth century, the aim had changed; parents sought to bend and mold their children's personalities. Corporal punishment still occurred, and Black Patch parents justified it by claiming it was the way to ensure that a child grew into a responsible moral adult. In reality violent forms of discipline taught children violence and contributed to its persistence in society.[16]

The connections between violence and religion in the Black Patch culture derives in part from the beliefs and values drawn from the Old and New Testaments of the Bible. The Second Great Awakening permitted converts to emphasize an individual's relationship with God. Each individual had to go through conviction—the realization of one's inherent sinfulness; wrestle with physical desires; and finally succumb to the second birth and surrender to Jesus. The conversion experience could be a long, agonizing struggle. For white men, especially, it was like a battle against one's sinful nature. A young man fought the evil within himself and emerged from the baptismal waters a believer. He could then go on to settle down in the community as a stable, hardworking farmer. If he did backslide, annual revivals offered the chance to renew his commitment and be forgiven. "Back then people were interested in the salvation of souls," Bob Parker, a white farmer recalled, "if there was a young person that wasn't a member of the church—they were sort of wild—a half a dozen people would go and talk to them during revival meetings." This urging might bring a sinner or backslider to Jesus and back into the community.[17]

For white women, the conversion experience was less a violent struggle and more a losing or surrendering of self and identity to Christ. Just as she became one with Christ, subject to his plan for her life, she later submitted to her husband's authority in marriage. She was expected to embrace her role as cheerful, willing servant to God, hus-

16. Theory on violent discipline is from studies by Alice Miller, *For Your Own Good: Hidden Cruelty in Child Rearing and the Roots of Violence*, translated by Hildegarde Hunnum and Hunter Hunnum; Philip Greven, *Spare the Child: The Religious Roots of Punishment and the Psychological Impact of Physical Abuse*.

17. Parker, interview; Bruce, *And They All Sang Hallelujah*, 63–70.

band, family, and community. Many women experienced conversion as teenagers, while boys waited longer, often until after marriage.[18]

Part of the wife's role involved bringing her husband to religion if he had not been converted. "He said I led him to be a Christian," recalls Eunice McCarty, about the words of her husband after he joined the Baptist Church. McCarty's parents reared her in a "good Christian home." They attended church regularly, her father served as deacon and "tithed all of his life," she says. McCarty's mother, Nancy Stovall, had led her husband to religion.[19]

White and black women transmitted religious values and morals in the Black Patch culture. Although they could not speak up or hold positions of authority in the church, they made up the majority of active members. Wives and mothers served as moral, pious examples of the community. They reared their children to follow godly, moral paths; sought to convert wayward husbands and sons; and gave succor to the needy.[20]

Before the Civil War, slaves and free blacks sought a conversion experience, called "mourning," which involved one's going away alone to contemplate one's life and sins and to pray for relief. Conversion usually followed this emotional trial. Camp meetings and revivals also spurred born-again experiences. The newly born then joined the community of believers whose religion served to comfort them during slavery and later, after emancipation, served as a conduit for struggle against social, economic, and political oppression.[21]

Churchgoing men and women possessed a fundamental faith in the inerrancy of the Scriptures. Upon the Old and New Testaments they based their system of morals, and they focused on the world to come rather than on the ills of secular society. Still, the church prescribed correct behavior for living in the world, usually designated as things the godly would not do, such as commit adultery, gamble, dance, or violate any of the Ten Commandments. Lives would

18. Elizabeth Price, interview by author, pen and pad, Southern Baptist Theological Seminary, Louisville, Kentucky, May 1987; Eunice McCarty, interview.
19. Eunice McCarty, interview.
20. Ibid.; *Cadiz Record*, March 2, 1908; Grace Smith Stovall, interview by author, Lyon County, Kentucky, July 16, 1987.
21. Raboteau, *Slave Religion*, 73.

be changed through the conversion of individual souls to the straight and narrow pathway to heaven. Ultimately, society would be transformed when reborn Christians set the example for others to follow in their daily living.[22]

Although Baptist, Methodist, and Church of Christ members testified to their belief in the teachings of Jesus, they acted upon the basis of years of study of the Old Testament god, Jehovah. Fatalism dominated—God, the wrathful authoritarian father, ruled their lives. Satan, the evil demon, vied with God for their mortal souls. Spiritual existence resembled a battle, a fight between the forces of good and evil. Old Testament commandments served as the model for morality in the Black Patch. Whites and blacks took such teachings as "an eye for an eye," literally and used them to justify brawling and even vengence. Their dualistic ideas allowed believers to deny responsibility for their own actions by blaming either God or Satan for their misfortunes. When mistakes were made, the loving forgiveness of Jesus saved them from damnation.[23]

The theology of blacks was based on Old and New Testament scripture. Preachers described a punishing God, who scrutinized his flock on Judgment Day, condemning sinners to hell to pay for their transgressions. But black ministers also compared their enslaved congregations to the children of Israel, who were freed by God and led from bondage by Moses. Black theology based on the New Testament told of Jesus the suffering child, a forgiving, loving savior. Both texts taught slaves that a better world existed elsewhere. Whites heard these sermons too, and they often expressed surprise at the good message and fine delivery of the slave ministers.[24]

Until the 1920s, life on the frontier and in the Black Patch remained difficult. The Old Testament God of wrath and vengeance fit

22. Bailey, *Southern White Protestantism*, 17–20; John Eighmy, *Churches in Cultural Captivity: A History of the Social Attitudes of Southern Baptists;* John Shelton Reed, *The Enduring South: Subcultural Persistence in Mass Society*, 59–60.

23. Eunice McCarty, interview; Bagget, interview; Parker, interview; Grace Stovall, interview; Gregory, "Origins of Violence," 9–14; Bruce, *Violence and Culture*, 18, 44, 48, 50, 64–66; Cash, *Mind of the South*, 79–82; Bailey, *Southern White Protestantism*, 3; Pete Daniel, *Breaking the Land: The Transformation of Cotton, Tobacco, and Rice Cultures since 1880*, 191–92.

24. Lucas, *History of Blacks in Kentucky,* 133; Mathews, *Religion in the Old South*, xv.

well in the precarious environment. An angry god might punish a farmer with a crop-flattening hailstorm or a barn fire. Black Patch people attributed tragedy to God's hand. Ferd Stovall believed the sudden death of his baby daughter was a punishment for his backsliding and moving away from the church. After the child's death, he vowed to return to the Friendship Baptist Church as a faithful member.[25]

Life itself could be perceived as an ongoing battle between God and Satan with the human soul as the trophy. Human rivalry and bloodletting reflected the symbolic struggle between Good and Evil. God and Satan fought, people fought, and individuals struggled against their basic instincts to preserve their souls. Popular hellfire-and-brimstone sermons emphasized God's actions toward sinners who refused to repent.[26] Harsh penalties, modeled on punishments of an angry God, were meted to violators of community standards. Elite and middle-class whites saw no contradiction in enforcing morals with violence.[27]

Theology, as it was understood by whites and blacks, influenced thought and action. Believers viewed God and the devil as powerful forces far beyond human reach or comprehension. One could never understand the mysterious hand of God in human affairs. The sole source of authority became the Bible—the written word of God. Here the truth lay, as Henry Baggett declared, "You're supposed to go by the Bible. And these folks are supposed to live by the rules." If one did not live by the commandments and fear God, one might become an outcast. Baggett continued, "And folks say 'Oh, you don't want a child to be afraid.' They have got to be afraid of something! Man or beast or God or something!" Without such terror, Baggett exclaimed with a pounding of his fist on his rocking chair, things could happen: "If I wasn't afraid of what'd happen to me if I didn't do nothing wrong, I'd just go out there and kill anybody that I didn't like! There's

25. Eunice McCarty, interview.
26. Bertram Wyatt-Brown, "Religion and the Formation of Folk Culture," in *The Americanization of the Gulf Coast*, vol. 3, ed. Lucien Ellsworth (Pensacola: Historic Pensacola Preservation Board, 1972), 24–26; Rufus B. Spain, *At Ease in Zion: Social History of Southern Baptists 1865–1900*," 9–14.
27. Lyon County Circuit Court, grand jury indictments, 1890–1920, circuit court clerk's office, Eddyville, Kentucky; Eunice McCarty, interview.

got to be something there that you'll be afraid of what'll happen to you in the hereafter!"[28]

Religion and violence were closely intertwined in the Black Patch culture. They symbolized the struggle between good and evil in individuals and in society. As the frontier receded, religion and morals as espoused by the Protestant churches, which were supported by elite and middling farmers, dominated, but that morality incorporated violence. Men of God did not hesitate to use violence, and society followed their lead. The Todd County Elkton *Register* commented on an affray between two Mt. Sterling rivals, Corneilison and Reid, by advising that Reid should have acted as a Todd County preacher did when a parishioner struck him—and knocked his attacker down. The *Register* further editorialized, "There is an unwritten law that must be obeyed as well as the law that is written, and it keeps many a rascal in his proper place."[29]

28. Baggett, interview; Lucas, *History of Blacks in Kentucky,* 120.
29. *Elkton Register*, quoted in Robert M. Ireland, "Homicide in Nineteenth-Century Kentucky," 150.

4

WAR IN ALL ITS HORROR

J uly is ended and the most horrible month ever. . . . War in all its horror! Brother against brother, friend against friend, the children of this great country fighting to destroy it," wrote Johanna Underwood in 1861. Although her family's Warren County plantation was worked by slaves, she remained a strong Union loyalist like her father, Warner Underwood. The consequences of taking such a stance in heavily pro-secessionist south central Kentucky became increasingly hard as the war came to the Black Patch. Johanna's father and uncle recalled, "The places in old Virginia, familiar and hallowed . . . by all the memories of their boyhood, now the scenes of bloody battles." The brothers mourned the division of their beloved country. "Poor old Uncle Henry says but little but as the news is read the tears roll fast down the furrows of his cheeks," Johanna observed. Warner commented to Henry one day, "It is hard brother that we are not younger men," and Henry replied solemnly, "Maybe it is best for us we are not." Johanna sensed the poignancy of the conversation. She realized "the dear old man was thinking he would be in the Rebel army and he knew Pa's loyalty to the Union could not be shaken." Black Patch folks, white and black, faced a time of anxiety, turmoil, political strife, and economic devastation never experienced before. The civil conflict ripped the region apart and escalated the violent tendencies of the Black Patch in a torrent of bloody chaos.[1]

The Black Patch region was perfectly situated for the clash of Northern and Southern armies. Union sympathizers in Kentucky at first hoped that the state could maintain neutrality. Warner Underwood thought the Union could be saved "if the border states stand firm." To reach that aim and "in the hope of saving Kentucky and

1. Johanna L. Underwood Nazro, diary, typescript, Kentucky Library and Museum, Western Kentucky University, Bowling Green, Kentucky, 64.

preventing her passing an ordinance of Secession, Uncle Joseph Underwood and a number of other prominent old men of the state who had retired from politics have again entered and been elected" to the Kentucky legislature, wrote Joanna. "They are trying to keep Kentucky *neutral*—but this is pretty hard in these trying times when every man, woman, and child is wrought up to the highest pitch of excitement."[2]

Keeping Kentucky in the Union would not be easy, Underwood knew. "The hardship of the position of Unionists in Tennessee and Kentucky, like Pa, Uncle Joe, and others is that they are just as much opposed to Lincoln and his policy as the secessionists are and Pa was a Bell and Everett Elector and did all in his power—to prevent Lincoln's election." Warner Underwood thought secession unconstitutional and he believed that "for that very reason all true patriots should stand true to the old flag and to the whole country." The elder Underwood opposed "secession *most*—out of his love for the south, for disunion will be her ruin—for if this is war—it will surely be in the South and the whole land desolated and laid waste and slavery will certainly go if the Union is dissolved." The elder statesmen, Johanna Underwood explained, hoped to keep Kentucky in the United States and work for Southern rights through the political system.[3]

In her view as well as her father's, the prominent men, the political leaders, tended to be loyal to the United States. Generational differences divided the people, however, she explained, because "many of these men have—wild reckless unthinking inexperienced sons—who make so much noise [about] secession as to almost drown their fathers [*sic*] wiser council." Class differences also appeared important to Johanna Underwood. In her estimation, "The unthinking hotheads and blatherskites are in for secession. They want change and excitement and 'War' (Warh) as that simpleton Bob Cox says." Cox, Johanna claimed, "never did a days honest work in his life—owns nothing and lives on Uncle Joe—(his brother-in-law)." While Johanna's Uncle Joe worked to preserve the Union, Cox trotted about the community on Joe's finest horse calling for secession. Johanna commented angrily that she would not be so tolerant. If it were up to

2. Ibid., 34–35.
3. Ibid., 16–17.

her "Mr. Robert Cox would have to secede from my home—pretty quick or keep his mouth shut."[4]

The Underwoods believed that the majority of Confederate sympathizers in Bowling Green came from the lower classes. Marion Henry, a young man staying at Mount Air with the Underwoods, returned with the mail one day and reported on the large pro-Confederate crowd that met the train. He declared that all the "'riff raff' in town was up there and when the train came in and when it started off they all yelled 'hurrah for Jeff Davis.'" The Underwoods believed Union sentiment dominated the county and Kentucky, but since "the Rebels have so many rowdies they make the most noise." Johanna added an incisive political comment that the Southerners had "the advantage of having admiration for the man Jeff Davis whilst the Kentucky unionists despise Lincoln and fear his policy." Black Patch whites had long seen social outsiders, or "riff raff," of the community as the troublemakers. Similarly, Black Patch Confederates described Unionists as the worst element in society. Defining opponents as the lower class helped people to justify their growing animosity.[5]

Even as the Underwoods worked for union, some Confederate sympathizers, a large group in the slaveholding southern section of the Black Patch, met in Russellville, Logan County, during October 1861 to forge constitutional ties with the Confederacy. Trigg Countian Henry C. Burnett led the convention in its move to declare Kentucky an independent state. The delegates set up a provisional government headed by the planter George W. Johnson and chose Bowling Green in Warren County as the capital. But the Kentucky Confederate alliance did not stand. The state remained in the Union, though citizens, especially those from Black Patch counties with large slave populations, such as Christian, Todd, and Logan, supported the Confederacy. White men from the region headed south to join Rebel brigades. Cautious elders worried about the war fervor of the young men. Logan County planter and Methodist minister George R. Browder wrote, "There is an alarming disposition in the minds of the boys to run away to the Southern army." In the fall of 1862, several neighborhood boys "from 15 to 17 years old have run away & enlisted and

4. Ibid., 35–37.
5. Ibid., 37–38.

even smaller boys are full of the spirit of war and their very natures seem to delight in hating the Yankees." Youthful Unionists also longed to join the forces. Johanna Underwood's brother left for the Federal camp immediately after his fifteenth birthday. "The dear brave boy with a man's courage and patriotism—He has been mustered in as 1st Lieut. in the 9th Ky infty and there will be no man in the regiment who will do his duty as a soldier better than this beloved brother." Fired with patriotism, Black Patch boys on both sides clamored for war unaware of the agonies to come.[6]

Among adherents of the Confederacy, the Black Patch tendency to distrust outsiders turned to hatred of the northern "invaders" when they seemed to threaten the homeland. Browder believed that the rash acts of the youth and the rising of disorderly elements of society were "great evil[s] & betoken[ed] an alarming recklessness in the coming generations." His thoughts reflected the Black Patch cultural tension between individualistic action and community well-being when he mused: "There is a great need of a firmer and more scriptural family government." Younger men who were anxious to fight before analyzing the consequences of civil strife threatened the Black Patch culture, which elders like Browder and Underwood had worked to build and unify. Yet another Black Patch cultural tendency—to respond to threats with violence—manifested itself among the younger generation. Depending on one's political views, one could side with either the Union or the Confederacy and still argue for the position of protecting one's home and way of life. Neighbors and friends saw the confounding issues of the war differently, dividing the Black Patch into factions. Some people staunchly supported the Union while others rallied around the new Confederacy, and still others wavered or sided with the group that best served their interests at a particular moment. Robbers and guerrillas arose from among these opportunists.[7]

As discord grew and war loomed, Black Patch whites agonized over sectional loyalties. Men true to the Union rushed to join the

---

6. Richard Troutman, ed., *The Heavens Are Weeping: The Diaries of George R. Browder, 1852–1886,* 136 (hereafter cited as Troutman, *Diaries*). Nazro, diary, 101.

7. Lowell H. Harrison, *The Civil War in Kentucky,* 20–21; Troutman, *Diaries,* 133, 136; Nazro, diary, 101.

forces of the United States. Joseph F. Anderson's farm near Hopkinsville, Christian County, served as a gathering site for Black
Patch Unionists. Between five hundred and one thousand men mustered to arms at "Camp Joe Anderson" under the leadership of Col.
James F. Buckner. A cavalry unit commanded by Capt. John W.
Breathitt was organized near Calhoun in December 1861. Soldiers
from Kentucky regiments fought at Sacramento, Kentucky; Shiloh
and Stones River, Tennessee; and Chickamauga, Georgia.[8]

After desperate attempts to forge a compromise, John C. Breckinridge left Washington and took leadership of the Confederate First
Kentucky Brigade, known as the Orphan Brigade, which Southern
secessionists organized on October 28, 1861, in the pro-South Black
Patch town of Bowling Green. The "Orphans," as the troops were
known, fought in every major battle in the western campaign from
Shiloh to Atlanta, suffering such heavy casualties that only 240 of
the 1,065 men who joined prior to Atlanta lived to surrender in
North Carolina in 1865.[9]

Many Black Patch whites struggled to decide their allegiance.
Tennessean Jeremiah W. Cullom wrote that "first my sympathies
were from the start with the South. But hoping that wise counsels
would prevail and the war be averted, I voted against separation
when that subject was brought before us in Tennessee." When fighting began, however, "Abraham Lincoln called for troops from my
state to fight the southern states. And from the hour I read his
Proclamation my mind was made up. I took sides with the South."
On May 25, 1861, Rev. Jeremiah Cullom joined the Twenty-fourth
Tennessee Brigade as a private despite some worry over whether a
preacher ought to be a fighter. Later, his fellow soldiers elected him
chaplain.[10]

For many Southern sympathizers, the decision to fight came, as it

8. Perrin, *Counties*, 183–89.

9. Thomas D. Clark, *Kentucky: Land of Contrasts*, 142–43; William C. Davis,
The Orphan Brigade: The Kentucky Confederates Who Couldn't Go Home, 35.
The Orphan Brigade was made up of Second, Fourth, Fifth, and Sixth Kentucky
Infantry and their accompanying artillery batteries.

10. Jeremiah W. Cullom Papers, Tennessee State Library and Archives, Manuscripts Division, Nashville, Tennessee, 25–29; Stephen B. Ash, *Middle Tennessee
Society Transformed 1860–1870: War and Peace in the Upper South*, 69–72.

did for Cullom, after the Union raised an army against them. They believed in fighting for defense of homes and land. Slaveholders or not, they believed a northern invasion could not be permitted without a struggle. Preserving and defending the hearth, homeland, and way of life from outsiders remained a Black Patch as well as a Southern tradition. Those who perceived the Union war aims as a threat to their livelihood, customs, and beliefs viewed the North's soldiers as alien aggressors. In the Black Patch, whites had long used violent means when serious threats arose. After the firing on Fort Sumter, former conservatives in Clarksville decided to secede, and in April 1861, they raised a bright Confederate flag over the county courthouse. Members of the religious community followed suit in July when the First Presbyterian Church of Clarksville sent word to church leaders to sever ties with their northern brethren. In Cheatham and Robertson Counties, Tennessee, officials organized local regiments to protect the area and initiated a census of weapons. The press urged unity.[11]

During the winter of 1861–1862, Ulysses S. Grant amassed an army in western Kentucky, near Paducah. That February, Grant's western campaign force broke camp at the confluence of the Ohio and Mississippi Rivers and pushed up the Tennessee and Cumberland Rivers to Forts Henry and Donelson in the heart of the Black Patch, inflicting a debilitating defeat upon the Confederate armies. Grant's forces then headed into middle Tennessee and captured the premier Black Patch tobacco market center, Clarksville, on February 19, 1862. On the eastern edge of the Black Patch, Union forces guarded the Louisville and Nashville Railroad, which crossed the Green River on its route to Bowling Green and Nashville, Tennessee. These Federal regiments invaded Nashville, forcing the city to surrender on February 24, 1862, and effectively ending Confederate control of the region for the remainder of the conflict. While Confed-

11. Ash, *Middle Tennessee*, 72–74; Gustavus W. Dyer and John Trotwood Moore, comps., Colleen Norse Eliott and Louise Armstrong Moxley, eds., *The Tennessee Civil War Veterans Questionnaires*, vols. 1–5 (Easley, S.C.: Southern Historical Press, Inc.), vol. 1: 168, 274, 277; vol. 2: 640, 656, 690, 702, 745, 758, 782, 795, 803; vol. 3: 1067, 1109, 1110, 1130, 1148, 1149, 1168, 1251, 1261; vol. 4: 1444, 1467, 1457, 1478, 1496, 1554, 1595, 1633; vol. 5: 1794, 1861, 1888, 1908, 1910, 2042, 2131, 2153, 2165.

erates occupied the area, Unionists suffered. When the North regained the Black Patch, rebel supporters faced trouble. Ultimately, civilians on both sides were victimized by robbing bands, guerrillas.[12]

Slaves knew of the approaching conflict and worried about the outcome. In the meantime, conditions deteriorated. Harassment by whites increased. In some towns and counties, vagrancy laws began to be strictly enforced to control blacks' movements. Slavery remained a reality through most of the war years. However, in areas controlled by Union forces, slaves freed themselves and joined the camp followers, causing serious logistical problems for the Federal forces.[13]

During the parts of 1861 and 1862 in which Southern forces held sway in the region, Unionists found themselves cast out and subject to persecution. "The feelings between the rebels and Union people gets bitterer and bitterer as the war goes on," wrote Johanna Underwood in April 1862. "Lizzie Wright sits on her porch just across the street and I on ours and merely the coldest of bows and never a visit now." Johanna's family plantation served as the Confederate camp in Warren County. She watched her beloved home destroyed as the soldiers foraged for supplies. She saw "the fields all trodden and fences being burned." But, she recorded in October 1861, "tonight as I looked out from my windows at the tents shining white in the moon light with here and there a camp fire and hear the various bugle calls from far off and near—there is something thrilling and beautiful in it all, in spite of the underlying and ever abiding sadness." The Black Patch people witnessed the realities of civil war as friendships cooled, families and kin divided over war loyalties, and society cracked along many tense lines.[14]

Black Patch slaves experienced increased hardships beginning in the summer of 1862. Both the Confederates and the Federals impressed black men, slave and free, for labor. Their women and children were left to fend for themselves, or they, too, were forced to work—as nurses, laundresses, or servants. The United States Army paid Unionist slaveholders for their servants' work, but if the master

12. Ash, *Middle Tennessee*, 83. For details on the Civil War in Kentucky and Tennessee, see Harrison, *Civil War in Kentucky;* and Robert E. Corlew, *Tennessee: A Short History*.

13. Lucas, *History of Blacks in Kentucky,* 146–49.

14. Nazro, diary, 87, 143–44.

was a Southern sympathizer, the slave received the wages. Kentucky blacks did most of the fortifying, trench digging, and other menial tasks for the Union forces in the state. Eventually, they also joined the army. At first, Kentucky was exempted from providing black soldiers. Then, in 1863, Lincoln permitted a census of Kentucky's draft-age blacks, which revealed that there were 1,650 free blacks and 40,285 slaves residing in the state available to fight. The U.S. government by 1864 also offered protection for slaves who volunteered. Three hundred blacks came to Bowling Green in a single month to offer their services.[15]

"There has been a very remarkable smoke or haze darkening the air all day—causing considerable curiosity and speculation," observed Logan County Methodist preacher George Richard Browder one July evening in 1862. "My heart is sad over the evils that threaten us. I fear Ky will be again the dark & bloody ground. Guerrilla bands are hovering over the state & enmity grows deeper and hatred intensifies as the federals increase their intolerance to Secessionists." The Black Patch people had long known violence, but the devastating social strife of a divisive war drove Browder to despair: "Oh the desolations of our country! When will our calamities end? Sick of war & its woes I turn my eyes to the 'Hill whence cometh my help'— and pray God to guide me & mine in peace & safety."[16]

Throughout the war years, all Black Patch residents suffered at the hands of the marauding guerrilla bands who showed loyalty to neither side. Soldiers fought battles and skirmishes in Hopkinsville in Christian County, Saratoga Church in Lyon County, and near Russellville in Logan County. The region had areas with abundant food crops, such as southern Christian, Todd, and Logan Counties in Kentucky and middle Tennessee, and it became a prime source of food and forage for the armies and marauding bandits. Kentuckians and Tennesseeans knew the meaning of brother killing brother.[17]

In communities where the majority of citizens were Confederates, the familiar violent methods of control were used against Union

15. Lucas, *History of Blacks in Kentucky*, 149–53, 155–58.

16. Troutman, *Diaries,* 117.

17. Harrison, *Civil War in Kentucky*, 43; Perrin, *Counties*, 174–78; Troutman, *Diaries*, 133; Clark, *Land of Contrasts*, 142–43; Ash, *Middle Tennessee*, 83.

loyalists, slaves, and free blacks to maintain unity. Racial violence escalated as rumors of slave revolts spread. Black Patch Unionists also employed violence to gain and maintain power and to subjugate the region's Confederate sympathizers.[18]

White men and women in the region who supported the Confederacy showed their belief in the rightness of their cause in various ways. George Browder's mother "took down the engraving of David slaying Goliath in the name of the Lord, & showed it to the soldiers who staid [sic] at her house last night." She used the religious illustration to bolster the confidence of Southern soldiers who had had their first experience in warfare. Black Patch whites had long accepted the Old Testament's warlike Jehovah as their God. Browder's mother believed, as did many others, that violence in his name was justified. The old woman, Browder continued, urged the soldiers "to trust in the God of David & seek help from him." They and many other Southerners believed that God sanctioned their cause. Not until the last devastating years of the war did they begin to doubt God's allegiance to the South.[19]

Men, women, and children used violence to protect and defend their homes. Mary Walker Meriwether Bell, Browder recorded, "acted very boldly telling the Yankees that she was willing to be killed if they desired—that her murder would fill up rebel ranks and that was her desire." She proclaimed her beliefs after fending off Union soldiers "with a Bowie knife and forbade them to ascend the stairs where she had hid her money." Mary Bell lashed out at the soldiers and "cut the guns & tried to stab the men with her knife & finally took [Major] Mansfields [sic] pistol from him & would have shot him with it, but he ordered her to be seized."[20]

"Days of Darkness!" exclaimed George Browder in September 1862, after he learned that a neighbor "Presley Herndon had gone to Henry B. Tully's house in a threatening attitude & that Tully had shot him, & killed him!" An anguished Browder wrote that "a grudge growing out of

18. Ash, *Middle Tennessee*, 76–79.
19. Troutman, *Diaries*, 133; Drew Gilpin Faust, "Christian Soldiers: The Meaning of Revivalism in the Confederate Army," 63–90.
20. Troutman, *Diaries*, 129. Mary Bell was from Christian County, Kentucky.

this war was doubtless the cause of this tragedy. I hardly ever hear a gun fire without feeling more or less anxiety and uneasiness."[21]

Browder learned that several neighbors had been taken by Southern troops. "B.K. Tully and his son Henry, & Henry's brother-in-law Joe Aingell—the last two being considered accomplices in the murder of Presley Herndon who is a confederate soldier," were seized on October 6, 1862, while Southern forces still held south central Kentucky. Tully had surrendered to the soldiers, Browder explained, and "it is generally supposed that Tully acted in self defence [against Herndon]—& rough using of him will bring bitter retaliation on Southern men if the federals get the power."[22]

Gangs of alleged Union men preyed upon Southern sympathizers. An incident occurred in Logan County when James Morrow and his men tried to seize a horse belonging to George Gray, a resident of Russellville. However, "Gray & some other Southern rights men resisted—& in the numerous shots that were fired, Burgher, a Lieut. in the Lincoln army was wounded by five different shots," wrote George Browder on July 29, 1862. Gray and another man also suffered wounds. Browder predicted, "this awful affair will cause trouble in our land. Morrow had been overbearing & insulting to Southern rights men—& his own party expected him to be killed." Political and personal divisions were widened by such incidents.[23]

That same July night, over four hundred Union soldiers entered Russellville. They soon established order, and Browder wrote, "Great suspense, anxiety and alarm prevail—& it is now believed that the country will be declared under martial law and probably the militia called out." Throughout most of the war the Black Patch remained under Federal military rule. Browder sensed the times to come when he wrote in July 1862, "I feel that evil days are at hand, but I trust in God for guidance and protection to me and all mine." Union control tended to be partisan, harsh, and disruptive. Southern sympathizers, and even some Northern loyalists, became embittered by the oppressive rule. The tough U.S. control, the ravages of the guerrillas, and the

21. Ibid., 131.
22. Ibid., 135.
23. Ibid., 121.

usual disturbances wrought by war incited increased violence in the citizens of the Black Patch.[24]

For loyalists, the presence of Federal soldiers brought relief from persecution. However, it came too late for the Underwoods, whose Mount Air plantation had been burned to the ground. Warner Underwood fled to Louisville, leaving Johanna and her mother in a secluded cabin. However, Washington friends of the former senator told Lincoln of the family's sacrifices, and the president made Underwood a consul to Scotland.[25]

Among slaveholders in the Black Patch, worries and fears about the loyalties of their slaves increased as Union control continued, and the South began to lose ground. "There are hundreds of negroes leaving their owners & going to the federals," George Browder wrote in June 1863. "I feel certain that my hired boy Henry has contemplated leaving. . . . Yesterday morning he was so insolent & insulting to my wife that I took him this morning & tied him, intending to whip him severely if he had not begged forgiveness & promised reform." Browder disliked such disruptions and wrote, "I regretted the occurrence but thought I was doing right." Many planters faced similar situations as the slaves acted to free themselves after hearing of Lincoln's Emancipation Proclamation. The large numbers of self-liberated blacks followed the Union forces in the region, camped near the Federal bases, and, later, established all-black communities near towns such as Birmingham in Marshall County. These activities ran counter to whites' ideas of how blacks should behave. Roaming, unemployed former slaves seemed a grave threat. The introduction of autonomous black settlements indicated how society might be reorganized after the war. Questions about how to control the former slaves in a free South agitated many whites. Problems arose when residents of the black communities found no economic support. Some turned to stealing local farmers' chickens and hogs. The actions of a few prompted whites to respond with anger and violence against many blacks. During the war years and Reconstruction,

24. Ibid., 122; Hambleton Tapp and James C. Klotter, *Kentucky: Decades of Discord, 1865–1900*, 1–2.
25. Nazro, diary, 149.

Black Patch whites quickly resorted to violence to shove blacks back into their "place" and restore white supremacy.[26]

George Browder, like other Southern masters, feared the consequences of the social and cultural changes that freeing the slaves would initiate. Large-scale tobacco growing demanded many workers, and the planters expected cheap, docile labor. Most could not foresee how their way of life could continue without slavery. Browder, more conciliatory than others, wrote, "If this war results in the liberation of all the slaves & the improvements of their condition, my heart and tongue will say 'Amen' & I shall think we of the South were wrong in our view that God designed them for bondsmen forever." On the other hand, he continued, "if the war results in the overthrow of abolitionism—the establishment of slavery in a quiet & peaceful government—I shall think that abolitionism warred against God's providence and was brought to confusion." Whatever the ultimate outcome, he knew, "If this thing be of God we cannot overthrow it."[27]

Robbing bands continued to roam, furthering the social and economic chaos of the region and adding to the anxieties of the citizens. George Browder wrote in July 1863, of bandits in the Black Patch who "have been plundering villages & country stores in this country," and added, "W. D. Boyer claims to have been robbed of $5000 worth of goods on Thursday night & Keysburg and Adairville also have been robbed." Browder judged that the "outrages in our midst are deplorable & alarming & we have no power to prevent it." Lives had been lost to the marauding outlaws. For example, he wrote, "Ed Small lost his life in pursuing them & citizens are afraid to resist— & yet rabid unionists charge the outrages on the citizens as aiders & abettors!" Browder disagreed with the Unionist evaluation. "I have heard nothing from any one but condemnation of such conduct. . . . I know to the contrary our citizens are better people."[28]

Sometimes depredations by guerrillas and escapes by slaves combined to the great dismay and fear of whites. On October 9, 1863, Browder wrote, "There was much excitement about guerrillas & a

26. Troutman, *Diaries*, 156; Tapp and Klotter, *Decades of Discord*, 7–8; George C. Wright, *Racial Violence in Kentucky, 1865–1940: Lynchings, Mob Rule, and "Legal Lynchings,"* 19–61.

27. Troutman, *Diaries*, 142.

28. Ibid., 159.

large stampede of negroes last night. Eight ran away from Dr. Stevenson and several from judge Edwards, but this is now too common to excite surprise." The guerrillas frightened whites and blacks when they swept into a neighborhood after dark. One band "robbed Gordonsville," Browder recorded, "& it is said they shot a man who was trying to escape them. They took off 3 horses from the school house . . . took Mrs. Blackford's negro *John* & also one of Mrs. Hawkins' but they escaped." Browder heard that some among the forty-two robbers had been shot by pursuers. Usually, however, outraged citizens who dared chase the bands were "threatened with death and house burning." Residents of the Black Patch would have agreed with Browder that "we are in peril & do not know what to do for safety."[29]

The occupation forces could do little to stop the guerrilla attacks on citizens. Often, Union attempts at justice only served to heighten local hatred of Federal rule. After guerrillas robbed and burned the home of George Hall, the U.S. officials ordered, according to George Browder, that "Southern rights neighbors should pay for it." The authorities were following the instructions of Maj. Gen. Jerry T. Boyle, U.S. Commander of Kentucky, who directed that damage to any loyal Unionists' property by bandits must be paid for by the disloyal Confederates of the community. Browder believed it unfair and "oppressive to require people to pay it who knew nothing of the raid & had no connection with it." Browder added, "I would willingly help replace his [Hall's] loss—but not by force—not to be considered a party to the crime." Nevertheless, soldiers arrived in the neighborhood to notify people of assessments to compensate Hall for his losses.[30]

Controlling the guerrilla bands probably lay beyond the ability of the Federal authorities or anyone else. Some of the bands had formed to shield their communities from other marauders. People often knew, approved of, and protected their own extralegal, but useful, neighborhood guardians. Some of these vigilante groups took advantage of the breakdown in law to rob, rape, and murder. Renegade bands of ex-soldiers, Confederate and Union, who were passing through the Black Patch, often added to the violence and confusion. For instance,

29. Ibid., 171.
30. Ibid., 172–73.

in May of 1864, George Browder exclaimed, "We here are overrun with robbers, who even in the broad daylight halt and rob men on the highway." Such gangs had been active in Logan and Todd Counties, stealing thousands of dollars and shooting one man who would not surrender his watch. Some gangs had formed before the war. One notorious Logan County outlaw turned to crime in the 1850s. George Browder described this outlaw chief: "Tom Morrow, once my neighbor & school fellow, now one of the most desperately wicked men in all the land." No one, Union or Confederate, cared for Morrow. His and other gangs' lawlessness only increased the level of violence, reinforced a disregard for authority, and added to citizens' fears and anxieties. Tensions created during these years contributed to the postwar animosities and hatreds that led to continued civil strife in the Black Patch during Reconstruction.[31]

"We heard the booming of cannon, & the peal of musketry," wrote Browder in April 1865, an appropriately military style of celebrating Union victory. "The rebellion is now fairly crushed," Browder conceded. "I think peace will soon follow & slavery be abolished all over the land. If such be God's will I cheerfully acquiesce." However, he continued ominously, "I think the northern states will yet be scourged, for unnecessary cruelties & oppression to the Southern people. There is great grief in the South & great exultation in the north to night [*sic*]."[32]

Emancipation had come to most Black Patch slaves by March 1865, and all were legally free by December of that year. However, the Lyon and Trigg Counties Freedmen's Bureau said that some owners continued to hold slaves until the summer of 1866. When one Logan County woman, Catherine Riley, attempted to claim her child from her former master, she was beaten. Blacks received little aid in such cases; courts in Logan and Warren Counties refused to act. The exodus of former slaves from farms led to a decline in labor, causing Kentucky tobacco production to fall 57 percent.[33]

The end of the war did not bring peace to either the Black Patch or

31. Ibid., 178; Ash, *Middle Tennessee*, 148–51, 163–66, 171–72; Hambleton Tapp, "Three Decades of Kentucky Politics, 1870–1900," (Ph.D. diss. University of Kentucky, 1950), 2–4, 9–13; Tapp and Klotter, *Decades of Discord*, 1–2.

32. Troutman, *Diaries*, 196.

33. Lucas, *History of Blacks in Kentucky*, 160, 182, 189, 206.

the South. Reconstruction and the years that followed it saw violence perpetrated by whites against freed blacks and against other whites, partisan conflict, kin feuding, and popular uprisings. The Civil War had inflamed the violent tendencies and habits already present in white society.

New Civil War heroes joined the ranks of the warrior pantheon in Black Patch folklore, making it still more militant. Whites were more inclined than ever to use violence as a tool for change—or for maintaining the status quo. Families honored returning soldiers after the war, thus creating local heroes and raising their exploits to the level of myth. Robert Penn Warren admired his maternal grandfather, an officer in the Confederate army and listened raptly to his war tales. Years later, Warren wrote stories that incorporated his hero. In "When the Light Gets Green," the young narrator's grandfather is a Captain Barden. Warren compares the captain's bearded countenance to that of Robert E. Lee. According to the story, during the Civil War Grandfather Barden served under General Nathan Bedford Forrest and narrowly escaped from Fort Donelson. Later he fought at Shiloh. In the story, the grandson asks how many enemy soldiers Barden killed and learns that his grandfather does not know. The boy wonders at the offhand response and concludes that his grandfather didn't kill any soldiers. He says that he "was just a captain because he never killed anybody, and I was ashamed." To kill an enemy, a threatening outsider, was an honorable deed. To fail at protecting one's family and home was a shameful thing.[34]

Christian County Union officer Gen. James S. Jackson gained prominence as commander of the Third Kentucky Cavalry. William Henry Perrin described the general as "one of Christian County's most gallant and illustrious representatives on the Federal side." Jackson commanded soldiers at Shiloh and Corinth, Mississippi. His brigade helped capture the Third Georgia Cavalry at New Haven, Kentucky. He died, wrote Perrin, "valiantly fighting, at the head of his brigade in the battle of Perryville, October 4, 1862." A promising career ended, but a legend began about Jackson, a man known "for his graceful form and almost feminine beauty of countenance." He

34. Robert Penn Warren, "When the Light Gets Green," in *The Circus in the Attic and Other Stories* (New York: Harcourt, Brace, Jovanovich, 1975), 88–93.

possessed the best of Southern attributes, wrote Perrin: "He had the manners of a Chesterfield, and was one of the most knightly soldiers who ever drew a sword. . . . He was the highest type of the Kentucky gentleman." Although he fought for the Union, Jackson symbolized the ideals of Southern elite males with "his exquisite grace and purest and noblest chivalry." Jackson had been "a Union man for the sake of the Union; and now, with his heart's blood he has sealed devotion to the flag." Thus, a battle hero was created who appealed to both Black Patch Confederates and Federals.[35]

In the chaotic aftermath of the war, a political vacuum left room for display of the full range of violent behaviors. Racial violence arose as a response to the freed people's efforts to live independently. The places where blacks worshiped, learned, and conducted political meetings became targets of white wrath, which was often expressed through mob action. Northern teachers in Bowling Green, Warren County, Kentucky received warnings from the Ku Klux Klan in 1868 to quit teaching in the blacks' schools and leave the Black Patch. In Cadiz, Kentucky, a mob beat a white who was planning to teach the freed people. Harassment continued after the turn of the century.[36]

Conflicts between black ex-Union soldiers and white former Confederate soldiers arose in the Black Patch. As many as 4,000 blacks had enlisted in the United States Army from Tennessee by October of 1863. Kentucky blacks, finally totaling 23,703, also joined the fight for freedom. In 1868, animosity toward the black fighters broke out in Logan County, Kentucky. Blacks who returned home to live only to be ordered to leave the county found jobs in the wool and flour mills at South Union, the Shaker farm and village. Again, the African Americans received threats, but they decided to stay in the nonviolent religious community. Whites from the area attacked and burned the black workers' cabins one August night in 1868. The Shaker leaders offered a five-hundred-dollar reward for the capture of the members of the mob, which only led to further violence. Whites returned to South Union September 2 and destroyed the uninsured Shaker mills. The Shakers' attempts to treat the ex-slaves fairly, pay

35. Perrin, *Counties*, 188–89.
36. Wright, *Racial Violence*, 35–36; *Hopkinsville Daily Kentucky New Era*, December 4, 1906.

them decent wages, and allow them to live in peace were not tolerated by Logan County whites. Violence, the traditional method of
oppression, ruined Shaker attempts at racial harmony.[37]

Ku Klux Klan members tried to force successful black producers
out of Todd County, Kentucky, in the mid–1870s. The *New York Times*
quoted one of the white attackers, who claimed, "We wanted to let
the poor white man have a chance." Class tensions between poor
whites and blacks would be a continuing problem in the Black Patch.
In Daviess County, Kentucky, white fears of the labor competition
the freed people represented led to mob action. A farmer was ordered to get rid of his black laborers, and mobs spread the word that
no one should rent to blacks. Race divided the groups, even though
poverty and powerlessness remained common experiences.[38]

The Civil War and Reconstruction years split the Black Patch,
causing political, social, and economic chaos, arousing new racial
tensions, obscuring class animosities, which were seen in the poor
whites' alliance with elite whites against poor blacks, and adding to
the cultural heritage of violence in the region.

37. Wright, *Racial Violence*, 30–40; Lester C. Lamon, *Blacks in Tennessee,
1791–1970*, 31; Lucas, *History of Blacks in Kentucky*, 166. Kentucky provided 13
percent of the 178,895 black union troops.

38. *New York Times* March 18, 21, 28, 1875, cited in Wright, *Racial Violence*,
33; Lucas, *History of Blacks in Kentucky*, 195.

*The farm woman's realm—working in the house, the yard, and the garden
and managing the poultry.*

*The farmer's realm—working in the fields, the tobacco barn, and the stables
and killing the family's hogs.*

Cutting and loading time in the dark-fired tobacco patch, Robertson County, Tennessee. Tennessee State Library and Archives. Conservation Department Photo Collection.

Black sharecroppers and white overseer in dark-fired tobacco at season's end, Christian County, Kentucky. University of Louisville Photo Archives. Arthur Y. Ford Albums Collection.

Black sharecropper family, Butler County, Kentucky. University of Louisville Photo Archives. Arthur Y. Ford Albums Collection.

White farmers with guns standing in a tobacco patch in Union County, Kentucky, 1908. University of Louisville Photo Archives. Arthur Y. Ford Albums Collection.

5

WORKING THE BLACK PATCH

E verybody worked," claims Edna Humphries, daughter of a Black Patch tobacco sharecropper. Men, women, and children worked in the tobacco patch, the cornfield, the chicken yard, the barn lot, and the house. Duties in each of these places depended on class, race, sex, age, and skill. The poorer the family, the more likely it was that every member of the household—no matter their age and sex—worked in the fields. Making a living depended upon each person's labor. "Children," Mary Emma Bleidt emphasizes, "were useful people when I grew up" during the early 1900s in Golden Pond, Kentucky.[1]

Whenever possible, however, the men and boys toiled in the fields, while women and girls worked in the house, dairy barn, vegetable garden, and chicken yard. Ideally, people wanted to keep the male and female domains separate. "They expected a man to run the family," explains J. Marcus Whitler, Jr. If women ever "overwhelmed their husbands, their husbands were considered by other men to be a weakling. Those men were not respected at all." On the other hand, "the woman was considered the mother of the home. She was supposed to be there when the kids came home from school. She was supposed to have the meals on the table on time." Sometimes, Whitler says, "in some homes, she even had to split wood, carry the wood in if there weren't any kids. Lots of instances she was the one that at least maintained three or four rows in the garden."[2]

1. Edna Humphries, interview by Nicolette Murray, tape recording, October 1, 1980, Western Kentucky History and Culture Collection, Jackson Purchase Oral History Project, Forrest C. Pogue Oral History Institute, Murray, Kentucky. Humphries was born in 1893. Mary Emma Bleidt, interview by David Sullivan, tape recording, July 9, 1976, Western Kentucky History and Culture Collection, Land between the Lakes Series, Forrest C. Pogue Oral History Institute, Murray, Kentucky.
2. J. Marcus Whitler, interview by *Owensboro Messenger-Inquirer,* tape recording, September 1, 1976, Kentucky Library, Western Kentucky University, Bowl-

Men took responsibility for and great pride in growing the primary cash crop of the Black Patch, the dark-fired tobacco that brought in the family's annual income. All farmers, black and white, land owner and tenant, shared the experience of tobacco growing. A man gained the respect and admiration of the community if he produced a fine crop. Black Patch men identified themselves as tobacco farmers. This shared experience and source of identity tied all elements of society together because everyone could converse on the growing, curing, and marketing of the crop. Everybody understood the joy and the pain of producing tobacco. However, there was also a subtle competition among growers and a ranking every season based on who had grown the best leaf and received the highest price. Farmers on the richest land probably won the competition most often. For tenants or owners on poor land, the tobacco money amounted to very little. Thomas Lee Askew, a white grower, recalled raising five acres and getting "only one hundred thirty-five dollars for it." That came to "no more than a dime a day," he says, but it was worth it if only to pay the taxes; "you can't grow nothing" like tobacco "that paid you to do it, but you had to do it to live."[3]

Women's work included "whatever needed doing," says Mary Emma Bleidt, a white farm woman, from the domestic chores of maintaining the household, to field work, and the secondary economic job of raising poultry for cash and trade, which provided the household with a regular weekly income. The people of the Black Patch describe the tasks of maintaining their farms, the process of growing a fine dark tobacco, which they learned from generations of forebears, and the raising of poultry by the women. Years of knowledge and experience on their farms gives them the ability to tell about the continuities and changes that occurred in Black Patch farm work from the 1880s to the 1920s.[4]

---

ing Green, Kentucky. Harriet Simpson Arnow, "The Pioneer Farmer and His Crops in the Cumberland Region," 310.

3. Thomas Lee Askew, interview by Jerry Herndon, tape recording, January 4, 1976, Western Kentucky History and Culture Collection, Jackson Purchase Oral History Project, Forrest C. Pogue Oral History Institute, Murray, Kentucky; T. H. Breen, *Tobacco Culture: The Mentality of the Great Tidewater Planters on the Eve of the Revolution*, 56–61, 66–67, 70.

4. Bleidt, interview; Eunice McCarty, interview; Daniel, *Breaking the Land*, 198–200.

From the earliest days in the Black Patch region until the late nineteenth century, the methods of cultivating tobacco changed very gradually. Sons learned the work of raising the weed and the art of curing it from their fathers. The older ones passed on the knowledge through descriptions and demonstration: during the long spring and summer work days, they worked in the field; in the autumn, by smoky fires at curing time; and in the deep cold winter, in the stripping barns.[5]

The life of Lyon Countian Joe Scott covers a remarkable span of years: he was born in 1886 and died in 1989. His work in the tobacco patch differed little from the work done by his pioneer ancestors one hundred years before. The same soils—silt and clay loams, and brown, yellow, or red subsoil—lying upon a chert stratum and a limestone base existed in the region with variations in richness. Poor, thin and rocky soils occurred near the uplands and between the Cumberland and Tennessee Rivers, the area inhabitants called "Between the Rivers." The most fertile potash soil lay in the limestone-based plains of southern Logan, Todd, and Christian Counties. These ideal soils, combined with the region's temperate weather, plenty of rain (averaging forty-seven to fifty-one inches per year), and high humidity, provided nearly perfect conditions for growing tobacco. "Well, I'm gonna tell you," Joe Scott begins, "I raised tobacco, raised it all my life. You work in tobacco and you got to work." The first task in tobacco production, preparation of the seedbeds, began in late fall or early winter. As Scott explains, "You had to build a big fire and burn your eyes out burning that plant bed."[6]

Clyde Quisenberry, an African American born in 1893, describes the way his father prepared plant beds on the level sandstone plateau of the Clifty upland in Caldwell County similar to the process of the colonial Virginia planters. Until about 1860, Black Patch farmers

5. Rick Gregory, "Human Factors in Tobacco Culture," 1986 (photocopy), passim; "Cultivation of Dark Tobacco," *Western Tobacco Journal* 28:15 (April 14, 1902); Arnow, "The Pioneer Farmer," 315–19; Daniel, *Breaking the Land*, 24–31; Breen, *Tobacco Culture*, 46–55.

6. Joe Scott, interview by author, tape recording, Lyon County, Kentucky, May 12, 1987; Rick Gregory, "The Crop and the Physical Setting," 1986 (photocopy), 9–10; Joseph B. Killebrew and Herbert Myrick, *Tobacco Leaf; Its Culture and Cure, Marketing, and Manufacture. A Growing, Harvesting, Curing, Packing, and Selling Tobacco* (New York: Orange Judd Company, 1914 [1897]), 25, Series UL (Frankfort, Ky.: Kentucky Geological Survey, 1927), 155, 173–74.

tried to use new or once-used ground for seedbeds and fields if it was available. The fields would be used for tobacco for two or three years and then wheat, corn, or oats would be planted in them. To begin preparing the seedbed, Clyde Quisenberry explains, "we'd have to go to the woods or a fence row and select us out a good rich place where the ground was rich and rake the leaves off. We would cut wood and lay [it] down and then set it to fire and burn the ground dry." The burning process aided in "killing the vegetation" and the insects. Next the men would "work the ground up with grub hoes. Work it down right smooth and then, after it cooled off, go back the next morning or evening and sow it." During the 1880s and 1890s, farmers mixed "the seed in ashes and sawdust like seeding a yard."[7]

Not until after the turn of the century did farmers gradually abandon the burning of plant beds and turn to a new method of mechanically steaming the soil to kill weeds and pests. Quisenberry describes this change in tobacco production. "We'd got to learn how to steam 'em with hot steam." To begin "a man would have a pan, a great big pan made with so many feet in it and we'd set it down," on the patch of earth chosen for the bed "and he'd run steam from a steam engine and scald the ground. We started doing that along in nineteen eleven and twelve." A lifetime neighbor of Quisenberry's, Robert Parker, describes the steamers' operation in their community and how farmers cooperated in the job. One man in the area owned the steam engine and equipment, which he moved from farm to farm. The steamer team "liked to move and stay there as long as they could. So three or four farmers would steam at the same place" with all their beds located on a single farm. This cooperation enabled the steamer to set up at one site and work more efficiently. Once the seedlings grew large enough to be transplanted, the farm families, neighbors, tenants, and, perhaps, hired hands pulled plants and enjoyed the camaraderie of the work.[8]

7. Clyde Quisenberry, interview by author, tape recording, Caldwell County, Kentucky, July 20, 1987; Charles S. Guthrie, "Tobacco: Cash Crop of the Cumberland Valley," 38–43; Gregory, "Human Factors in Tobacco Culture," 27–35; Killebrew, *Tobacco Leaf*, ch. 7, 8, and p. 302; Sauer, *Geography*, 147; Daniel, *Breaking the Land*, 194.

8. Quisenberry, interview; Robert Parker, interview by author, tape recording, Caldwell County, Kentucky, July 15, 1987.

Sowing the beds usually began in the late fall. In the days before 1920, explains Lyon County farmer George McCarty, "they felt like if they didn't get their plant bed burned and sowed by mid-February," they might not have tobacco plants grown by spring. "But," he continues, "there's been a change in that now. I usually sow my plant beds around the twentieth of March." Over the years, farmers noticed that "plants that came up stayed too long on the bed" if sown in the fall, "and they'd blossom out a lot" before transplanting. However, if you planted in warm weather, they grew stronger and "blossomed out bigger."[9]

Ruston Flowers recalls how his father carried out the next step in the planting process, the sowing of the tiny seeds. Flowers grew up on a large thriving farm in Logan County called Fair View, where the elder Flowers grew eighty-five acres of dark tobacco with the labor of ten black tenant families and his own five sons. "When [we] sow[ed] the tobacco beds," Flowers explains, "we used one table-spoon full of tobacco seed to a hundred yards and that's a hundred square yards. That tablespoon full of tobacco seed is, well you've heard of a mustard seed, it's a lot smaller."[10]

Flowers was a boy in the 1920s, when a change came to the way tobacco was sowed. Instead of ashes "we'd mix those seeds in fertilizer, and then [we'd] take and sow them out in the latter part of February or the first of March." The next step "after you got your beds sowed, you would take a canvas and stretch it" over the seedbed and "anchor it down with . . . poles on the edge of the bed, and then we stretched the canvas from one pole to another. We'd take twine string and put a rock in the canvas and tie the twine string around the rock." After that, "we'd take a wooden stob and drive it in the ground and take this string and put over that wooden stob and that would keep the canvas tight. Now that was up until about 1955 or sixty and then they started coming out with nylon canvas. Before that it was cotton." The change to the synthetic fabric brought progress to tobacco cultivation, Flowers claims, "because your plants will grow faster under the nylon because it's warmer."[11]

9. George H. McCarty, interview by author, tape recording, Lyon County, Kentucky, March 10, 1987.
10. Ruston Flowers, interview by author, tape recording, Lyon County, Kentucky, June 20, 1987.
11. Ibid.

Once the farmers had planted the seeds, they returned to stripping the previous year's crop and to their wintertime farm duties, such as repairing harnesses, clearing out brush, rebuilding fences, or carving new cedar tobacco pegs to use when setting the plants in the spring. After the seeds sprouted, more time was required for their care. "When the plants come up," Flowers says, "you have to water them. If you don't have enough rainfall, you should water them at least once every week." Growers, like the Flowerses, who had the money and labor to do the job in dry years would "saturate that bed with water, and it takes about a hundred or hundred and fifty gallons. We carried it in wooden barrels on sleds. We used a tow sack to tie over the top of the barrel to keep the water from sloshing out."[12]

After the seedlings matured to "around five inches tall, you'd take the canvas completely off the bed and you'd wrap that canvas up and use it the next year and you let mother nature toughen that plant" to survive the move to the tobacco patch. Pulling plants and setting was a back-straining job in which nearly all members of the farm family—men, women, and children—participated, as well as hired laborers if the family could afford them. First, as Ruston Flowers explains, "you pull the plants and you try to pull them with a stem as big as a pencil." Experienced workers instructed novices on how to pull the plants out of the dirt with the roots intact by digging the fingers down by the stem and gently tugging the seedling loose. Workers held the plants in one hand with roots neatly aligned so they would be easy to drop in the field later. Bunches of plants were laid aside on sacks or baskets for transport to the field. During the pulling of plants, everyone talked, stories and jokes were told, and young children who needed training were cajoled into working.[13]

Prior to setting, workers prepared the tobacco patch carefully for the new crop. Orvil Oatts, a white Christian Countian, details the process. First, "people'd rake the tobacco patch up and then get in there and disc it, drag it down and then get ready to set it. They laid it off both ways with a mule and a little plow called a coulter. Then when they'd lay this off both ways that checked it about four feet

12. Ibid.
13. Ibid.

apart, every stalk, every plant of tobacco would be about four feet apart."[14]

Sharecropper and tenant women and children worked the tobacco with the men. Children, particularly boys, missed school when all hands were needed, and some worked all year. Even white middling farm women entered the fields at peak laboring times, and their children worked after school. "They'd draw these plants off the bed and then they'd drop 'em on a hill" in the new field. "They made these little [hills by] taking a hoe and a little old amount of fertilizer—just what you could hold between your two fingers." Until about the 1920s, Oatts says, "people was afraid that fertilizer would ruin that tobacco."[15]

Next, working in stages, a woman or a child walked down the field rows, dropping the tobacco seedlings one by one onto the hills, followed closely by peggers and setters. Men nearly always performed the tasks of pegging, using a short, wooden, pointed stick to make a hole in the hill, and setting, or transplanting, the seedling. If there had not been a "season," a period of spring rains to moisten the soil, another child followed along to douse the plant with a cup of water.[16]

"May, early in May, by hand," George McCarty says was the time for setting. "You cultivated it with a mule and didn't use very much fertilizer. The idea was back in that day that [if] you used very much fertilizer you'd burn your tobacco up. That wasn't a fact, but that was the way they understood it at that time."[17]

Farmers adopted mechanization slowly and erratically to the cultivation of tobacco. Some tasks, such as cutting, never became mechanized. There were several reasons for this. First, plenty of cheap labor—provided by families, tenants, and hired hands—was available. Second, only humans could handle the tobacco leaves gently enough to prevent damage. Prime leaf must be free of blemishes, tears, and discoloration to bring the best price, and no mechanical setters existed until after 1945 that satisfied the farmers' stringent requirements. Mechanical setters became popular after World War II,

14. Orvil Oatts, interview by author, tape recording, Christian County, Kentucky, September 12, 1987; Killebrew, *Tobacco Leaf*, 299–300.
15. Oatts, interview; George McCarty, interview; Killebrew, *Tobacco Leaf*, 299.
16. Oatts, interview.
17. George McCarty, interview; Killebrew, *Tobacco Leaf*, 299.

according to Ruston Flowers. "I guess it was in the fifties. It's still not mechanized. It's still a hand crop." Individual farmers bought the machines, which were first pulled by mules and later drawn by tractors. Sometimes families or neighbors shared a setter. They pulled plants together and took turns helping one another set the tobacco in the fields. Wealthy planters with plenty of croppers or tenants owned at least one setter for use on their own lands.[18]

Women, white and black, joined the men in the fields regularly. Louise Freeman of Lyon County remembers that she "started working on a farm by the time I was ten years old and I worked on the farm until I was seventy." She did all the tasks. "Pegged it out with a peg, I set it, I dropped the plants, and then I've suckered it. I never did cut any tobacco, but I've helped house it, and I helped strip."[19] Black and white women express pride in their ability to work the tobacco in the fields in addition to tending to their household duties. They saw themselves as co-producers, along with their husbands, of the family's livelihood.

Children learned as they worked and watched others. For those who stayed on the farm, work in the fields was a vital part of their education. As George McCarty, a boy who later inherited the family's farm remembers, "You followed along, they say, your father's footsteps and did what you were able to do as your capabilities were and just gradually grew into it." For some children, farm work made up the bulk of their education. Marginal farmers with poor land and no help, tenant farmers, and sharecroppers often held children out of school to work in the crops. In the early 1900s, less than 50 percent of Kentucky's school-aged children attended the often substandard one-room schools in their neighborhoods. Some tobacco farmers considered schooling beyond the elementary grades a waste of time. More practical knowledge could be gained through farming itself.[20]

18. Flowers, interview; George McCarty, interview.

19. Louise Freeman, interview by author, tape recording, Lyon County, Kentucky, July 16, 1987.

20. George McCarty, interview; Henry Eugene Baggett, interview by author, tape recording, Robertson County, Tennessee, July 14, 1987; Humphries, interview; Scott, interview; Gregory, "Human factors in Tobacco Culture," 38; Harriett A. Byrne, *Child Labor in Representative Tobacco-Growing Areas*, United States Department of Labor, Children's Bureau Publication No. 155 (Washing-

Most farm children worked on the farm and in the fields because their labor was vital to the family farm economy. Even children of larger planters, as Ruston Flowers recalls, worked alongside the croppers. Although the work was demanding and monotonous, "I guess we just accepted it. Course, when I was a boy I was more interested in getting out of work than in work. I enjoyed being in the fields with the other workers. There was a lot of kidding going on, always a lot of fun. Even though it was back-breaking work, you could have fun with it. I imagine that the companionship is what I like about it."[21]

After the setting, George McCarty continues, "tobacco would grow until . . . about the Fourth of July. From the first to the fifteenth of July, they topped it," removing the seed buds, or "buttons," before they flowered to keep the plants from developing into leafy, tall stalks. This forced the plants to grow eight or ten broad leaves instead. Orvil Oatts describes the repetitive cultivation of the maturing plants. "It's a one-mule outfit. . . . I'm telling you about years ago." To begin "you'd scratch that tobacco, it ain't big enough to plow. But you can do it when the leaves ain't that large. And then you go to plowin'. Plow it until it was ready to top. Then the next thing was to top it," followed by repeated suckering—or removal of the subsidiary shoots, called "suckers"—which sprouted after the topping.[22]

Finally, the everlasting round of worming, which was dreaded by all, commenced, and "you'd try to catch your worms off it and everything else." Few farm people forget the hated job of removing worms and insects. "I couldn't do much with those worms," recalls Grace Smith Stovall. "I'd push them off and then take my stick and hit them." During the hottest days of summer, a constant round of plowing, suckering, and worming continued for over a month after the topping process had been completed.[23]

George McCarty says about his family's farm, "At the time I first remember, it was ten or twelve acres. See, at that time, all the suckers

ton, D.C.: United States Government Printing Office, 1926), and "Child Welfare in Kentucky," in *Bulletin of the State Board of Health of Kentucky* 9:11 (Frankfort, Ky.: State Journal Company, 1919).

21. Flowers, interview; Gregory, "Human Factors in Tobacco Culture," 37–38.

22. George McCarty, interview; Oatts, interview; Killebrew, *Tobacco Leaf*, 307–10.

23. Robert Stovall, interview by author, tape recording, Lyon County, Kentucky, March 10, 1987; George McCarty, interview; Killebrew, *Tobacco Leaf*, 310.

had to be pulled by hand; consequently, there couldn't be a big acreage." Commonly in the Black Patch "the biggest acreage an individual would have would be six acres because they would sucker an acre a day. A single man was routinely expected to sucker an acre of tobacco a day. If he suckered six days a week, he'd get that six acres suckered." The following week the farmer repeated the suckering or the worming.[24]

Farmers increased their acreage by increasing the labor force. Wealthy farmers employed hired hands, sharecroppers, and tenants. Middling farmers managed by putting their wives and children into the fields when their labor was needed. However, middling farmers tried to keep their wives and daughters out of the fields as much as possible. Wilma McCarty Marshall, daughter of a middling farmer who had about a hundred acres and one tenant family, recalls that, when she worked in the tobacco, her mother made her wear a bonnet and long sleeves to prevent her skin from tanning. Appearances were important, and tanned, rough skin made a girl look like a sharecropper's daughter.[25]

"Worms had to be picked by hand at that time," George McCarty continues, talking about the years before the 1940s. "I first remember picking worms at eight years old. Didn't pick a lot of worms, but I still had to be there. You caught them and rubbed their heads between your thumb and forefinger to kill them and dropped them on the ground." Some economy-minded farm wives instructed that the worms be collected and fed to their chickens.[26]

When each farmer determined that his tobacco was ripe, sometime in August or September, cutting time began. In Christian County, says Orvil Oatts, "you cut it in the old time way. You'd take a tobacco knife [and] first cut the stalk right down the middle" from the top down in one swift movement. "And then you'd cut that off, turn it up and set it up like that and let the sun shine on it until it wilted. Then you'd hang it in the barn on a stick. Everybody worked, the whole family, they's big enough to work, they worked."[27]

24. George McCarty, interview.

25. Ibid.; Wilma M. Marshall, interview by author, tape recording, Jefferson County, Kentucky, May 29, 1987.

26. George McCarty, interview; Gayle F. McCarty, interview by author, tape recording, Union County, Kentucky, August 25, 1987; Humphries, interview.

27. Oatts, interview; Killebrew, *Tobacco Leaf*, 310–18.

"Back in the early, early days," says George McCarty, "the tobacco stalks were split and that split, then, was hung" over a hand-rived tobacco stick. "Back in the early period of my thinking they hung nine plants to a stick. The tobacco then probably averaged less than a thousand pound to the acre. When I first remember talking to people making a good yield, they made twelve hundred pounds. To the best of my knowledge now there's a lot of them that make 2,500 and 3,000 pounds to the acre. Where back in that early day they hung nine plants to a stick, they hang five or six now, because the plants are so much bigger." The change has come because of "better farming techniques, fertilizer, chemicals to keep down weeds. The only chemical we had in the early days was a gooseneck hoe." And he exclaims, "Did I have to hoe tobacco? I grew up on the farm to do that!"[28]

Women did double duty in the house and field during cutting season. Louise Freeman, a neighbor to McCarty, cooked the big harvest dinners and also helped house the tobacco. First, she says, the men "cut it and put it on a stick and let it wilt and haul it to the barn. I usually handed it off the wagon to somebody and they put it up." Freeman takes great pride in her skills as a farm woman and her ability to care for home, children, garden, and poultry while doing the field work of tobacco cultivation. She compares herself to the sturdy pioneer women who could cut firewood and then use it to cook a wholesome meal. Her family farm consisted of less than two hundred acres in Lyon County—making the Freemans middling farmers—and the labor of all the women and children was necessary for it to succeed.[29]

At Fair View, Logan County, Ruston Flowers compares his family's work style to that of families in another community. "We'd do like the Mennonites do. Everybody helps each other." The Flowers son and the black cropper families "cut the tobacco and put it on the stick and put it on the scaffolds. Then it wilted [and] it would turn yellow." After the leaves wilted so that they could be handled without breaking "you'd take it out and put it on wagons. When I was a kid we'd use steel rimmed wagons. You'd load a wagon and take it to the barn and hang it up into the barn onto the tier poles." Once the

---

28. George McCarty, interview; Killebrew, *Tobacco Leaf*, 316–18.
29. Freeman, interview.

loaded, mule-drawn wagons arrived at the tall, airtight barns, the men "always hung it about six inches apart on the tier poles." These tiers "were in the center of the barn and the barn was usually eight tiers to the top."[30]

Hanging the tobacco in the tin-roofed barns was an arduous, steamy-hot task. Men from neighboring farms, friends, kin, tenants, and hired hands cut and housed the weed. Men competed, taking pride in being the best cutter or housing men in the area. Robert Parker describes the competition in Caldwell County during his younger days in the 1920s and 1930s: "Two of us in our country were called the 'brag' housing men. An older man named Cook had been the brag man until I come on and then he faded a little bit and everybody admitted I was the fastest." After thinking a moment Parker went on, "I reckon I liked to cut it better. I was always an expert tobacco cutter and I was considered the fastest man in the barn there was in this part of the country. I usually worked at the bottom and they put two men on the wagon when I was working in the barn."[31]

Housing tobacco required four to five hands. As Louise Freeman describes the work, she handed the sticks of tobacco from the wagon to a man standing on the barn floor. The floor "man" then passed it up to the man on the first tier, who handed it up to those located on the upper tiers. Gradually, the men filled the barn from the highest to the lowerest tier pole with the dark leaf. Everyone exercised great care in this task. "That was a process that you had to be quite particular at," George McCarty stresses, "because number one, if you got it too close, it house burns. If you didn't [get it] hung on the tiers in good shape, why, a stick might fall out and cause you to burn down your whole crop of tobacco."[32]

Housing began in the hottest month of summer, when the heat in the tin-roofed, tightly constructed barns could smother a man. Men on the upper tiers suffered the most, and accidents resulted. Clyde Quisenberry remembers in the 1910s when his "daddy got so hot that he fell out of the barn once. He was housing and he'd hauled some sawdust in there and that sawdust kept him from hitting that hard-

30. Flowers, interview; *Western Tobacco Journal*, April 14, 1902.
31. Parker, interview.
32. George McCarty, interview; Killebrew, *Tobacco Leaf*, 318–19.

ware when he fell. It was bound to have broken him up if it had'nt been for that." The intense heat and physical labor left "him wringing wet with sweat, it was running all over him. His body shaking and his britches just as wet as if they'd poured water all over him."[33]

Each stage of dark-fired tobacco production required skill, but the firing of the year's crop was the most demanding and dangerous task. "In the early days," George McCarty recalls, "this would be just at the very beginning of memory—they put the tobacco really closely in the barn and they would take two mules and drag logs into that barn and set those a-fire so that they could control the way they burned." Men and boys "would stay with the tobacco barn probably three days and two nights. They didn't leave the barn except to go to the house to eat. And they cured the tobacco quickly."[34]

"When they built the fire under the tobacco at that period of time and fired it for three days and two nights," McCarty says, "they cured the dickens—stalk, stem, and all. They had it very hot in there." Farmers used various woods for firing; all believed the one they favored worked best. "Preferably," says McCarty, "you burned hickory or oak—there was more heat to it. They were after heat in this period. I've heard people talk about going in the barns and laying their hands on the posts so hot you couldn't hold you hand on it."[35]

The age-old way of curing was abandoned over the years. "In the mid-thirties, they developed the soft-cure method. They began to use sawdust and wood enough to keep the sawdust a-fire and only moderate heat, and at the same time, they kept the humidity high. Back in 1933, '34, and '35, my Dad and the fellow that lived here who was named Emmit Gray, would take a water hauled to throw in those barns to keep the humidity high."[36]

Farmers claim that although firing was difficult work, it was a source of pleasure. Quisenberry says, "When you started to firing you'd have to stay in the barn when it started to smoke. I've come out with smoke in my eyes to where I'd have to put a wet rag over it. I went down after it was fired and it'd break through. I've went down

33. Quisenberry, interview.
34. George McCarty, interview.
35. Ibid.
36. Ibid.

there to put dust on it to cool them down and I got out to the end I'd be so hot I'd fall." Ruston Flowers remembers the pleasant times from his boyhood: "We don't watch the fires like we used to." But then "somebody stayed at the barn all night long." To make a resting place "they took a plank. Everywhere a post came down to the ground they usually had a pretty good size rock for that post to sit on and the rock was used for this plank to lean up against and you would make a pallet on that plank, and that's where you would sleep during the night right in the middle of the barn." Fun times began at sundown during the nightly fire-watch. "When we were kids we used to take potatoes and put them in the edge of the fire," Flowers says, "and bake those potatoes. You used corn the same way and leave it in the shuck and roast it. Other words, if you didn't have a little fun along the way, it was drudgery."[37]

During the firing time, everyone in the Black Patch feared a crop-destroying blaze. "You had to cut it and put it in the barn," says Joe Scott, "then you had to fire it. I thought that a-many and a-many a-time how foolish a man is to work his life away a-putting a big crop by and then put a big fire under it. He don't know whether he's gonna get [it cured] or whether he's gonna lose the whole thing or not." Never did an autumn firing season pass without a loss of barns in the neighborhood. "There'd be two or three fellers burn up their barns of tobacco. All they made all year and then burn the whole barn up. Burn up everything up. Burn up a whole year's work."[38]

Fear of burning up the year's cash crop was so strong that people woke in the night in a cold sweat. One boy, Leslie Markens, dreamed that a fire broke out in his tobacco barn. It was after midnight when he awoke from the dream and bounded out of bed to check the tobacco. To his amazement a fire had begun, but his dream had warned him in time to save the crop, and the story made the front page of the newspaper.[39]

Firing all night long was tiresome, Floyd Bell admits, "but I'd worked a year making the crop, that was a year's work tied up in it, and I'd try to make it the best I could. That was my pride to make a

37. Quisenberry, interview; Flowers, interview.
38. Scott, interview.
39. *Princeton Twice-A-Week Leader*, October 22, 1920.

good piece of tobacco." Bell was a young tenant farmer in the 1930s.
A fine crop of tobacco brought respect to any man in the Black Patch.
It showed his hard work, patience, skill, and experience, qualities
that Black Patch people believed assured prosperity.[40]

Not only have production methods changed since pioneer days, so,
too, has the plant itself. The type of tobacco people hoped to produce
before the 1920s was a less-weighty leaf used for snuff and chewing
tobacco. Manufacturers reacting to the demands of the European
market wanted the thick, smoky, chewy leaves that pleased the foreign imbibers of plug tobacco, cheap cigars, and snuff. Currently,
George McCarty explains, "snuff is produced out of thinner stuff
than that. They still have the same grades of tobacco that they had
years ago, but these grades are not the same tobaccos that they were
then." Also, the declining demand for chewing tobacco and snuff
in the 1920s in favor of cigarettes, which require thin mild, light-
leafed tobacco, meant the importance of dark varieties decreased. Beginning in the 1930s, most Black Patch farmers began to produce
air-cured burley for smoking tobaccos in addition to their dark crop.
Gradually, McCarty asserts, "there has been a change over the
years."[41]

Black Patch tobacco cultivation made its greatest transition after
the turn of the century. The changes might seem small and insignifi-
cant to outsiders, but for the growers, such improvements as chemical weed and pest killers, mechanical setters, and modern fertilizers
profoundly changed the business of growing tobacco. They made the
field work easier. They made it possible for parents to leave children
in school instead of holding them out to sucker and worm the weed.
Because of the improvements, farmers' wives began to work fewer
hours since their labor was no longer required in the fields. Finally,
the reduced labor requirements and the decreased demand for dark-
fired tobacco also meant fewer tenants and hired hands were needed.
During the years after World War I, the landless left the Black Patch
for jobs in cities like Louisville, Detroit, and Chicago.[42]

40. Floyd Bell, interview by author, tape recording, Lyon County, Kentucky,
July 20, 1987.
41. George McCarty, interview; Killebrew, *Tobacco Leaf*, 291–92.
42. For a comprehensive discussion of tobacco production and history consult

Women who helped in the fields returned to their houses at noon to prepare the hearty midday meal that the hardworking farmers needed. Afterward, while the men rested a while before returning to the afternoon's chores, women cleaned up and turned to domestic indoor work. During peak cutting season or during stripping time, women worked all day in the tobacco along with the men. Beulah Ryan recalls such busy days when "she did everything a man did in the fields, except mow," and she did it "in a dress," because Deuteronomy says women should never wear pants and she would "never consider" such a thing, although she often wore a man's old shirt over her dress to keep from getting "blistered and sun-burned."[43]

In addition to field work and housework, women cared for their families. Mothers, rather than doctors, usually tended to children's ailments. Many remedies were made from tobacco by-products. For instance, warm tobacco smoke blown into a child's aching ear soothed the pain, and a chew of tobacco applied to a throbbing bee sting took away the swelling.[44]

Although all family members weeded, hoed, and tended to the vegetable garden, the women were responsible for ensuring that enough food would be available for meals. They served fresh vegetables while the garden thrived and canned produce to use in the winter months. They used tobacco stalks to fertilize the garden soil. Old hand-rived tobacco sticks no longer needed in the fields might be used to tie up tomatoes and beans in the garden. Black Patch women let nothing of value go to waste.[45]

Tobacco could be used for pleasure as well. Farmers chewed twists of tobacco they made from their own crop. Chewing left the hands free for other work, numbed hunger pangs, and kept the mouth moist during hot days in the dusty fields when the water jug ran dry.

Wrightman W. Garner, *The Production of Tobacco;* W. F. Axton, *Tobacco and Kentucky;* Lewis C. Gray, *History of Agriculture in the Southern United States;* and Nannie M. Tilley, *The Bright Tobacco Industry, 1860–1929* (Chapel Hill: University of North Carolina Press, 1948).

43. Beulah Ryan, interview by Sammy Fisk, tape recording, May 5, 1977, Western Kentucky History and Culture Collection, Land between the Lakes Series, Forrest C. Pogue Oral History Institute, Murray, Kentucky.

44. Eunice McCarty, interview.

45. Ibid.

Women used snuff, which they kept in dainty tins. A sassafras sprig that was frayed at the end was used as a brush to dip snuff. After the turn of the century, fewer young women took up the habit of their mothers and grandmothers. After the 1920s when women began to smoke, Black Patch people disapproved of both habits. Even today Baptist women like Eunice McCarty call using them sins.[46]

Important regular income for farm families of all classes and races came from women's raising and selling of poultry or their trading of eggs and fowl. Throughout the year, as the cycles of the "thirteen-month" cash crop of tobacco passed, women participated in and supervised the care of poultry. While the tobacco money came once a year, the egg money came every week or two, providing a regular income or credit line at the general store.[47]

"I packed hundreds of eggs to the store in a basket and exchanged" them for due bills, recalls Mrs. O. C. Wells. "We usually had enough eggs to pay the bill" for the week's groceries, the flour, sugar, coffee, soda, and other items farm families could not grow. W. T. Ahart, a general store proprietor, recalls his son, Seldon Ahart accepted the eggs and issued due bills—credit slips, which customers used to purchase supplies in the store. Hucksters would come and buy once a week from the general store or "we shipped them [eggs and chickens] out on boats" on the Cumberland River.[48]

"The Hen More Important, Financially, Than the Country's Wheat Crop," the Cadiz *Record* announced in 1905 to no one's surprise. Myrtle De Priest took as many as thirty dozen eggs a week to trade and that "helped feed us." Nancy Ramey Stovall raised chickens, recalls her daughter, Eunice McCarty, "and when she had more eggs than she needed to buy groceries they'd give her a due bill. She'd

46. Ibid.
47. Ibid.
48. Mrs. O. C. Wells, interview by Tina Ratterree, tape recording, June 10, 1976, Western Kentucky History and Culture Collection, Calloway County Folklife Series, Forrest C. Pogue Oral History Institute, Murray, Kentucky; Eunice McCarty, interview; Mabel Farmer, interview by Susan Lindauer, tape recording, February 6, 1976, Western Kentucky History and Culture Collection, Calloway County Folklife Series, Forrest C. Pogue Oral History Institute, Murray, Kentucky; Seldon Ahart, interview by David Sullivan, tape recording, August 16, 1976, Western Kentucky History and Culture Collection, Land between the Lakes Series, Forrest C. Pogue Oral History Institute, Murray, Kentucky.

bring the due bill home and put it up in the cupboard and save them. One time," McCarty says, "she bought a chair." She spent them "more than just on food." Women also received substantial sums of money McCarty says, for hens, which they sold in the fall. "I've sold as high as seventy-five dollars worth of old hens to get them out of the way for the pullets. And I'd take that money," she says, laughing, "I'd think I had some money then" and bought "whatever we needed for the children. Usually buy clothes for the children." In this way, women controlled some money in the family. However, the use of due bills restricted their shopping to one store.[49]

Men, too, recognized the importance of women's chicken and egg income. The due bills from egg trades, Ruston Flowers says, "took the place of the income of once a year," when farmers received the tobacco money. "So the egg money and the milk money and all was used for the running of the household." With it, he says, they bought "sugar, coffee, essential things like that and the rest of the food on the farm was either raised or grown on that farm." Store merchants shipped eggs from the Black Patch to distant cities. "T. H. Fuqua of Canton, Trigg County," a Cumberland River town, shipped "forty-eight cases with 17,000 eggs," the largest amount ever from his store, in 1906 to Pittsburgh, Pennsylvania.[50]

Raising chickens occupied a woman every day. If she had no children, she did all the work herself, from feeding the birds and gathering eggs to cleaning out the hen house periodically. If she had children, as soon as the youngest could lift a pan of chicken feed, he or she began to help with the poultry. One Lyon County woman, Eunice Stovall McCarty, learned about poultry raising from her mother. "I started out [and] did it just like she did." During the many years she raised chickens, she made changes and improvements, which she explains while narrating the tasks involved.[51]

"I have Buff Orpington eggs for sale at $1.00 per setting of fifteen," Mrs. Harold Jacob advertised in the Princeton, Caldwell County newspaper in March of 1908, when Eunice McCarty's mother was order-

49. *Cadiz Record*, December 21, 1905; Eunice McCarty, interview; DePriest, interview.

50. Flowers, interview; *Hopkinsville Daily Kentucky New Era*, March 5, 1906.

51. Eunice McCarty, interview.

ing eggs to start the new season. In 1920, a setting of fifteen eggs still sold for only a dollar. "During the 1930s," McCarty says, "poultry houses began selling eggs for hatching or live chicks by mail order." Before then, McCarty set the eggs to hatch in the nests of hens old enough to "mother a brood" in early March. "I put about sixteen eggs under each hen." In about three weeks, the chicks pecked their way into the world to be hovered over by both the mother hen and the farm woman.[52]

The woman's tasks were to keep the chicks well fed, warm, and dry. Before the advent of the electrically-heated tin brooder house, which used a light bulb, in the 1940s, "the old hen had to do all the taking care of the chickens," says McCarty. If the weather got cool, the "hen would spread her wings out and they'd [the chicks] go get under her wings." Women provided shelters, or coops, for the brood hens, which "were like an A-line house." The men made the frames and "women would take those and put boards on top of them so [they] wouldn't leak." Also, McCarty says, "we'd have little feed coops made out of tobacco sticks so that little chickens could get in there between the slits and the old hen couldn't get in and eat up their feed."[53]

Feeding the chickens, McCarty says, was a delicate, time-consuming task until the late 1920s, when commercial feeds became available in the region, because in "those days we would get corn meal and cook corn bread without any seasoning in it, put it in a sack and let it get dry." Once dried, children "would crumble it on lids and planks, for the birds to peck. At least twice a day watering had to be done because "if chickens don't get water they won't lay eggs because a chicken's egg is about two-thirds water." In very cold weather, mothers sent their children to break the ice on the water troughs several times a day.[54]

Although hens cared for their chicks, emergency situations arose that demanded the woman's time. A sunny quiet afternoon, McCarty recalls, might be interrupted with the "whoop" of an old hen who had spotted a hawk intent on stealing a young one. The hen's warn-

52. Ibid; *Princeton Twice-A-Week Leader*, March 1908.
53. Eunice McCarty, interview.
54. Ibid.

ing brought the little chicks near, and they "would just flatten down in that grass as flat as they could and get under her wings." The squawk of the hen also brought McCarty outside to grab the "single-barreled shot-gun on the back porch," which she fired to scare away the predator.[55]

"If it commenced to coming up a cloud, look like it was going to rain," the woman had to work to shoo the chickens into their coops. Some knew to go to their coops during a spring shower, but "some of them if you didn't come and drive them up, they would squat down out there and if it rained hard enough it would drown some of the chickens" nestled under the hens' wings in the mud puddles. Sometimes the hens were not discovered before the downpour hit, McCarty recalls. "One time a bunch of chickens went down on the bluff and we couldn't find them." Finally, "we heard the old hen clucking and we went out there and those chickens were laid out on the ground practically drowned." McCarty, her mother, and her younger brothers "brought them in the house and wrapped them up good and rubbed them and built a little fire in the wood stove and laid them in the oven and they began to move and came out of it." Lost chicks, McCarty emphasizes, meant less income later.[56]

Besides tending to the chickens' physical needs, women maintained the chicken house and yard. McCarty estimates that she spent at least two to three hours every day working around her two hundred chickens. When each of her children turned six or seven years old, he or she joined the others in doing much of the work, which McCarty directed. For instance, one weekly chore involved cleaning the henhouse. "We'd take an old broom and sweep the roost out and clean the pen good," then "shovel out the manure and take it and throw it on the garden by the bucket-full, and then I'd take a slack lime and throw in there and sanitize it." Finally, she doused the coop with a toxin she had made of juice from the stalks of tobacco to deter lice and mites.[57]

"In the spring of the year we began to have this hen's nest grass, I don't know actually what kind of grass it was. We never did call it

55. Ibid.
56. Ibid.
57. Ibid.; Marshall, interview.

anything but hen's nest grass, but it grew in the old gullies." Before "the weeds and the green grass began to grow, I'd take tow sacks and go take it up by the handfulls" to use in the hen's nests along with some crumbled tobacco or cedar chips. Springtime also meant the buildings had to "be white-washed inside and out" to clean the buildings and make for a neat appearance. Faded, unkempt out-buildings on a farm, McCarty explains, indicated a "lazy good-for-nothing" farmer.[58]

When the chickens got sick, women did the best they could to cure their ailments. Chickens sometimes got the "limber neck from eat-ing maggots or drinking bad water," recalls McCarty. She, like her mother, treated the affliction skillfully. "She'd take a broom straw, or a chicken's wing feather and dip it down into turpentine and ram that right down the chicken's throat and right back up." The turpen-tine killed the germs like a medicine would have. McCarty tried to prevent waterborne disease by putting a few drops of turpentine in the water troughs, however, too much of it "made the chicken's flesh taste like turpentine." When there was no disease, there was some-thing else to do. McCarty claims, "you had to work with them all the time on one thing or another."[59]

All the work and care paid off as the chickens matured and began to lay eggs. Children gathered the eggs every day, taking care not to crack the eggs or get pecked by angry hens. Women stored the eggs, except for those the family ate. Each Saturday, McCarty says, she packed the eggs for her husband to take to the general store, where he traded the eggs for supplies and brought home due bills for any leftover credit, which they saved for later purchases. Women pro-vided a weekly income that was essential to making a living, but in McCarty's claim that "it helped out," she reveals the woman's belief that her work was subordinate to the men's work. Income from chicken sales and egg trades augmented the family income and enabled them to buy essentials, like flour or sugar, as well as a few luxuries.[60]

Women's work with chickens and eggs provided a welcome regular income to the family each week. Myrtle DePriest received about

58. Eunice McCarty, interview.
59. Ibid.
60. Ibid.

thirty cents a dozen in the 1930s and 1940s for her cartons of eggs. She would have "about thirty dozen a week." This income added up to about nine dollars worth of due bills each week, which, she claims, was not a paltry sum. For comparison, female workers in the Eddyville Cumberland Shirt Factory made just eighteen cents an hour, or about seven dollars for forty hours of labor each week. Often, George McCarty says, the egg and chicken income kept the middling farmers out of debt to the merchants. Even tenant farmer's wives raised a few chickens for food and sale, and they, too, were sometimes able to avoid debt.[61]

The livelihood of Black Patch farm families depended on the work of all members of the family. The Kentucky tobacco crop of 1919, for example, brought farmers $116,424,639, while the total income for women's chicken and egg production amounted to $9,238,447. The total amount cleared on the two allowed many Black Patch families to procure a modest living. Along with tobacco, poultry "was part of your livelihood," claims George McCarty.[62]

Black Patch farm families organized their lives around the "thirteen month crop" of dark-fired tobacco and ordered their society on the basis of family, hard work, and religion. Tobacco provided a cohesive element in society because it was something everyone in the region depended upon. Most farmers who grew it took pride in their skills and knowledge of dark tobacco cultivation, despite the demanding nature of the work and the uncertainties inherent in farming— the entire tobacco crop could be destroyed by bad weather, poor handling, or fire. Henry Baggett recalled the words of a song he used to sing at church, "life is like a little mountain railroad." Tobacco people's living is hard, he says, and requires people who do not fear work, but who do fear God because, "there's got to be something there that you'll be afraid of in the hereafter."[63]

61. Ibid.; Myrtle DePriest, interview by author, tape recording, Lyon County, Kentucky, July 22, 1987; George McCarty, interview; Bell, interview.

62. United States, *Fourteenth Census* (1920), vol 4, part 2, *Agricultural Reports for the States; The Southern States*, 384–434; George McCarty, interview.

63. Baggett, interview; Breen, *Tobacco Culture*, 21–23, 56.

6

A WORLD OF VIOLENCE

Robert Penn Warren, of Guthrie, Todd County, Kentucky, wrote of the "world of violence" he knew during his boyhood in the Black Patch. It was a world, he recalls, in which one "accepted violence as a component of life. . . . You heard about violence, and you saw terrible fights . . . not violence of robbery, you see; it was another kind of violence in the air: the violence of anger." The violence Warren recalls was so pervasive a part of the Black Patch culture that "there was some threat of being trapped into this whether you wanted to or not and being stuck with it." Violence remained a constant, inescapable element of daily life in the region; there was racial violence, domestic violence, fighting among adolescent males, and murder. These actions worked to validate force as a means to an end, thus perpetuating the cycle of violence in the culture.[1]

After the disruptions of the Civil War, the region's people tried to reestablish old social structures and adapt to the changes wrought by the conflict. Violence against the newly freed slaves began soon after the war and continued into the early twentieth century. Racial violence served as a tool that whites used to control blacks politically, socially, and economically.

African Americans in the region were granted precarious status as an out-group that could mingle with whites of all classes only according to precise but unwritten and unspoken rules. Within the black community young children quickly learned the racial etiquette since all adults in the black neighborhood possessed the authority to discipline children, especially when they interacted with whites. In this way African American adults educated their children about the segregated society of the nineteenth-century South.[2]

1. Robert Penn Warren, quoted in Daniel Joseph Singal, *The War Within*, 346; John G. Miller, *The Black Patch War*, 48.
2. Lula Bell Hollowell, interviewer unknown, tape recording, n.d., Kentucky De-

White violence, or the threat of it, lay like a fog over the black communities. An elaborate social etiquette developed from of Old South customs with new Jim Crow adaptations, which created a superficial "harmony" between the two races. African American men, in particular, had to maintain attitudes of social deference, obsequiousness, and emotional control when in the company of whites. Any hint of "uppityness" on the part of a black man in the social, political, or economic arenas could raise the ire of whites. Far more serious were reports of black men's "actions" toward white women; to express interest in a white woman could lead to the hangman's noose. Lynch law was not unknown in Kentucky and Tennessee, where hatreds and rivalries caused by the Civil War contributed to the tumultuous postwar years. Regulators, Loyal League activists, and Ku Klux Klansmen, some of whom Democratic officials accepted and even allied with, carried out lynch law in the state until the early 1870s. Across the South, the decade of the nineties saw a horrific number of lynchings. During the 1890s, 82 percent of the country's lynchings occurred in the South, and between 1889 and 1918, the proportion rose to 88 percent. The Black Patch experienced its share of this violence.[3]

Most lynchings in the Black Patch took place in Kentucky. Christian County, Kentucky had the largest black population in the state. Montgomery and Henry Counties in Tennessee had the greatest number of black citizens in that section of the Black Patch, each with between 30 percent and 50 percent of blacks in the total population. Elite whites sought to control their laborers. Political, economic, and social restrictions worked to this end. Whites who were not dependent upon the black workers resented the economic competition they provided and wanted to rid their communities of all African Americans. Methods ranging from paternalism to threats, intimidation,

---

partment of Libraries and Archives, Kentucky Oral History Commission, County Tapes, Trigg County, Frankfort, Kentucky. Hollowell, the granddaughter of slaves, grew up on the Broadbent farm in Trigg County, Kentucky.

3. Tapp and Klotter, *Decades of Discord*, 377–85; statistics are from Joel Williamson, *The Crucible of Race: Black-White Relations in the American South since Emancipation*, 117; Pete Daniel, *Standing at the Crossroads: Southern Life in the Twentieth Century*, 56; George Brown Tindall, *The Emergence of the New South, 1913–1945*, 172.

and attacks were employed to reach these goals. Logan County lynch-ings began with the first-known incidence in the autumn of 1883. By 1895, thirteen lynchings had taken place there.[4]

A few Black Patch white citizens hated the practice of lynch law. Owensboro attorney George W. Jolly declared that lynching "was a disgrace to Kentucky. It is one of the most deplorable events that has transpired in the history of this state." Citing the recent lynching of Allen Mathis, a black man charged with assaulting a white woman, Jolly stated that "it was nothing more nor less than the mob captur-ing the court and the strong arm of the law clasping hands with Judge Lynch. Mathis deserved hanging, but it should have been a legal execution," under Section 1197 of the Statutes. Jolly took a risk in so openly criticizing mob justice. Few others dared to make simi-lar remarks, because popular opinion supported the lynching of blacks accused of rape.[5]

Evidence that the majority of citizens disagreed with Jolly's views came to the fore when white hysteria reached a fever pitch in Russell-ville, Logan County, in 1908. White citizens were aroused by the murder of James Cunningham of Allensville, who had been killed by his black employee, Rufus Browder. Browder had been taken to Bowling Green in Warren County for his safety; however, four blacks—John Bouyer, Joe Riley, and brothers John and Virgil Jones—were confined in the Russellville jail on minor charges. Frustrated whites mobbed the jail and dragged the men, who were clad only in their underwear, out onto the main street, where a crowd waited. The mob took the victims to the Hangman's Tree on Armstrong Street and lynched them. Three other victims of a lynch mob had died at the same tree in 1897. One man told what happened after the 1908 lynching: "Well, my grandaddy told me that after they cut them guys down, they unwound the rope and sold it for fifty cents an inch."[6]

4. Joseph H. Cartwright, *The Triumph of Jim Crow: Tennessee Race Relation in the 1880s*, 25–27; Wright, *Racial Violence*, 72–73.

5. *Cadiz Record*, January 25, 1906; *Hopkinsville Daily Kentucky New Era*, January 22, 1906; *Hopkinsville Daily New Era*, August 8, 1906.

6. Granville Eugene Cates, "Folklore from Logan County," MSS 1980–87, Folk-lore and Folklife Collection, Department of Library Special Collections, Folklife Archives, Western Kentucky University Library, Bowling Green, Kentucky; Rev-erend Edward Coffman, interview by Virginia Gray, tape recording, November 22,

Following the lynching, the black victims' families took the bodies away for burial. Mary Lou Saunders, a child at the time, recalls that her parents did not allow her to go to Armstrong Street, because they were very upset about it, as "we all were at the time." Blacks believed Night Riders, who were operating in the Black Patch in 1908 during the Black Patch War of 1904–1909, called the "tobacco wars" by the locals, were involved in the lynching. Some whites were disturbed by the violence too. Mrs. Hal Mays, a resident of Russell-ville, claims that a white rural mail carrier was so haunted by his involvement in the mob action that he later committed suicide. Quiet individuals who would never commit a crime when alone might be caught up in crowd hysteria and moved to unbelievable violence.[7]

Eventually the murder suspect, Rufus Browder, returned to Logan County under the guard of Sheriff Tom Rhea and a militia contingent. The Logan County sheriff "resented the efforts of the militiamen to sur-round" the captive and threw two of the soldiers off his wagon. Peace prevailed; Browder arrived at the jail safely, and no lynching occurred.[8]

While violence was a constant part of the lives of the Black Patch people during the nineteenth and twentieth centuries, there were distinct forms of violence. Each has a unique and often complex source arising out of the cultural, social, economic, familial, and personal situations of the participants. The ramifications for society were sometimes obvious, but many subterranean effects of violent behavior percolated through the cultural structure of the region. Everyone in the Black Patch was influenced by the violent culture. Although many people never committed violent acts or became victims of them, no one was immune to the social and psychological effects of life in a violent culture.[9]

Violence began at home. Discipline for children, including spank-

---

1966, Folklore and Folklife Collection, Department of Library Special Collections, Folklife Archives, Western Kentucky University, Bowling Green, Kentucky.

7. Mary Lou Saunders, interview by Virginia Gray, tape recording, November 22, 1966; Judge Homer Dorris, interview by Virginia Gray, tape recording, November 22, 1966; Mrs. Hal Mays, interview by Virginia Gray, tape recording, November 22, 1966. All of the above are in the Folklore and Folklife Collection, Department of Library Special Collections, Folklife Archives, Western Kentucky University, Bowling Green, Kentucky.

8. *Cadiz Record*, August 13, 1908.

9. Based on oral histories and examination of newspapers including the *Cadiz*

ings and beatings, were common and accepted. Children who suffered whippings learned to use violence to control others. Biblical sources, whites and blacks believed, condoned violent forms of punishment. Eunice McCarty cited Proverbs 22:6, "Train up a child in the way he should go: and when he is old he will not depart from it," as proof that God favored corporal punishment. Folk sayings also supported the use of force with disobedient children. McCarty recalled that her mother, Nancy Stovall, often declared "Don't spare the rod and spoil the child," when she punished her children. If McCarty's mother could not determine the guilty party after some childish prank, she threatened, "I'll whip you both and I'll get the right one." She also got the innocent one and taught both children the power of arbitrary justice and violence.[10]

In cautious statements, some women discussed the harshness of husbands toward wives and of parents toward children. They recalled sensing that their mothers seemed to fear their fathers. Black Patch adults, white and black, recalled that as children they feared their fathers as they had learned to fear God at church. The strict rule of authoritarian fathers created fear and awe in the children. One Black Patch farmer's son, James R. Glass, recalled that though his father could be fun-loving, he could also be "severe in the discipline of his children, having been thoroughly indoctrinated in the belief that the rod was a very efficacious instrument in bringing to obedience refractory boys and girls." Glass recalled that on a "cold November morning when the ground was frozen and the frost lay thick on the cornstalks, we were rushed out early . . . to gather corn." During the work, Glass, dressed scantily and without gloves, began to suffer from the chill air. "My hands grew so cold that they became quite numb, and I could not keep up my row. I suffered untold agony . . . was shivering from head to foot, and began to cry." He was also tormented by fright because of his father's tough methods of discipline. "I was afraid that he might punish me for breaking down."[11]

Record, Hopkinsville Daily Kentucky New Era, Hopkinsville Kentuckian, Princeton Twice-A-Week Leader and the Clarksville Leaf-Chronicle.

10. Eunice Stovall McCarty, letter, June 18, 1991. See Miller, For Your Own Good; Greven, Spare the Child.

11. "Autobiography of James R. Glass," unpublished, c. 1912, original owned by Odell Walker, Kuttawa, Kentucky.

While young James Glass continued to whimper uncontrollably, he remembers that his father "scolded me, ridiculed me, threatened me, and tried to minimize my suffering." Finally, the boy was ordered back to the house. Glass mused that "if he had been kind and forbearing with me, I would have enjoyed the permission, but as it was, I was miserable, for I felt that I was practicing a fraud" rather than truly suffering the effects of the intensely cold weather. Such verbal abuse, as well as the use of switches at home and at school, instructed children in the culturally acceptable ways of violent behavior.[12]

Violence against women and children very seldom was discussed, not because it rarely occurred, but because people considered it a private family affair. Few people discussed such incidents, and when they did, they only alluded to domestic troubles in other families, not in their own. However, several cases are recorded. In July 1904, Mack Hern shot and killed his father, Jim Hern, in a saloon in Hopkinsville after a family quarrel. Mack Hern revealed the root of the trouble when he declared, "I would kill two fathers if they talked about my mother like he did." One of the worst insults any man could hear was the impugning of his mother's character, especially by his father. Ideally, Black Patch whites idolized their women as moral, self-sacrificing, gentle beings, who should be defended at all costs by the males in the family. Mack Hern defended his mother's virtue against her husband, Mack's father. No doubt a long history of verbal and possibly physical abuse led Mack to the extreme action of committing murder.[13]

The same summer in Todd County, a white woman, Minnie Mitchell, died at the hands of her husband, R. L. Mitchell. Her "throat [was] cut from ear to ear." R. L. Mitchell was arrested for the killing, but he denied his guilt and acted quite "demented," according to officials commenting for the local paper. The coroner spoke to an elderly black woman who lived just one hundred yards from the Mitchell residence, and she reported hearing scuffling and "fussing" before the killing. The coroner recorded evidence of a fight in his report. Other records in the case no longer exist, but the death alone is proof enough that violence against women on lonely farmsteads in

12. Ibid.
13. *Hopkinsville Daily Kentucky New Era*, July 5, 1904.

the region was not uncommon, although it was often well hidden and silence prevailed. "That's not something we talk about much," warned one woman.[14]

Women reading the county paper in 1904 saw confirmation that the courts still considered them subject to their husbands' authority. Judge John J. Riley upheld the old English custom of wife beating in a case in which a Squire Smith came to court in Lexington, Kentucky accused of abusing his wife, Annie Smith, after he had seen her talking to another man. Judge Riley dismissed the case, demonstrating to all women their subordinate status in society.[15]

Violence within black families occurred as well. In the summer of 1905, George Johnson, a laborer in Christian County on the George B. Starling farm, killed his wife. Jurors found Johnson guilty and recommended a life sentence. Abuse of women and children did not usually lead to murder; rather, levels of violence ebbed and flowed in the privacy of homes, and domestic disputes often went unreported.[16]

A case exemplifying the complex social and economic roots of domestic violence against women occurred in Christian County at Sharpe's Field in the summer of 1906. Just a week after giving birth, Mrs. Wint Berry died from a beating inflicted by her husband. Apparently she arose from bed only three days after the baby came and quarreled with her husband. He struck her in the stomach with his fist, and she fell to the ground unconscious and never revived.[17]

Lawmen arrested Winchester "Wint" Berry for the murder. Berry claimed innocence and gave his side of the story: He had been preparing to go to town to get groceries on the morning of Tuesday, August 7, and was about to leave when his wife came to the door. He told her to go back inside, and when he returned home later in the day, he found her unconscious. Berry's six-year-old stepdaughter, Eulace, saw the events differently. She stated at the trial that Berry struck her mother with a "large pan in which she was making bread and struck her with it in the side and in the stomach with his fist." Flour flew on Mrs. Berry, the walls, the floor, and on Eulace. Then

14. Ibid., August 15, 1904; Eunice McCarty, interview.
15. *Hopkinsville Daily Kentucky New Era*, June 7, 1904.
16. *Hopkinsville Daily Kentucky New Era*, March 8, 1906; *Cadiz Record*, February 16, 1905; *New Era*, August 8, 1906.
17. *Hopkinsville Daily Kentucky New Era*, August 9, 1906.

Mrs. Berry ran out of the kitchen door. The little girl began to cry, she said, "because I couldn't do anything else." She said that thirteen-year-old Johnny Humphries, who lived with the family, told her not to tell or someone would get arrested. Instead, she should say that her mother had suffered a fit. Young Humphries denied this and claimed he had instructed the child to tell the truth.[18]

The Berry "family was almost poverty stricken," despite their work as tenants, a situation that could lead to tension and violence. County officials requested that the Kentucky Home Society of Louisville take the couple's children, who ranged in age from six years to three weeks. Wint Berry, who, at age sixty, was much older than his wife, testified that he suffered from an asthmatic condition and "was attacked by a smothering spell" at times. He claimed that one of these spells hit him on the morning following the arrival of the baby. Mrs. Berry left her bed to wait on her husband and then continued her usual household duties. Neighborhood conjecture suggested that economic and familial problems and tensions brought on by the birth of the baby and Mr. Berry's ill health might have led to the argument, which escalated to a fight and resulted in the killing of Mrs. Berry. The court convicted Wint Berry of voluntary manslaughter, but he did not live to serve out his sentence. He died in jail in late September 1906, as a result of heart trouble and bronchitis.[19]

This tragedy reveals the darker side of life in the region: poverty; lack of opportunity for single women, which often forced widows to remarry quickly; lack of health care, which allowed ailments to drag on and led to family tension; little or no maternity care for new mothers; and the isolation of farm life, with no neighbors to help out in emergencies could contribute to stress, a sense of hopelessness, and domestic violence.[20]

In the Black Patch, where the culture rested upon the unquestioned authority of an Old Testament God from whom the earthly husband and father derived his role in the family and society, it is not surprising that fathers resorted to harsh measures when challenged or disobeyed. Some women recognized that their subordinate

18. *Cadiz Record*, January 5, 1905, August 11, 1906, August 14, 1906.
19. Ibid., September 26, 1906, September 29, 1906.
20. Ibid.

position in society sometimes left them dangerously unprotected. When Percy J. Luster of Elkton, Todd County came to trial for murdering his wife, the courtroom was packed with spectators, many of whom, the paper noted, were women. These white women left their daily chores to witness the fate of a wife killer. Luster remained adamantly silent, declaring only that "they can twist my arms, or burn me at the stake, but they cannot make me tell a thing." Whatever the cause of the Lusters' marital dispute, the community's women, by making themselves present, demonstrated their knowledge of the plight of all women in society.[21]

Violence and killing among family members happened with disturbing frequency. Conflict broke out between fathers and sons, cousins, uncles and nephews, and among in-laws. Arguments, long-held grudges, and explosive anger prompted tragedies such as the 1905 Sumner-Dixon murder.

"Killed His Cousin," proclaimed the bold headline of the Trigg County paper in January 1905. "Matt Sumner, age twenty-four, son of the late James Sumner and half brother of Ed S. Sumner of Cadiz, was shot and killed on Friday, December 30, 1904, by his cousin Claude Dixon, age twenty-two, son of Bob Dixon of Futrell in the Land Between the Rivers." The paper, as was customary, pointed out all the family relationships of those involved. "Dixon is the grandson of T. J. Dixon, of Donaldson and Ed Ross of near Golden Pond. . . . Sumner's father being a brother of Dixon's grandmother."[22]

The sole witness to the shooting, Clyde Sumner, reported that he, Matt, and Claude all spent the night prior to the killing with Matt's mother. During the day the young men went to visit a neighbor, Sterling Adams, who lived about a mile and half from Matt's mother's place. "The boys were all drinking, and Matt began to curse Claude. Adams asked Clyde to take Matt away" however, the cursing continued and "both went out to the wood pile and there engaged in a fisticuff." Eventually the cousins were separated, and Clyde and Matt left.[23]

Once they had gone down the road a short distance, Matt stopped

21. *Cadiz Record*, September 7, 1905.
22. Ibid., January 5, 1905.
23. Ibid.

and asked Clyde to take him to Sam Ford's home. The route to Ford's farm passed Claude Dixon's residence. Clyde consented to accompany Matt to Ford's if he promised not to start any more trouble with Claude. Despite his promise, once they reached the Dixon farm, Matt resumed the verbal exchange with Claude. "Clyde caught hold of Matt to hold him, and finally threw him down and put his hand over his mouth" to stifle the curses. At that point "Claude Dixon came out the gate with pistol in hand and told Clyde to get off of Matt if he did not want to get shot as he was going to kill Matt." Clyde released his grip on Matt and lunged toward Claude to stop him from shooting, but Claude fired and Matt ran behind the stable. Dixon followed and shot again. Matt had turned and headed toward his cousin when a third shot rang out. "About that time they clinched and fell, Matt on top, and he began to cut Dixon with his knife. Dixon shot twice more, killing Sumner."[24]

After the murder, Claude went to Johnny Adams's place. Deputy Sheriff Shoemaker arrested him there and locked him in the Cadiz jail. He was held over in court with a five-hundred-dollar bond. Dixon claimed he had acted in self-defense. A few months later, Claude and two cell mates escaped from jail. Dixon remained at large until summer, when he was found in Mississippi. That fall Claude Dixon received a sentence of thirty months in the state penitentiary at Eddyville for the murder of his kinsman.[25]

Violence among young men, black and white, usually followed a similar pattern. Old grudges, questions of honor, insults to one's family or women were settled by physical combat. Simple arguments could lead to serious confrontations. "Gus Johnson and John Southall, two negro laborers on the farm of E. D. Jones, near Church Hill" in Christian County came to blows over the job of hitching a mule for the day's work. With no other weapons available, the men used lumps of coal and a stick in the battle, and one suffered a fractured skull.[26]

Drinking, gambling, and other vices enjoyed at social gatherings led to confrontations, even murder. Ed Greenway received a sentence

24. Ibid.
25. Ibid., March 2, 1905, September 14, 1905.
26. *Hopkinsville Daily Kentucky New Era*, November 22, 1904.

of five years in the state penitentiary for voluntary manslaughter in the killing of Oscar White at a "negro festival at Pee Dee in 1905." The shooting occurred early one Sunday morning after a Saturday night barbecue where, the paper explained, much "drinking [was] indulged in." Among youths, episodes of violence arose over arguments during games. Two boys in their teens grew incensed over a marble match. One of the boys, Lee White, got a shotgun and fired two shots at his rival, Hunter Carlos, hitting him in the legs. Both were brought to justice: Carlos was fined ten dollars, and White was held for trial. Another murder occurred near Pee Dee at Guire's Chapel schoolhouse in June of 1907, when Jim Dawson shot Jim Terry in the head during a gathering. Time and time again, incidents of black on black violence caused by poverty, frustration, and the effects of racial oppression occurred in the community, adding to the level of violence in the region.[27]

In some instances, conflicts occurred, tempers flared, then cooled, and profuse apologies were offered, but aggression later resumed and escalated, resulting in injury or death. In one case, a baseball game played in Kuttawa, Lyon County, Kentucky, ended in death for Newton Riley. Riley and the elderly Al Tumblin quarreled after the game with "an exchange of very uncomplimentary epithets." The verbal dispute ended in apology; however, later that evening, Tumblin walked into a drugstore where Riley stood and shot him down. Tumblin took revenge for the younger man's insults and attack. By satisfying his wounded pride with an act of vengeance, Tumblin restored his sense of self-esteem and manhood.[28]

Law officers sometimes used excessive force in their work. A grand jury indicted Marion Stagner, a former constable of Long Hollow district, in Trigg County, for malicious shooting—or shooting without due cause—during the arrest of a suspect. In a similar case in Lyon County, Marshal William McCullom received a fine of fifty dollars for the malicious shooting and wounding of Dr. A. P. Purdy of Kuttawa during an arrest. Purdy had "had trouble with the police

27. Ibid., March 8, 1906; *Cadiz Record*, June 29, 1905, December 13, 1906; *Hopkinsville Kentuckian*, June 13, 1907; *Hopkinsville New Era*, August 3, 1904; *Cadiz Record* May 4, 1905, August 31, 1905.

28. *Cadiz Record*, June 18, 1908; Rick Gregory, "Origins of Violence," 1986 (photocopy).

Judge" and resisted McCullom. Violence occurred at all levels of
society in the Black Patch, and no one remained isolated from its
effects.[29]

Prominent white men in the community died as the result of seemingly trivial disputes. Jeff Prewitt of Caldwell County suffered fatal
wounds when Bob Mills crushed his head during a fight over the
cutting of a bee tree on Prewitt's farm. Prewitt had shot at Mills
once before receiving his injuries. In this case, Mills was jailed. Few
murders went unnoticed by the law initially, even though grand
juries might refuse to indict or cases might be dismissed. Refusal to
indict or convict often revealed community sentiment in favor of a
defendant. As one Black Patch resident said, some people deserve
killing. If the community decided a death was justified, they would
not convict the killer. People from all classes in the Black Patch
resorted to violence in situations when insults, disputes, or differences of opinion aroused anger. Hezekiah Malone shot George Flynn
for trespassing on his land. Neighbors in the Buffalo community,
near Cerulean in Trigg County, were greatly excited by the affair
since "both men [were] among the county's best citizens."[30]

Relations between landowner and tenant resulted in physical conflict when tensions escalated. Gip Griffin, a thirty-five-year-old newly
married cropper, "shot and clubbed" seventy-year-old Henry Warner,
who later died of the wounds. "The men had disputed about the
working of stock and parted in anger," the paper reported. This
conflict exemplifies various aspects of tenancy that could be frus-
trating and demeaning to the cropper. Often landowners closely supervised the work of tenants, who resented being watched. Landless
men waited longer to marry because of their financial situations.
Griffin had just wed at the relatively late age of thirty-five. He was
responsible for a family, yet had not achieved the ideal goal of land
ownership and still fell under the control of a much older landowner,
who apparently did not allow much independence in work decisions.
Such power over tenants' lives and labor was common. Landowners
prevented tenants from getting extra food by "cutting down all the
fruit trees" near the tenant house. Contracts between land owners

29. Ibid.
30. *Cadiz Record*, April 19, 1906, October 24, 1907.

in the George A. Washington family of Robertson County, Tennessee, and their black sharecroppers reveal strict supervision of labor. These practices created dependency that sometimes led to resentment, anger, and violence. However, the powerlessness could also produce apathy and hopelessness. Violent behavior in these cases might be directed toward people other than the landlord, such as relatives or neighbors.[31]

Violent incidents seemed acceptable and normal because people grew up witnessing such acts. H. W. "Son" Bennett, who grew up near Dycusburg on the Cumberland River in the early 1900s, saw one murder and listened to the beating of his uncle during the Night Rider violence. In addition, he knew of two other killings in the town, neither of which went to trial. Whites condoned these killings, and grand juries refused to indict. Community-endorsed violence and justice prevailed.[32]

Malevolent behavior, vandalism, and boyish pranks were also very common in the region as they were in the South as a whole. Often bearing the brunt of such attacks were institutions of authority in the society, such as the church and the school. Adolescent and young adult white men committed these acts at community gatherings. Nearly any political meeting, religious revival, neighborhood party, or school social could be the setting for random shooting sprees outside the gatherings, loud talk, crude jokes, and bouts over honor among the young men. Preachers suffered abuse during their sermons and grew angry when they found their horses' manes and tails sheared off after a night meeting. Gradually during these years the traditional authority of the small community churches began to erode. The practice of policing the community through church hearings still continued into the teens with some regularity, especially in cases of a moral nature. Members tended to abide by these church rulings only when necessary to maintain their status within the neighbor-

31. *Hopkinsville Daily Kentucky New Era*, August 19, 1904; Christopher Waldrep, "Planters and the Planters' Protective Association in Kentucky and Tennessee," 570. The subject of powerlessness is discussed in John Gaventa, *Power and Powerlessness: Quiescence and Rebellion in an Appalachian Valley*.

32. H. W. Bennett, interview by author, tape recording, Crittenden County, Kentucky, September 19, 1988; Thomas Bender, *Community and Social Change in America*, 100; Tapp and Klotter, *Decades of Discord*, 408.

hood. Those who cared little for the church's sanctions ignored the rulings.[33]

Political meetings attracted local rowdies especially if the meetings included blacks. During December of 1906 in Todd County "while Sen. R. R. Grady was addressing an audience of colored voters in the colored Methodist church in behalf of the prohibition cause, someone shot through a window." Just a short distance away another "party of ruffians about the same time stoned the Colored Baptist Church, where Rev. Mr. Widgett, a white preacher was speaking for the same cause." Although the guilty parties in these cases were not apprehended, some believed whites were involved. Since black voters in other precincts in the 1890s had voted against prohibition, perhaps these incidents were warnings against a similar vote. The violence also intimidated black voters in a period when southern whites were struggling to take the franchise away from blacks.[34]

Rowdy behavior among male youths was nothing new. Religious services had always been the scene of rambunctious, irreverent antics on the part of backwoods folk. However, by the late 1800s, the ritualized camp meetings in the Black Patch witnessed only the deeds of youthful male transgressors. In this culture males were permitted, even encouraged, to sow wild oats, and "to kick up a commotion," during their teens and early twenties. Until men married and began the serious business of running farms and supporting families, people tolerated wild behavior. Being saved, or born again, meant the youth passed into adult manhood, where hard work, dedication to family and farm, and values of morality, honesty, and a strong religious faith were revered.[35]

Protracted meetings held in the late summer in every Black Patch county attracted nearly as much devilish behavior as worship. "Kirkmansville News" in the *Hopkinsville New Era* called attention to the

33. Trigg County, grand jury indictments, 1904–1908, boxes 6–10; Macedonia Baptist Church records, Department of Library Special Collections, Western Kentucky University, Bowling Green, Kentucky; Lyon County Circuit Court, Eddyville, Kentucky, indictment of James Brindly, no. 318, May 1905.
34. *Hopkinsville Daily Kentucky New Era*, December 4, 1906. Some blacks continued to vote throughout the teens and twenties. Clyde Quisenberry, interview, says he always voted with no problems.
35. Eunice McCarty, interview.

wild activities in the revival season of 1912. "There has been quite a good deal of pistol shooting in and near this place for about two weeks during a protracted meeting at the Christian Church" in the Kirkmansville neighborhood in the north west corner of Todd County near the Christian County line. On "Monday night four young men were a little bolder than common and did not wait to get out of town before they began to shoot." They began firing their weapons in front of Lea A. Gates's house, and bullets screamed over the heads of children playing near, striking an apple tree and another house. Such harassment of the revival-goers, along with a thunderstorm, which knocked down the tent, did not prevent the evangelist from having a successful evening. The Reverend C. Denson baptized thirty converts when the meetings ended.[36]

Congregations might witness vengeful murder, as happened near Hico in Calloway County. Fred and Clarence Jones teamed up to shoot Will Lewis at a baptizing in Jonathan Creek because of an old grudge. Some said the white men had quarreled about a woman. Whatever the motive, Lewis died with eight bullet wounds, and the community saw yet another instance of brutal violence enacted. No place proved sacred when personal vendettas were carried out.[37]

In addition to the individual acts of violence, a tradition of violent behavior existed within one kin group or family. Certain family names appear repeatedly in court records and in oral accounts. For instance, members of the Farmer family, of Lyon County, appear frequently in the court records for arrests and grand jury indictments from 1910 through 1930 for disturbing the peace, liquor violations, adultery, and carrying concealed weapons, among other things. Neighbors remember the tenant family and its lawless behavior. Emily Street recalled that Mark Farmer stole chickens from her mother's flock. Her father, Frank, suspicious of Mark, had his shotgun ready one night in case the chicken house was raided. When he heard the cackling of hens, he ran out and fired buckshot in the direction of a shadow he saw in the henhouse. Later, Mark Farmer visited the doctor, a friend of Frank's, to have shot removed from his backside. The Farmer boys participated in fights at local social events and

36. *Hopkinsville Daily Kentucky New Era*, September 19, 1912.
37. *Cadiz Record*, September 17, 1908.

dabbled in moonshining. Mark Farmer also appeared before the grand jury to hear indictments for immoral conduct with an underage female.[38]

Connected to the families with unfavorable reputations were whole neighborhoods that were notorious. Often a group of families, all of whom possessed "poor" characters, lived in the same neighborhood. It is unclear whether the families tended to congregate together due to a natural affinity or whether they were forced together because they had been pushed out of law-abiding communities due to their bad behavior. Orvil Oatts, a white landowner in Christian County recalls, "You have to go in certain sections," to locate the rough neighborhoods. "They was some around. Up in there around Allegree and back in there in Higginses, they's always cutting one another up and fighting." In some places "used to be they'd fight one another, and brothers fight one another and ever thing else." Oatts suggests that some of the violent characters came from Tennessee, which he regards as a rough place. The reasons for these pockets of violence, Oatts believes, is the people "didn't believe in God. Didn't believe in nothing. Laws of the land didn't mean any more to them than nothing. . . . They's their own law. You still have a lot of them today." White class tensions are revealed in the characterizations of these neighborhoods. The areas with unfavorable reputations, such as Fruit Hill, were in the hilly section of northern Christian County, where poor soils, poverty, and isolation prevailed.[39]

Fruit Hill in Christian County, Lamasco in Lyon County, and Guthrie on the Tennessee-Kentucky border stand out in residents' minds as rough locales. Newspaper reports of fights, arrests, and lawlessness in and near Fruit Hill substantiate the community's rough reputation. "Bloody Deeds Stop Dances, Young Farmers Full of Whiskey, Quarrel and Use Pistol and Knife," cried the headlines of the Christian County paper in July 1904, after a melee involving the four whites at Fruit Hill. That same summer one elderly farmer was

38. Trigg County Circuit Court Records, 1895–1935, Kentucky Department for Libraries and Archives, Public Records Division, Frankfort, Kentucky. The names in this case have been changed at the request of the interviewee. Lyon County Circuit Court Records, Eddyville, Kentucky, *Commonwealth of Kentucky v. Mark Farmer*, August 22, 1919.

39. Oatts, interview.

murdered and another seriously wounded in separate incidents in
the neighborhood. Court records of arrests and indictments of Lamasco
men for disturbing public worship, carrying concealed weapons, random shooting, brawling, and liquor infractions support oral sources'
descriptions of the place. "It's always been a rough place" from the
late 1800s until the 1970s, recalled one farm woman who belongs to
the Baptist Church in Lamasco. She claims that boys heard stories
of older men's fights and "carrying-on" and liked to do it themselves.
In effect, they consciously continued what they viewed as a tradition
of disruptive behavior. Also, she claims, many of the rowdy men
never attended church and lacked morals taught in Sunday School—
the morals and values of the middling, church-attending whites.[40]

The single largest subregion in the Black Patch that possessed a
notorious reputation was the region between the Cumberland and
Tennessee Rivers. The people of the area considered themselves close-
knit, law-abiding folk. Some residents noticed the violence of the
area and commented that people from "outside and inside" caused it.
Seldon Ahart grew up at Golden Pond, a little community a few
miles west of the Cumberland River. His father was the "magistrate
or constable" there for about fifteen years from about 1910 until the
mid-1920s. Ahart says most of the arrests made in Golden Pond
"were made for fighting."[41]

Residents living beyond the subregion point to the activities of the
people, derisively called "river rats," such as moonshining, immoral
behavior, violence, and murder, to prove their claims that it is lawless country. Court records do indicate a higher incidence of violence
in the area. That the Between the Rivers people deny this indicates a
difference in opinion about what constitutes lawlessness, immoral-
ity, and an acceptable level of violence in a society.[42]

40. *Hopkinsville Daily Kentucky New Era*, July 18, 1904, June 24, 1904, August 19, 1904; Lyon County Circuit Court Records, grand jury indictments, 1890–
1940, Eddyville, Kentucky; Eunice McCarty, interview.

41. Ahart, interview.

42. Katie Forsythe, interviewer unknown, tape recording, August 14, 1978,
Kentucky Department of Libraries and Archives, Kentucky Oral History Com-
mission, County Tapes, Lyon County, Kentucky. See Matthews, *Neighbor and
Kin;* Durwood Dunn, *Cades Cove: The Life and Death of a Southern Appalachian
Community, 1818–1937.*

Many factors contributed to higher levels of violence in the Land Between the Rivers. First, a subculture with different values and levels of toleration of violence arose among the majority of people. This developed due to the isolation of the area where, Floy Millers says, "not much moving in and out" occurred and where everything across the rivers seemed like "foreign soil" to Land Between the Rivers inhabitants.[43]

Class position also played a role. Poor land supported only subsistence agriculture supplemented by other work, such as timbering, working at the iron mills, and illegal alcohol production and sale. These people in their oral accounts admit that the area has a poor reputation, yet they take pride in their rough, independent, sometimes illicit means of making a living. Outsiders' opinions of the Between the Rivers communities are scorned, yet antipathy exists, and perhaps a subconscious sense of inferiority persists. This sense, along with the tensions wrought by poverty, hardship, authoritarian religious beliefs, and disrespect for the law, created a subculture of increased acceptance of violence.[44]

Another disruptive and sometimes violent influence in the Land Between the Rivers involved river traffic and the transient population it brought to the port towns, which added to the rowdy image of the area. Finally, the iron industry that operated in the area attracted outsiders, single men (the majority of whom were African American), and other allegedly disreputable characters into the Between the Rivers communities. Center Furnace, an iron industry village consisting of eighty to eighty-five dwelling houses and the furnace operations, earned a rough reputation. Trouble of various sorts, including brawling, shootings, and "lawlessness," went on from the time the furnace opened in 1905. As for the residents and workers, "as a general thing, it is a pretty hard class of people."[45]

43. Floy Miller, interview by David Sullivan, tape recording, June 29, 1976, Western Kentucky History and Culture Collection, Land between the Lakes Series, Forrest C. Pogue Oral History Institute, Murray, Kentucky.

44. Harry McCarty, interview by author, tape recording, Lyon County, Kentucky, March 9, 1987.

45. *Hopkinsville Daily Kentucky New Era*, August 1, 1904; *Cadiz Record*, February 27, 1908; *Commonwealth of Kentucky v. John W. Kelly*, testimony of J. P. White.

The nearly palpable atmosphere of violence in which Black Patch people lived and died seemed normal to them. Their preachers told them that a harsh God sanctioned violence and its use by fathers against wives and children. People who grow up in violent cultures become socialized and desensitized to the use of physical force. It becomes an acceptable method of instilling discipline, obedience, and control. The powerful always have the tool of violence available for use if needed. In the Black Patch, physical force had become an acceptable method of dealing with recalcitrant people of all races, classes, ages, and sexes. Violence was used against relatives, friends, enemies, and outsiders and justified by references to the Scriptures, practical effectiveness, and the need for law and order. A rich seam of violence—like coal in rock—ran through the culture of the Black Patch. That violence could be drawn on in times of economic and social distress.

7

A BATTLE OF JUSTICE
AND PATRIOTISM

I am an humble farmer. I was raised on the farm and have made tobacco all my life," declared Charles H. Fort, president of the Dark Tobacco District Planters' Protective Association of Kentucky and Tennessee and elite planter in Robertson County, Tennessee, before the 1904 United States Senate hearings on the relief of tobacco growers. "I came here for the poorer classes of my people, and they have not anything—have not enough money to buy groceries for their families even" because of the sharp drop in the 1904 tobacco prices.[1]

"Now, you may not know it," Fort explained, "but tobacco is the most slavish crop—and the dark tobacco is the worst. . . . We have to work fifteen months in a year on a crop of tobacco." Although he identified himself as a tobacco farmer, his wealth in land and his control of labor lightened his burden of physical toil. Charles Fort had black croppers to perform the backbreaking labor of tobacco production. Still, as an elite planter who took his paternalistic role seriously, he saw hardships and pain suffered by the laboring classes, black and white, during the crisis. He spoke compassionately for them in distant Washington, for which he received admiration and respect. Poor farmers could not travel so far nor speak so eloquently for the tobacco producers' cause. Fort fulfilled his role as planter and community leader by aiding the people of the Black Patch in their time of need.[2]

Charles Fort, a leader in the farmers' cooperation movement in the Black Patch counties, spoke of the tobacco situation and con-

1. Congress, House of Representatives, Subcommittee on the Internal Revenue Committee, *Hearings on the Relief of Tobacco Growers*, Fifty-Eighth Cong., 2d sess., February 4, 1904, and February 25, 1904 (Washington, D.C.: United States Government Printing Office, 1908), 39.
2. Ibid., 36–39; Waldrep, "Planters and the Association," 569; *Western Tobacco Journal*, February 6, 1910.

veyed to the Senate committee his perspectives on the plight of tobacco growers. He focused on the six-cent tax that had been placed on tobacco to finance the Civil War. Removal of the tax, he argued, "would benefit the poor people and the negroes who are dependent." It would also benefit the wealthy planters, who did not intend to lose their power in the economic crisis. The lower classes in many ways were dependent upon the elite, like Fort, who owned the land, mules, and equipment. The wealthy also had access to education, which led to high status and political power. People in the Black Patch believed that status and wealth inevitably led to power and prestige. For those who doubted this natural hierarchy, the real power that the elite held could be wielded roughly. Usually the social network of reciprocal relations between rich and poor and kin and friends and the tradition of deferential manners, racial etiquette, and religious beliefs about one's personal responsibility for failures, moral and economic, prevented overt conflicts.[3]

Charles Fort explained to the committee the way in which the classes coexisted to maintain the status quo, which he envisaged as best for the Black Patch. "In our country we have an ignorant class of laborers who know nothing except what they learn from us. We white people teach them all they know and take care of them." Fort, a southern paternalist, firmly believed that he helped and uplifted the blacks through teaching them the art of tobacco cultivation and the habits of labor on his plantation. From his perspective, he carried out a worthy mission. Fort continued, "I have a negro on my place who has never known anything else in his life. His mother was my black mammy. I went on his bond for a thousand dollars for shooting a negro once, and he came clear." In this way Fort kept a good laborer in the "family," and through intercession with the law indebted his black tenants to him and furthered the dependence of the powerless on the powerful. Fort stated that "these negroes are afraid of the revenue law and they are afraid of the Federal laws. They have no way of getting help if they get away from their own people," their white landlords.[4]

3. *Hearings*, 36–39; Waldrep, "Planters and the Association," 569; Dyer and Moore, comps., Eliott and Moxley, eds., *Tennessee Civil War Veterans*, 1261–62, 1467, 1794–95, 2042–43, 2162–63, 2179.
4. *Hearings*, 36–38.

Some blacks may have accepted the paternalistic system as the safest situation. Few opposed it openly, but some showed their displeasure by moving to Mississippi or elsewhere. Those who remained displayed the effects of an oppressive racial environment in their violence toward one another, such as domestic violence at home, when the young men fought at festivals and resorted to drinking and other behavior judged disorderly by the legal system.[5]

When Fort spoke before the congressmen in Washington, his region was facing the worst economic downturn since the Civil War. The crisis had been long in the making with roots in the immediate postwar period. Although the Black Patch had had a diverse agricultural base centered on three crops—tobacco, wheat, and corn—prior to the 1860s, this situation began to change in the 1870s. In 1872, tobacco accounted for 20 percent of the total crop value and ranked first as a money crop in Kentucky, with wheat ranking second. Thereafter, tobacco and wheat production increased substantially. Tobacco production increased from 15,000,000 pounds to 149,017,855 pounds during the 1870s. Wheat prices recovered then stabilized, leaving tobacco the unchallenged money crop in the Black Patch.[6]

Although dark tobacco had been the main cash crop since the early 1800s and had tied the growers to the world market economy, the increased production of the plant after the Civil War made farmers even more dependent as they gave up self-sufficiency for the cash economy. Gradually, in the postwar period they became entangled in debt, tax, and mortgage problems. The industrialization of the United States accelerated, affecting Americans everywhere. Black Patch producers, like other southern and western farmers during the 1880s and 1890s, searched for solutions to their complex problems. They had joined the Grangers, the Greenback party, the Farmers' Alliance, and the Populist party. In addition, they set up local tobacco organizations to address specific Black Patch concerns. Knowledge gleaned from these earlier efforts influenced the founders of the Dark Tobacco District Planters' Protective Association of Kentucky

5. Survey of county grand jury indictments and court records shows black male violence of this type.
6. Edward F. Pritchard, Jr., "Popular Political Movements in Kentucky" (senior thesis, Princeton University, 1935), 25–28.

and Tennessee (PPA) designed to address the crisis of 1904, when tobacco sold for three cents a pound or less, or as the farmers observed, "3-2-1 and a 'cussin.'"[7]

Black Patch producers cited specific factors that they believed caused the crisis. Many pointed to the importance of changes in tobacco marketing. "A few years ago a good market [in the Clarksville district], a good trade and a good deal of competition" existed, argued Charles E. Barker of Pembroke, Christian County. "We could put our tobacco on the open market, with an auctioneer to sell it, and we would have fifteen and twenty men bidding." By 1904, however, things had changed: "We have only one man to make a price on it, and he refuses to go into the market at all." T. E. Justice of Cheatham County, Tennessee, detailed the new market workings in 1904, when his county "was divided into three distinct districts by the Regie dealers, and a buyer . . . was by them placed in each one of these districts" in the county. Each buyer had "positive instructions to keep within the district assigned him, and not enter that of either of the other buyers." County purchasing districts "were laid off and bounded by certain public roads, prominent streams in the county," and no buyer crossed the lines. Cheatham County farmer G. W. Frazier, who owned "a farm through which the Neptune and Halfpone Road runs, having two tobacco barns, one on either side of said road," was visited by a buyer. The contents of one barn was sold, but when Frazier asked the buyer to offer a price on another barn's contents, the agent declined, "saying it was out of his territory, and that the road was the line of the district." Growers across the Black Patch told similar stories and became increasingly frustrated with the dealings of the tobacco companies.[8]

What the farmers perceived as a loss of competition was due in part to the workings of the American Tobacco Company, which was owned by James B. Duke, and two foreign businesses, the Italian

7. Ibid.; Rick Gregory, "Desperate Farmers: The Planters' Protective Association of Kentucky and Tennessee, 1904–1914" (Ph.D. diss., Vanderbilt University, 1989), 59; Henry Harrison Kroll, *Riders in the Night*, 25.

8. *Hearings*, 4; J. E. Justice, attorney at Ashland City, Tennessee, to A. O. Stanley, Henderson, Kentucky, August 23, 1907, Stanley Papers, Department of Special Collections and Archives, King Library North, University of Kentucky, Lexington; W. H. Hook to A. O. Stanley, August 1907, Stanley Papers.

Regie and the British Imperial. The foreign buyers purchased 80 percent of the Black Patch leaf and practiced schemes similar to Duke's trust as described by Charles E. Barker: "The whole region has been cut up into districts . . . and agents of each [tobacco company] go around the districts and pick out just such as they want, and we have to take what they offer or leave it alone." The changed marketing methods disturbed warehousemen like R. E. Cooper of Hopkinsville, who had grown up on a farm and had been selling tobacco for growers for seventeen years. Cooper recalled the days when eight different firms operated warehouses in Hopkinsville. During that time, farmers sent their leaf in huge wooden hogsheads from which buyers drew out samples and then sold it on the open market. "At that time we had from forty to fifty buyers in our market . . . and each of those buyers represented a distinct and separate manufacturer or country at that time," Cooper said. But since the domination of the three tobacco companies, "instead of forty to fifty buyers, we are without a tobacco market at all. The American Tobacco Company sends Mr. Norman Smith . . . who has charge of all four of the markets . . . instead of competitive bids the Trust buyers offered only one price."[9]

Price-fixing eliminated competition among the remaining three tobacco buyers. J. E. Justice reported that the "buyers, previous to going into the field to buy the 1903 crop, had instructions given them as to the prices to be paid for the different grades" of tobacco. Italian Regie buyers would travel the countryside offering low prices to the farmers. Later, American Snuff Company men would pass through offering still-lower prices. A. O. Dority bought tobacco in Christian County, Kentucky, during the difficult years of 1901 through 1904 as an agent for the Italian Regie and later for the American Snuff Company. While buying for the Regie in 1901 and 1902, Dority "was instructed not to go out of my allotted territory," and no others bought in his district. He had similar instructions when he worked for the American Snuff Company. Prices for good tobacco had never been so low. For the first two years, Dority stated, the "average price was about $4.90, including my commissions, and I bought the best

9. *Hearings*, 3–14, 18–21; Christopher Waldrep, 24–26.

tobacco in our country." The next two years were worse, the "prices averaged $3.67," far below the cost of production.[10]

Besides the new marketing methods and the machinations of the trust buyers, the Black Patch producers faced other problems during the depression. Increased production flooded the market with tobacco between 1889 and 1899 as poundage doubled from 488 million pounds to 868 million pounds. Besides nationwide overproduction, Black Patch farmers confronted strong competition from North Carolina and Virginia. The eastern growers increased production in North Carolina from 36 million to 127.5 million pounds between 1889 and 1899, while Virginians increased their output from 48.5 million to 123 million pounds. Kentucky's production, in contrast, dropped from 314 million pounds to just 221.8 million pounds in the same decade.[11]

Compounding these problems was a market war on chewing tobacco, which reduced prices for Black Patch leaf; a decreased demand for dark tobacco on the foreign market (one-third of dark tobacco production had been for foreign buyers); and a change in the use of tobacco by Americans from chewing tobacco to mild smoking blends, which did not use the strongly flavored dark variety. The majority of farmers were unaware of or uneducated about these trends in the tobacco industry. They only knew that they were losing ground, sometimes literally, their children were raggedly dressed, and the situation seemed hopeless. For these farmers, Duke Trust and the Italian Regie became the focus of all their frustration and anger. Getting rid of the monopolies, they believed, would save the Black Patch way of life. Two connected movements arose to address the farmers' plight: first, the Planters' Protective Association in 1904, and later, a secret force of vigilantes, known as the Possum Hunters, the Silent Brigade, or the Night Riders.[12]

In response to the problems besetting the Black Patch, Charles Fort and other elite men from the region organized an association of

10. J. E. Justice to A. O. Stanley, August 23, 1907, Stanley Papers; A. O. Dority of Pembroke, Christian County, Kentucky, 1907, excerpt from a report written by an unidentified person from Dority's affidavit, which was sent to Stanley, Stanley Papers.

11. Axton, *Tobacco and Kentucky*, 83–87; Gregory, "Desperate Farmers," 69.

12. Axton, *Tobacco and Kentucky*, 84–87.

tobacco growers as a joint-stock company, because the laws of Kentucky did not allow for incorporation of a cooperative. These men, Charles Fort of Robertson County, Tennessee; Charles E. Barker of Christian County, Kentucky; Frank Walton of Todd County, Kentucky; J. B. Jackson of Logan County, Kentucky; and Polk Prince of Montgomery County, Tennessee, became the only shareholders in the association.[13]

County civil districts lay at the base of the three-tiered organization. Tobacco producers in each of the Black Patch county civil districts elected a district chair. The district chairmen elected a county chair, and after a majority of the county's producers joined, the county chairman could apply to the association. Together, the county chairmen served as the executive committee. The executive committee, combined with the elected officers of the association, met as the board of directors, which dealt with the cooperative's business. The board elected officers each year, beginning at the 1904 Guthrie, Kentucky, meeting, when Charles H. Fort became president; Charles E. Barker, vice-president; Frank Walton, secretary-treasurer; and Felix Ewing, a wealthy Robertson County planter, chair of the executive committee. The association called for all tobacco growers, landowners, and sharecroppers, blacks and whites, to join. When 70 percent of the region's producers had allied, operations would begin. Growers pledged to sell their crops through the association, which possessed the sole right to determine the time of sale, the price, and the purchaser. The association served its members by grading and selling their tobacco, which was prized into hogsheads and stored in association warehouses. The cooperative published a newspaper, the *Black Patch Journal*, to inform, propagandize, and arouse the populace to the association's cause. Speakers fanned out across the region to explain the PPA goals and methods.[14]

"By corrupt practices . . . the farmer was induced to believe that the murderously low price of tobacco was occasioned by over production," explained an association member in 1906. "Competition was

13. Gregory, "Desperate Farmers," 75.
14. Ibid., 76–80; C. Vann Woodward, *The Origins of the New South, 1877–1913*, 386–87; Miller, *Black Patch War*, 104–19; James O. Nall, *The Tobacco Night Riders of Kentucky and Tennessee, 1905–1909* (Standard Press, 1939).

absolutely destroyed, and lands which our ancestors had snatched out of a wilderness and bequeathed to us as our heritage forever" were divided into districts by "Lord Tobacco Buyer" who took "our crop, not at its value, but at a price fixed by a greedy and merciless combine." Although tobacco growers appealed for relief through legal channels, they received no help. So "driven to the last extremity, we appealed to that power that is higher and more potent to the law, that power that nerved the arm of Cromwell to strike . . . the shackles from the English people." The same "power that nerved Patrick Henry to proclaim freedom . . . the power of an oppressed and enslaved people, of the race of blue-eyed Anglo-Saxons." Patriotic Black Patch men should fight the "robber trusts" and do "a battle of justice and patriotism against greed, to break the manacles of commercial slavery and elevate and ennoble the man who earned his living by the sweat of his face."[15]

Charles Fort became president of the association, but the spark of leadership came from "the largest planter in Robertson County, and perhaps the world, Felix Grundy Ewing," known as the "Moses of the Black Patch." Ewing first "issued a call to the planters of the 'Black Patch' to assemble at Guthrie, Ky., on September 23, 1904, to organize a planters' association," and risked his health in his dedication to the cause of the Black Patch tobacco growers. Fort and Ewing hoped the association could attract the support of all Black Patch growers, large and small, who would pool their crops in PPA warehouses to compel the trust to pay reasonable prices for the dark tobacco leaf and end "the 'Black Patch' poverty, desolation and commercial decay." The elite founders intended to preserve their place in the Black Patch society and direct the dealings with the trusts.[16]

Farmers did not join the association solely for economic reasons. Many white growers joined because of their belief in the cultural ideal of uniting as a community to oppose an outside force like the Duke Trust, and to preserve a way of life they held dear. They deferred to the community leaders, Ewing, Fort, and other wealthy

15. "History of the Planters' Protective Association," *The Black Patch Journal* (August 1908); the *Journal* was printed in Springfield, Tennessee. See also Nall, *Night Riders*, xiii–37; Gregory, "Desperate Farmers," 70–112, 113–50.

16. *Black Patch Journal*, August 1908; *Hopkinsville Daily Kentucky New Era*, September 24, 1906; Gregory, "Desperate Farmers," 81–86, 95.

planters, who led the association. Joining the PPA seemed the best way to both gain high tobacco prices and preserve the orderly community. White tenants and sharecroppers sometimes shared this view of the community. They thought that with better tobacco prices they could save money and eventually purchase land and rise to landowning status. The association appealed to African American tobacco growers to join the ranks and promised them equal treatment in the handling and sale of their crops. Since black farmers suspected that they had been discriminated against on prices, the association offer looked reasonable. In Montgomery County, Tennessee, they organized a PPA affiliate.[17]

Black Patch people, however, also held values that contrasted with collectivism. Individualism, freedom of choice, and independence were also components in the Black Patch value system. Tobacco growers with an individualistic temperament or worldview opposed joining their neighbors in the association. Collective action smacked of loss of control and individual liberty. These farmers proudly called themselves "independents." Some, such as William McCarty of Lyon County, had personal reputations as "cussedly" independent men who went their own way, deferring to no one and joining no organization, not even the church. McCarty's refusal to cooperate with the association was characteristic of his life and attitudes. The depression and the rise of the PPA and the Night Riders starkly revealed the differing worldviews inherent in the culture and the tensions between them.[18]

For the members of the PPA, however, the key to success lay in majority cooperation among all producers. Approximately 70 percent of Black Patch growers joined the association to pool tobacco at the peak of the movement. However, the organization required more than 70 percent participation for success. Part of the problem lay in the association's inability to give full cash advances to the farmers for crops being held for future sale. Also, trust agents struck at the association's weakest point by offering higher prices to independent farmers, which, in turn, widened the rift between association mem-

17. *Clarksville Leaf-Chronicle*, August 15, 1905, August 30, 1905, September 7, 1905, September 23, 1905, September 26, 1905, September 30, 1905, October 2, 1905; Gregory, "Desperate Farmers," 86–89, 90, 94–95. Gregory says the association was portrayed like a crusade between Good and Evil.

18. George H. McCarty, interview.

bers and the independents, who were nicknamed "hillbillies," after the male goat, by those loyal to the association. The PPA orator, Joel Fort, the "Warhorse of the Black Patch," gave a "rip-roaring speech on 'Goats' which brought many growers into the Association and made some of the Hill-billies froth at the mouth."[19]

The Planters' Protective Association, however, attracted members from all classes in the Black Patch. Newspapers estimated that as many as twenty-five thousand people attended a barbecue held in Guthrie, Todd County, in 1904 to rally support for the growers' cause. At the second annual gathering, in September 1905, ten brass bands led the parade. During this event, Jane Washington Ewing, the wife of the association's general manager and daughter of George A. Washington, the wealthiest tobacco grower in Robertson County before the Civil War, presented a hand-sewn white-silk banner with a green tobacco leaf in the center to the organization.[20]

Women and men of both races numbering in the thousands flocked to the anniversary rallies held in 1905 and 1906 to show their enthusiasm for the association and enjoy the festivities. As farmers began to pledge their crops to the PPA, figures of support were gathered. Statistics claimed that the organization gradually increased its control of tobacco sold from about one-fourth of the total crop in 1904 to over one-third in 1905, one-half in 1906, and by 1907 it controlled more than three-quarters of the hogsheads produced that season. Concurrently, during these years, the total amount of tobacco grown in the Black Patch declined, significantly affecting the old problem of overproduction.[21]

19. Gregory, "Desperate Farmers," 86, 110. Christopher Waldrep, 567; Axton, *Tobacco and Kentucky*, 88–90; Nall, *Night Riders*, 88; Archie Green, "Hillbilly Music: Source and Symbol," 204, 223; Nannie Laurara Fortson, collected by D. K. Wilgus, Todd County, Kentucky, 1947, Western Kentucky Folklore and Folklife Collection, Department of Library Special Collections, Folklife Archives, Western Kentucky University, Bowling Green, Kentucky.

20. *Black Patch Journal*, August 1907; *Clarksville Leaf-Chronicle*, September 25, 1904; *Hopkinsville Daily Kentucky New Era*, September 30, 1904; *Western Tobacco Journal*, September 26, 1904; Gregory, "Desperate Farmers," 70–71; Marion Williams, *Todd County*, 60; Miller, *Black Patch War*, 36–37.

21. Nall, *Night Riders*, 37–40; *Black Patch Journal*, August 1908; *Hopkinsville Daily Kentucky New Era*, August 8, 1906, and September 24, 1906; N. E. Green to A. O. Stanley, August 17, 1907, Stanley Papers; *The Tobacco Planter's Yearbook*,

Despite a great outpouring of spirit and support, the independents blocked success. Since frontier days, Black Patch whites had valued the independent life that yeomen farming permitted. Even those who scarcely experienced true independence, such as the tenants and sharecroppers whose numbers increased over the years following the Civil War, claimed to enjoy and fiercely defended their right to independent decision making. "I was a sharecropper, I didn't own no farm," explained Clarence Head, who was also the son of a tenant farmer. The aspects of sharecropping he appreciated most included "being independent. The landowner, the one I worked for, they didn't come around trying to tell you how to farm as long as you did right and worked the farm and give them what was coming to them." Head raised tobacco on halves and gave two-fifths of his corn to his landlord. Sometimes he raised cattle supplied by the owner and received a half share in the stock. "It was an independent life. It was respectable. You could be honest, if you had a good name. I had no trouble renting." Although all sharecroppers did not have as positive an experience with the often oppressive system, many strived to achieve a sense of independence.[22]

During the struggle between pro- and anti-association farmers, Logan Moore, a Crittenden Countian, wrote, "We people that think we have the right to sell our tobacco to whom we please are visited regularly by bands of night riders that apply the torch and whip without mercy." P. C. Boren declared that "I was Borned Raised and Lived in Trigg C. Ky. all of my life. Want to Bee a free man live in a free country and Have and See my neighbors have a Free Happy Home," rather than be coerced by association members into joining a cooperative movement that might limit individual freedom. Feelings of resentment at being forced to cooperate with association goals ran strong.[23]

1908 (Guthrie, Kentucky), 6–7; Waldrep, "Planters and the Association," 569; *Cadiz Record*, January 5, 1905.

22. Clarence Head, interview by Karen Owen, tape recording, Owensboro, Kentucky, July 29, 1986, *Messenger-Inquirer* Collection, Folklore and Folklife Collection, Department of Library Special Collections, Folklife Archives, Western Kentucky University, Bowling Green, Kentucky.

23. Head, interview; Logan Moore to A. E. Willson, March 23, 1908, Willson Papers, Manuscripts Collection, Filson Club Historical Society, Louisville, Ken-

For the independent growers, combining with others in an association or pool threatened their sense of freedom. They feared losing control over their crops, the sales method, and the prices—the few things that they perceived they had power over. On the other hand, those in the association knew it was vital to the Black Patch for all farmers to join in the cooperative effort. They viewed the independents as a threat to the very existence of the Black Patch economy and culture. "Old Shanks," the pseudonym of W. P. Anderson of Keysburg, Kentucky, wrote in the *Black Patch Journal* concerning the association's efforts against the Tobacco Trust, citing the third chapter of Judges where "Ehud thrust his dagger so deep into the flesh of old fat King Eglon that he could not get it out." Similarly the association had attacked the trust, and victory seemed near "in spite of the hillbillie" who "the Good Lord ought to apologize for making." The independent, according to "Old Shanks," was so "infernally selfish that he would steal the baby's candy and eat it." Association members looked upon the independents' refusal to cooperate as selfish, contemptible behavior.[24]

Independent farmers spoke of their freedoms and liberties and claimed these values gave them the right to stand apart from the association. However, PPA members saw their goal as a sort of independence movement and compared it with the American Revolution. "The Colonies had their tories and the Association has its hill-billies," wrote G. B. Bingham. He was not trying to "justify or encourage acts of lawlessness growing out of the planters' movement, but merely to show that when people are denied their rights, and are victims of a devilish conspiracy to rob them" the legal niceties may fall to the wayside. Bingham denounced illegal, violent tactics to force independents to join the ranks of the association, but he reminded readers of historic rebels whose action from "Bunker Hill to Yorktown in a certain sense was a lawless one." Despite the association leaders' call for unity and warnings against violence, the division between members and nonmembers erupted into the Black Patch War—nearly

tucky; P. C. Boren to A. E. Willson, October 29, 1908, Willson Papers. The name "Boren" is obscured in the document. An *r* appears to be the correct letter.

24. "'Old Shanks,' [W. P. Anderson] Must Keep the Pledge," *Black Patch Journal*, n.d.; *Cadiz Record*, August 29, 1907.

four years of vigilante action against independents, Tobacco Trust agents, and trust property.[25]

The economic crisis of the early 1900s brought to the surface the divisions between the two worldviews that existed in the culture: the idea of neighborly community cooperation as embodied in the association's goals and rhetoric, and the individualistic tendencies as held by the independent farmers. The first emphasized cooperative work in time of need, and the other favored separate individual effort. In prosperous times the differences between the two did not cause any problems. Farmers could approve of and participate in collective work in times of distress, as after a barn-burning, when neighbors came to help a man rebuild, or when "if anybody gets sick they went and worked your crop."[26]

In contrast, the independent, individualistic cultural attitude remained dominant among the farmers who resisted the association's methods and goals. The split between the poles of behavior common in the Black Patch culture created a rift between the two groups of tobacco farmers and contributed to the rise of the Night Riders' vigilante activity. As has been noted many times before, violent response to economic ills, value conflicts, and threats already had a long history in the region.[27]

The division between independents and association members surfaced in personal neighbor relations, group activities (Night Riders), and even within families. Strained relations brought on by the split were evident in Trigg County during the 1906 wheat-threshing season, a job that traditionally required a community effort. Neighbors helped one another at wheat threshings because the work involved expensive machinery, many laborers, and time. Customarily, one man in the neighborhood owned a steam-powered wheat thresher and went from farm to farm in the sweltering July heat to thresh crops. Usually the thresherman received a percentage of the wheat from the job to cover the cost of the machine, fuel, and attendants.

25. Judge G. B. Bingham, "An Encouraging Article," *Black Patch Journal*, n.d.; *Cadiz Record*, May 30, 1907, June 16, 1908; *Hopkinsville Daily Kentucky New Era*, December 25, 1907; *Hopkinsville New Era*, January 8, 1908.

26. Scott, interview; Eunice McCarty, interview; See Erikson, *Everything in Its Path*.

27. Scott interview; Erikson, *Everything in Its Path*, 79–93.

People greatly anticipated threshing as a social event as well as a time of collective labor. Men worked the thresher and brought in the crop. Children helped as best they could. Women prepared huge noon meals of fried chicken, ham, fresh vegetables, syrupy fruit cobblers, pies, and cakes. Sometimes they held a quilting party for themselves. However, during the 1906 season, the traditional community effort was marked by tensions between association members and nonmembers. Neighbors refused to help one another if they disagreed on the tobacco dispute.[28]

"Buckner Cherry, a good Association man . . . sowed wheat last fall on his father's farm on the Linton Pike," reported the local paper. Buckner's father, Henry, a white farm owner, was, in 1900, living with his wife, Ider, and their three children. By 1906, Buckner was twenty years old and his father forty-eight. Henry Cherry, however, "being an outsider or 'hill billy' as we term them, there arose a dispute about who would thresh" the wheat. Father and son divided the crop into 225 shocks each, and the elder Cherry's wheat was processed by one thresherman while Harrill and Clark, association threshers, did young Buckner's grain. PPA members from the neighborhood "began to flock in to help and soon there were twenty-six wagons there," and they quickly had the wheat loaded. During a wheat-threshing season before the divisive period, the father and son would have threshed together.[29]

Word of the association men's help for their fellow member during the threshing season spread across the county. The pro-association *Cadiz Record* printed the names of the fifty men who worked Buckner Cherry's wheat crop to publicize the benefits of association membership and also inform the community of the loyal association members. Of the fifty men listed, at least ten were between the ages of fourteen and twenty-seven, members of Buckner's generation. These were young men, like Buckner, still living and working on their fathers' farms. Six of the men were between the ages of thirty and forty-eight, perhaps friends of the elder Henry Cherry but associa-

28. *Cadiz Record*, July 26, 1906; Ruston Flowers, interview by author, tape recording, Logan County, Kentucky, June 20, 1987.

29. *Cadiz Record*, July 26, 1906; Thomas Jones, comp., *Trigg County 1900 Federal Census*, 145–46, Special Collections, Forrest C. Pogue Library, Murray State University, Murray, Kentucky.

tion members who chose to help the son and spurn the independent-minded father. One black man, Ernest Savillis, a boarder and laborer on the Joseph J. Elliott farm, helped also. The association claimed to welcome all tobacco men including blacks, and in this instance it did so.[30]

The association promoted a policy of shunning the hillbillies, like Henry Cherry, who refused to cooperate. Sympathetic newspapers such as the *Clarksville Leaf-Chronicle* published the names of independents. Association leaders read the lists at their meetings and called for members to shun the hillbilly families. Business owners and professionals who refused to support the association also found themselves ostracized and their establishments boycotted. The editor of the pro-association Clarksville newspaper queried his readers, "Can those who don't sign expect to remain part of the community, can they expect to borrow meat or get help to thresh wheat, kill hogs, or roll logs?—NO."[31]

Family and neighbor conflicts intensified during the uprising of the violent branch of the association, whose members came to be known as the Night Riders. The cultural proclivity for violence in the face of threats to one's person, family, home, economic way of life, and culture combined with the Black Patch tendency to organize collectively and the region's tradition of populism to produce nearly four years of vigilante violence known as the Black Patch Wars.[32]

30. *Census*, 145–46.

31. "History of the Planters' Protective Association," *Black Patch Journal*, n.p.; Gregory, "Desperate Farmers," 106–7; *Clarksville Leaf-Chronicle*, April 6, 1905.

32. Edward F. Prichard, Jr., "Popular Political Movements in Kentucky" (Senior thesis, Princeton University, 1935).

8

TAKING CARE OF THE COUNTRY

I was twenty-one years old and I joined 'em right here, and I didn't want to join 'em," recalled Joe Scott about his initiation into the secret order known as the Night Riders. "They'd been around three or four years before it ever got really bad." Lyon County tobacco growers had held their first meeting on December 20, 1906, to form a branch of the Planters' Protective Association two years after the organization's founding in Robertson County, Tennessee. Due to a number of farmers balking at joining the PPA, Lyon Countians, along with residents of Trigg and Caldwell, participated in large numbers in the vigilante actions of the Night Rider movement.[1]

Scott joined the group partly because of his fears. People who refused to cooperate with the secret band might be whipped or worse. Rumors warned of the deadly fate of two men who had talked too freely about the Night Riders, and everyone knew of the whippings the band inflicted upon those who defied them. Scott's other reason had to do with the poor conditions of tobacco farmers and their families, who barely survived.[2]

"I raised tobacco, put it up and housed it and sold, and it brought three cents a pound," not a living wage, recalled Scott. "Finally, the Trust agents sold the crop across the water [in Europe] and they'd get forty or fifty or eighty cents a pound" for the plants, an unfair profit, Scott believes. "Now you talk about farming—you gonna sit down and talk about them mob doings—you gonna blame me for getting up in it? I was taking care of the country as well as I was myself." Before the association's efforts and the Night Riders' action, Scott says, everyone "was afraid they'd lose their homes, their tobacco barns and everything else.[3]

1. Joe Scott, interview.
2. Ibid.
3. Ibid.; Eddyville, *Kentucky Herald Ledger*, September 14, 1988.

After Scott became an active member of the Night Riders in Lyon County, he helped initiate others into the group. He forced the blindfolded newcomers to hold a skull to remind them of their fate if they breathed a word about the Silent Brigade's plans or actions. Such rituals and the terror instilled by the Night Riders when they administered whippings, resulted in a lingering fear among the people of speaking openly of the Black Patch War.[4]

The secret order that Scott joined arose in Robertson County, Tennessee, in October 1905, when thirty-two association members met not far from general manager Felix Ewing's estate, Glenraven, at the Stainback schoolhouse. These men founded a group called the Possum Hunters and adopted the "Resolutions of the Committee of the Possum Hunters Organization" to guide their efforts in coercing independent farmers into the association. Bands organized on this model spread to other Black Patch counties, and nearly four years of intimidation, vigilantism, and well-planned military raids on the tobacco market towns of Princeton, Hopkinsville, and Russellville followed. However, throughout the years of upheaval, the Planters' Protective Association denied any connection with the Night Riders and continuously condemned the organized violence of the nocturnal bands.[5]

G. B. Bingham, an association supporter, concluded that when people "are victims of a devilish conspiracy to rob them under guise of law, the restraints of law are subverted to a certain extent." Although "many things have occurred which every law abiding man should regret . . . it is to be hoped nothing more will be reported." Night riding should end, he said, since riders "can only bring disrepute" to the association cause. Violence ought to be avoided because "it is the part of true men to bear with patience all this and be comforted with the knowledge that right will triumph" and peace will be pure "because nothing will have been done to mar the serenity of a good conscience." Not all Black Patch growers had the patience to wait. Violence could be a useful tool, an instrument they

4. Scott, interview; other interviewees talked about the Night Riders but asked to remain anonymous; *Commonwealth of Kentucky v. Hugh Wallace*, Trigg Quarterly Court Records, Kentucky Department for Libraries and Archives, Public Records Division, Frankfort, Kentucky.

5. Gregory, "Robertson County," 341–58; Gregory, "Desperate Farmers," 113–27, 128–50; Nall, *Night Riders*, 43.

did not hesitate to use. Across the region growers joined the Night Rider bands, threatened independent farmers, brandished whips, and spread terror. Initially, the terrorism was directed at the recalcitrant independents; later, under a second distinctive phase of night riding, violence was directed at blacks who seemed to threaten the social and economic status quo. As the *Clarksville Leaf-Chronicle* editor wrote, the farmers' struggle was "a war, war means fight, and fight means kill."[6]

By November of 1905, newspapers in Tennessee and Kentucky were reporting the depredations of the Tobacco District night riders. Mott Ayers, Kentucky State Fire Marshal, warned Governor Augustus Willson that the trouble would escalate unless the association condemned the violence. Ayers cited the burning of the rehandling house of Chestnut Brothers in Trenton, Todd County, Kentucky, on a December night in 1905, and a train hold-up in Todd County on December 12, 1905, when several men affiliated with the tobacco trust were threatened. Ayers continued his report with incidents of independent farmers' plant beds being destroyed. Once the movement of the 1905 crop to market ended, the violent activities stopped, resurging during the marketing of the 1906 crop. Rice Brothers, tobacco rehandlers, lost their Kelsey, Caldwell County, warehouse to fire on November 12, 1906. On the same date unknown parties dynamited the rehandling house owned by the Baptist Seminary at Eddyville, Lyon County, Kentucky.[7]

From the 1906 season until 1909, violence swept the Black Patch counties as Night Riders sought to force the independents into the association ranks. Although the Night Rider action began as a violent defense of a higher cause—the preservation of the Black Patch through cooperative efforts of farmers to raise prices—it also came to include other organized violent activities to intimidate blacks, enforce morality, and carry out personal vendettas. A hierarchy of oppression weighed down upon the tobacco growers. All farmers,

6. Bingham, *Black Patch Journal*, August 1907; Gregory, *"Desperate Farmers,"* 124; *Clarksville Leaf-Chronicle* January 31, 1905. The *Leaf-Chronicle* was a pro-association newspaper.

7. Mott Ayers, *First Annual Report of the State Fire Marshal* (Kentucky, 1907), 19–21, Willson Papers, Manuscripts Collection, Filson Club Historical Society, Louisville, Kentucky.

rich and poor, black and white, suffered from the effects of the market and the trust. Middling and tenant farmers also faced the power of the elite planters, while the poorest whites and blacks lived under the combined oppression of class and race. Night Rider violence provided a cover for each group of whites to work out its specific resentments and frustrations.[8]

The most dramatic undertakings of the Night Riders were the militarily precise raids on the regional tobacco towns. Actual loss of life was minimal and accidental, but the terrorism proved very effective. Citizens of Princeton, seat of Caldwell County, Kentucky, first heard the hoofbeats of the Night Riders' horses on the evening of November 30, 1906, "when masked men rode into the town, captured the police officers, seized the Central Telephone Station and proceeded to burn two large tobacco stemmeries" owned by J. A. Stegar and J. G. Orr. These rehandling houses held dark tobacco owned by the trust. The farmers struck directly at James B. Duke's American Tobacco Company by destroying property and displaying their skill and organization. Later, the Night Riders successfully raided Hopkinsville in Christian County in 1907 and Russellville in Logan County in 1908. Other market towns, such as Clarksville, Tennessee, feared such an attack, but none occurred.[9]

Night visitations and smaller scale raids characterized the Night Rider activities. Farmers from Lyon, Trigg, and Caldwell Counties visited Henry Bennett in early February 1908, and "they whipped him. They just pulled him up around a sapling and jerked off some limbs and wore him out. They whipped him until he couldn't get his breath," recalled Joe Scott, who numbered among the men in the raid that night. "I thought they was going to kill him. And they did like to kill him too." The Night Riders called upon Bennett, owner of

8. Ibid.

9. Ibid., 18–20; *Princeton Twice-a-Week Leader*, December 1–6, 1906; *Cadiz Record*, December 1–6, 1906; *Hopkinsville Daily Kentucky New Era*, December 1–6, 1906; *Clarksville Leaf-Chronicle*, December 6, 1906; *Paducah Evening Sun*, December 1, 1906; *Hopkinsville Kentuckian*, December 4, 1906; *Louisville Courier-Journal*, December, 1, 2, 12. The raid on Hopkinsville occurred in 1907. *New York Times*, December 8, 1907. Meacham, *History*, 341–59. The raid on Russellville came in late 1908. *Hopkinsville Daily Kentucky New Era*, January 3–4, 1908; *Clarksville Leaf-Chronicle*, January 3, 1908; *Western Tobacco Journal* 35:1 (January 6, 1908).

a tobacco warehouse, store, and saloon in the Cumberland River town of Dycusburg, because previously "they told him to not buy no more tobacco and he was gonna kill every one of them and he cussed them—ever thing and ever body."[10]

Besides independents and association members who broke their pledges, the Night Riders hated those who dared threaten them or who talked about their secret activities. Old grudges, personality clashes, and hints of class antagonism figure in the Bennett case. Some locals had long resented Bennett's prosperity and behavior. His personality grated. Joe Scott knew Bennett before the tobacco troubles arose. "I'd hauled tobacco over to Henry Bennett. I though a lot of old Henry, but he was the wickedest fellow. He never drove a horse without cussing it. He'd cuss you out, but then he'd turn right around and let you have ever dollar he had if he wanted to let you have it." Scott also recognized Bennett's wealth. "He had a big saloon and owned the biggest part of Dycusburg—him and his daddy. And he had the big warehouse there and a big farm right across the creek." Then when the association asked Bennett to stop selling to trust buyers and the Night Riders repeated the request only to be cussed, trouble arose. Bennett "was just one of these bull-headed kind of fellow—you couldn't do nothing with him. He had his way. He had money. He just thought his money'd be more" helpful in saving him from the violence.[11]

The severe beating the Night Riders inflicted on Henry Bennett led to his selling out and moving from the Black Patch to Metropolis, Illinois, where other refugees fled. Poor health due to his injuries caused much pain and hardship for Bennett and his wife. She wrote that "no one knows better the vengeance meted out . . . for I have seen with my own eyes their hellish work." Moreover, "not only have I gone through with that" and the traumatic move out of state, "but have sat by the bedside of my dear husband and administered to his mutilated body the soothing hand of a dear wife."[12]

10. *Cadiz Record*, February 6, 1908; *Bennett v. D. A. Amoss, et. al.*, Case #1970, October 30, 1908, Records of the United States Circuit Court for the Sixth Circuit, Western District of Kentucky at Paducah, Federal Archives Record Center, Atlanta, Georgia; Scott, interview.

11. Scott, interview; Nall, *Night Riders*, 103–4; *Cadiz Record*, February 6, 1908.

12. Mrs. H. B. Bennett, letter to the editor of Caldwell County's *Princeton Twice-A-Week Leader* n.d., vertical file, George Coon Library, Princeton, Kentucky.

Mrs. H. B. Bennett, however, fixed a keen eye on her home county and wrote a letter to the Caldwell County newspaper to urge people to vote for Hugh Lyon, the "Law and Order and the whole Republican ticket," despite the fact that she had been a lifelong Democrat. She condemned the Night Riders although she distinguished "five classes" of men among them. "One class is for gain, another class is through fear, another class for the hellish work, another for jury purposes and another class have given the whole thing away." Many joined, she said, as a Night Rider she knew had admitted, to "save his scalp." And there were a "number of good citizens" as well. Now she urged voters to end lawlessness so that never again would she, or any woman, have to sit "by my husband's pallet in the woods" to watch him while he slept. No longer would women have their "poor little children crying and looking you in the face and saying 'Mama, do you reckon they will kill papa tonight?'"[13]

Henry Bennett filed suit in federal court in October 1908, naming the alleged leader of the Night Riders, Dr. David Amoss, and over one hundred suspected Night Rider members as defendants. Although he sued for $100,000, he received $100 for medical expenses and $15,000 for his business losses. The alleged Night Riders in the suit denied all charges and produced alibis as to their actions on the night of the raid. Their control of juries and public opinion protected them for a time.[14]

Sadly for Mrs. Bennett and other family members, health complications set in that, she claimed, led to Henry's death two years later on October 20, 1910. She defiantly ordered the words "Killed, By the Night Riders" engraved on her husband's tombstone. Some of the secret order's members considered wiping out those words but decided it would arouse too much emotion against them. They grew concerned because by 1909, lawsuits against their actions were being filed and brought to trial.[15]

13. Ibid.

14. *Bennett v. Amoss;* the defendants had to pay the costs. Similarly, in the Hollowell case the defendants first tried to transfer their property to others to avoid payment, but soon they realized they would go to jail if they did not pay. They decided to share the costs, with people paying according to their ability; Nall, *Night Riders*, 175.

15. Scott, interview; Henry Bennett tombstone, Dycusburg, Kentucky; Odell

From the independents' point of view, they had followed the American tenets of the work ethic, individual effort, and fairness and believed they should be free to pursue their interests without fear of mob attack. Anna Imogene Bennett West wrote that her father, Henry, "dealt with his fellow man and he had acquired a small fortune by his own industry. He had bought tobacco from these (Night Riders) in the best of times and in the worst of times." He did not join the association, and "a law abiding citizen" was not required to join. Her view of the events reveals that after receiving a warning and a bundle of switches, the "small red-haired Irishman, who, no doubt, drank some whiskey occasionally," visited an Eddyville saloon frequented by "some of the leaders of the Night Riders," where he "challenged them to a physical encounter, one by one," which they declined. Bennett's challenge antagonized the Night Riders, but Anna Bennett West believed her father had simply tried "to protect the sanctuary of his home, his family and his business" within the bounds of the law.[16]

The nephew of Henry Bennett, H. W. "Son" Bennett, had huddled in his home just down the road from his uncle's place, listening in horror to the brutal beating. "We could hear him all around here. They told him that if he didn't holler they'd kill him, and they whipped him with thorns and tore a piece of his ear." Son Bennett believes the Night Riders' brutality resulted from his Uncle Henry's attitude and fearlessness. "He wasn't afraid of nobody." When the Night Riders arrived, guests at Bennett's house claimed he was gone, but the guise didn't work, and Bennett "grabbed a Winchester pump gun and went out with the words, 'they may get me, but I'll get some of them.'" The mob then "took him out there on the side of the road and whipped him and some of the Night Riders asked him, 'You know who we are?'" And, according to Son, Henry Bennett defiantly retorted, "I know ever damn one of you."[17]

Bennett later told his daughter, Anna Imogene, who in turn passed it on to her cousin, Son, that Henry believed "if he hadn't said noth-

---

Walker, interview by author, tape recording, Lyon County, Kentucky, August 25, 1988; Nall, *Night Riders*, 105.

16. Anna Imogene Bennett West, *Lyon County Herald Ledger,* June 13, 1979.
17. Bennett, interview.

ing they wouldn't have whipped him." That same night the raiders beat W. B. Grove, Bennett's factory foreman and Son Bennett's future father-in-law. "He lived up on top of the hill in Dycusburg and I seen them bring Mr. Groves down here to the branch and whipped him there." The Night Riders burned the Bennett warehouse and destroyed Son's father's tobacco patch too. Son Bennett cried when telling the story of his uncle's ordeal, and his animosity toward the Night Riders remains strong. "There was about as many whiskey drinkers and cutthroats in it as there was anywhere in the United States."[18]

A few nights after Bennett received his flogging, the Night Riders ventured forth on the muddy winter roads to call on A. H. Cardin, another independent tobacco dealer, one who refused to sell through the association, at View, his farm near Fredonia. Cardin's large house sat atop a little knoll under the shady branches of a stand of sugar maples enclosed by an iron fence, far surpassing other country homes in the county. Located on the farm was Cardin's tobacco factory. After discovering the Cardin family absent, the Night Riders burned the house and the factory, which contained 35,000 pounds of leaf. Besides his obvious prosperity in the troubled times, Cardin incurred the wrath of the Night Riders because he had served in 1905 as an interim chairman for the association but ended the affiliation to conduct his business independently from the association. Earlier, in 1887, Cardin had been the Union Labor party's gubernatorial candidate. He was a well-known, wealthy member of the upper strata of the Black Patch society, who chose to profit at the expense of the middling and poor farmers who made up the association, or so the Night Riders believed.[19]

Although the Night Riders' primary goal involved achieving 100 percent membership in the Planters' Protective Association, some members carried their culturally embedded racial prejudices to the extreme in individual and collective acts against blacks in the region, enforced morality on neighbors behind the Night Rider mask, and carried out personal vendettas based on old grudges. As Son

18. Ibid.; Walker, interview; Nall, *Night Riders*, 103–5; *Cadiz Record*, February 6, 1908.
19. Nall, 103–5.

Bennett claimed, sometimes during these chaotic times "cutthroats" took advantage of the opportunities to do their own violent deeds.[20]

Black Patch whites believed that African Americans were inferior humans—lower in status and in need of supervision. Racial prejudice permeated the culture. Whites accepted it as the natural order, citing the Bible as evidence. Elite whites who depended upon black labor used violence to control their workers and preserve their power. Whites who did not manage black labor employed violence to intimidate blacks who challenged the white-imposed caste system by rising socially or economically. They often sought to drive all blacks away to gain land and jobs for whites. In the Black Patch, as in the rest of the South following the Civil War, segregation grew and white violence against blacks occurred with mounting frequency.[21]

Violence against blacks began before the Night Rider years. In 1904, a negro, Wash Childress, was attacked by whitecappers, beaten up, dunked in a pond, and partly hanged because he allegedly took part in a series of meat house robberies in the county. Childress denied the charges, and the mob released him without forcing a confession. "Childress told the circumstances to Judge W. T. Fowler, but had no evidence to implicate anyone and so no action could be taken." Typically, blacks had little hope of recourse in the legal process since whites seldom confessed or came forward with evidence.[22]

During a shooting spree on "the streets of Cadiz last Saturday night . . . the houses of several negroes near the corporate limits . . . were shot into, but fortunately no one was hurt," reported the local paper. Trigg County blacks, like others throughout the South, experienced the horror of random violence characterized by no apparent motive except a lack of respect for blacks' rights to a safe environment. But the blacks of Cadiz suffered such acts quietly. Lynchings occurred in the tobacco counties and were usually reported by the press in an effort to warn about consequences of breaches of racial etiquette.[23]

Racism occurred at all levels of society, which operated to sanction

20. Ibid., 116; Scott, interview; Parker, interview.
21. See Wright, *Racial Violence.*
22. *Hopkinsville Daily Kentucky New Era,* April 6, 1904.
23. Ibid., June 6, 1904, August 30, 1904.

violence against blacks. In a dispute between Republicans and Democrats in Caldwell County over jury selections, an editorial pointed out that juries "worked to the interest of the white man and not the negro element of the Republican party." However, "had it been otherwise, or at the dictation of one who had by his acts and practices placed himself on the level of the negro, the juries would be made up of negroes." The county, though, "has never been humiliated along these lines and by the eternal she shall never be so long as the good and fair-minded people are at the helm of justice and right." As long as whites held this opinion, blacks would remain subject to persecution and violence especially in times of economic decline and upheaval.[24]

In contrast, Christian County allowed its large population of blacks to vote and sit on juries. The first grand jury that included blacks was chosen in March 1885. Black voters, who strongly supported the Republican party, elected a black man, Edward W. Glass, to the Hopkinsville city council and kept him there for twelve years until 1907. By 1898, blacks held several elected offices: James L. Allensworth served as county coroner, "Kinney Tyler, Deputy Jailer; John W. Knight, Constable; J. C. Lyte, Pension Examiner; William Leveritt, County Physician."[25]

Social and demographic changes spurred by the economic crisis in the Black Patch led to white planters' concern about cheap available labor in the counties, which relied heavily on black farm labor. The black population in Kentucky had decreased from 17 percent of the total population to about 13 percent by the turn of the century. Whites who did not depend on black labor remained unconcerned about the decrease or applauded it. Those dependent on black labor worried.[26]

Black sharecroppers and tenants felt the effects of the 1904 tobacco price drop first. Some chose to answer the calls of plantation agents in search of hands. Gano Henry left Christian County, the newspaper reported, for "Itta Bena, Mississippi, with twenty colored men who will be employed on cotton plantations." More laborers and their families headed for the Deep South. Others went west. Thirty-five "colored laborers and rock workers" left the Black Patch to mine

24. *Princeton Twice-A-Week Leader,* June 24, 1904.
25. Meacham, *History,* 209, 228; Tapp and Klotter, *Decades of Discord,* 93.
26. Tapp and Klotter, *Decades of Discord,* 61.

in Princeton, Missouri. The Christian County school census showed a "net decrease of 52," stated Superintendent Katie McDaniel. "This decrease is entirely among the colored people and it is probable that it is due to the fact that so many colored families have moved to Mississippi." Employers of these marginal black workers would have preferred them to stay in the region to provide a ready labor pool when the tobacco economy improved.[27]

Christian County authorities, undoubtedly pressed by the "Farmers Not Pleased with Hands' Exodus to Cotton Fields," sometimes acted to halt the movement. Officials charged Jordan Beckner, a black man, with breach of peace and fined him thirty dollars and costs. Beckner's "offense really consisted in inducing a farm hand who was under contract to Mr. S. H. Ward of the Casky neighborhood to go and work the cotton." Beckner had earlier worked for Mr. J. H. Winfree of Christian County before leaving for the cotton region. A white agent, T. H. McNeill, also faced charges for exporting labor to Mississippi, but the court dismissed his case.[28]

White planters perceived the loss of black laborers as a threat to their economic system, which depended on cheap workers in the labor-intensive tobacco industry. The exodus also seemed to be an affront to the planters' sense of noblesse oblige. Blacks should remain deferential and loyal through the bad times. However, by 1906, when nothing else looked promising for attracting labor, Christian County planters were offering higher wages for tobacco cutters. To further assist the growers in procuring willing workers in the critical cutting season, Hopkinsville city officials passed an ordinance against vagrants. The new law, the paper warned, would be "rigidly enforced. The farmers are begging for hands to save their crops at from $1.00 to 1.50 a day and board, and every man who wants work can get it." Therefore, "idlers and loafers must go to work or leave Hopkinsville." The first to be arrested, a white man, chose to leave the city rather than pay the eleven-dollar fine.[29]

Charles Fort, testifying before the Senate committee on the tobacco situation, spoke of the plight of the blacks in his county, al-

27. *Hopkinsville Daily Kentucky New Era*, April 18, 1904, June 20, 1904.
28. Ibid., March 4, 1904, March 15, 1904, March 17, 1904.
29. Ibid., September 3, 1906, September 7, 1906.

though he spoke from the wealthy planters' point of view. "A good crop for one hand," according to Fort, would be about three acres. On his farm he did not "work anything but negroes . . . and they have women and children, and they all work, and manage to work about three acres to the hand—that is to the man." Despite his language, Fort's blacks worked as families in the fields. The women and children were subsumed under the term *hand* or *man*. Yet without the work of the women and children, the acreage could not be produced, the cropper family would not survive, and Fort would not have been a successful, wealthy planter.[30]

The association did not appeal specifically to blacks in the tobacco region to join, but neither were they discouraged. Blacks apparently joined because of genuine interest, or through a desire to go along with the landlord who had joined, or due to the owner's coercion. When the Night Riders became active, they called on tenants, white and black, to demand affiliation with the association as one group did when "they visited the farm of J. D. Coleman, near Peedee, and called the several tenants on the Sypert place and advised them not to attempt to make a crop with Mr. Coleman." Another tenant who received the nocturnal visitors reported his tobacco had already been pledged to the association. The Night Rider "leader told him to be sure that no mistakes was made about it." Sometimes croppers and tenants got into trouble when landlords took all the crop to a non-association warehouse. Night Riders did not always take the time to determine who controlled the marketing of the tobacco.[31]

One lodge of Night Riders, seeking to rid Christian County of black sharecroppers, sent a note to Robert Rives, an association member, to let him "know that you are not to have any negro croppers for next year." Furthermore, "if you think anything of your back you had best ter git rid of them negroes and tell all of your neighbors and friends." Night Rider lodges consisting of white men from the northern reaches of Christian, as well as from Trigg, Caldwell, and Lyon—where the black population was low and racial hatred high—hoped to rid the region of the competition of black labor and give

30. *Hearings*, 23, 30–31.

31. *Hopkinsville Daily Kentucky New Era*, February 18, 1908, March 16, 1908, January 21, 1908, February 4, 1908; Gregory, "Desperate Farmers," 86–87.

poor whites a better chance at getting tenancy contracts in the depressed tobacco economy. Benevolent paternalism applied only to blacks, such as Tom Wright of Cerulean, Trigg County's first black federal court juror, who conformed to whites' standards of behavior. Even the local paper boasted that Wright was the wealthiest black in the county, who "had the utmost respect of his white neighbors."[32]

The *Paducah News-Democrat* first picked up stories and reported the Night Rider warnings, "Skidoo loafing, thieving negroes, skidoo." Threats were being sent to "dozens of negroes with bad reputations" in Lyon and Livingston Counties. African Americans reportedly were hastening out of Grand Rivers, Kuttawa, Eddyville, and the surrounding vicinity. The Paducah paper blamed the victims and attributed the problems to blacks stealing mules.[33]

The Trigg County branch of the Planters' Protective Association spoke out against all Night Rider violence. They resolved that no more force should be used for a period of one year and to call citizens to halt "anonymous letter writing, whether in regard to the employment of negro labor . . . or to gratify personal spite." The PPA reminded whites that "the negro has been true, and no instance is known where he ever violated his pledge, and the association is honor bound to protect him." Elite officials who headed the county associations spoke from their class interests of preserving the cheap labor force and also out of their paternalistic view of their role as guardians of blacks. Nevertheless, the racism of whites compounded by economic difficulties, prevented peaceful dealing with black farmers and iron industry laborers.[34]

Eventually, Night Riders, or those claiming to be members, operating in the counties of Trigg, Lyon, and Caldwell, areas of lower association membership and the central area of Night Rider activity, began to attack whites and blacks. "Night Riders swooped down upon Eddyville, 300 strong, Sunday morning at 1 o'clock and horse-whipped four white victims and six negroes." They were then ordered to leave the county "under threat of death." The paper re-

32. *Hopkinsville Daily Kentucky New Era*, January 1, 1908.
33. *Paducah News-Democrat*, January 16, 1908.
34. *Hopkinsville Daily Kentucky New Era*, January 16, 1908; *Cadiz Record*, November 15, 1908.

ported that "the raid was not altogether in the interest of the tobacco association as only one of the men," J. W. Bradshaw, the PPA tobacco prizer, has any "connection with the tobacco business." In fact, Bradshaw had offended the Night Riders by operating a poolroom in conjunction with his association business. The other white victims, Police Judge C. W. Rucker, "who has had the name of being a bad man about fighting," former City Marshal Leslie Woods, policeman Press Fralick, and saloon porter Grace Robertson, were either attacked because of their opposition to the Night Riders or their involvement in illegal alcohol sales. One report commented that this raid was like a "regulating party," rather than a tobacco Night Rider activity.[35]

One of the black men, a recently arrived school teacher, George Gordon, who was whipped on the banks of the Cumberland River that evening, later received an apology because he had been beaten by mistake. However, the Night Riders ordered the other blacks to leave Lyon County; Gordon could remain. Flogging the innocent men supposedly served as an example to others who might contemplate stepping out of their place or violating community morals by selling alcohol.[36]

The Silent Brigade also spoke to Lyon County Judge W. L. Crumbaugh and reminded him that he was safe only because of his previous good relationship with the PPA. Crumbaugh, along with the county prosecutor, William Krone, actively spoke out against the Night Riders and sought to bring them to justice. Crumbaugh informed Governor Augustus E. Willson of Kentucky that the juries were full of Night Riders. In normal times, Lyon County jurors refused to indict blind tigers, illicit alcohol sellers, or the young men accused of disrupting church services. During the troubled times, Crumbaugh claimed, juries acquitted men accused of crimes as long as they supported the Night Riders.[37]

Another incident happened one March night, the paper stated,

35. *Princeton Twice-A-Week Leader*, February 18, 1908; *Hopkinsville Daily Kentucky New Era*, February 17, 1908; Nall, *Night Riders*, 108–10; *Cadiz Record*, February 20, 1908; *C. W. Rucker v. D. A. Amoss, et al.*, Case #1933, Records of the District Courts of the United States, Federal Archives Center, Atlanta, Georgia.

36. *G. W. Gordon v. D. A. Amoss, et al.*, Case #1938, Civil Docket, United States Circuit Court, Paducah, Kentucky, Volume H, 1908; Nall, *Night Riders*, 108–9.

37. *Hopkinsville Daily Kentucky New Era*, February 17, 1908; W. L. Crumbaugh to A. O. Willson, November 19, 1908, Willson Papers.

when "Night Riders, masked and armed, and estimated to be about twenty-five in number, rode into Benton" where Circuit Judge William and Marshall County jury members slumbered in the hotel. The Silent Brigade "going to the negro part of the town, ordered all negroes to leave." This action followed an alleged period of lawlessness in the county, which some whites blamed on the blacks. In reality, whites sought to rid the Cumberland and Tennessee Rivers iron industry of its black laborers.[38]

Shortly before the Benton raid, "150 masked men" had entered another Marshall County town, Birmingham, to restore order, as they perceived it. The white mob "shot up the place and wounded John Scruggs, colored, and several members of his family, and whipped five negroes." The judge and jurors, in fact, were in Benton to investigate the earlier raid that had occurred in the river town, Birmingham. Seventy-five of the Birmingham blacks sought refuge in Paducah, after being given ten days to pack up and leave. One white Birmingham man claimed the blacks in the town were lawless drunks and troublemakers who deserved being run out, a standard rationalization among whites to justify racial violence.[39]

Following the raid, Tom Chiles and Marvin Farley were arrested for their part in the affair and for whipping a black sharecropper. The cropper, Steve Whitfield, the paper editorialized, "is a very troublesome and insulting negro and his presence in that community had become very obnoxious. He would take great delight in abusing . . . and annoying white people until they decided his conduct had reached its climax." Furthermore, "most people commend the action." The two white men were tried under the old Ku Klux Klan law and found guilty. Dr. Emilus Champion, a white Lyon County physician, was convicted for his role in the Birmingham raid and served time in the Kentucky State Penitentiary.[40]

38. *Paducah News-Democrat*, March 16, 1908.

39. Ibid.; *Cadiz Record*, March 19, 1908; *Hopkinsville Daily Kentucky New Era*, March 20, 1908, March 24, 1908; Anonymous, interview by author, pen and pad, Lyon County, Kentucky, summer 1987; *Cadiz Record*, July 16, 1908.

40. *Hopkinsville Daily Kentucky New Era*, January 31, 1908, February 11, 1908; *Cadiz Record*, February 20, 1908, July 9, 1908. For a detailed analysis of the night riders led by Champion see Christopher Waldrep, *Night Riders: Defending Community in the Black Patch, 1890–1915*, 142–52.

Whites' racism, economic stress, and the opportunity afforded by other activities of the masked Night Riders, permitted some whites in the Black Patch to persecute and harm the lowest class in the society, the black members. That little public outcry met these racially motivated attacks only shows the extent of racism in an era of intense racial strife in the South and the nation. Any possible condemnation of these acts was squashed due to the fear of Night Rider revenge.[41]

One case reveals how black sharecroppers were treated in counties experiencing a labor shortage. Rob Wood, a prominent young white Christian County farmer, wrote a threat letter to Louis Dawson, "a colored cropper on the adjoining farm." Assistant Postmaster Gus Breathitt "testified that on February 11, between two and three o'clock, he saw Mr. Wood enter the post office and mail a letter which bore two one-cent stamps." Since Wood was under suspicion for having mailed threats, Breathitt looked at the letter in the box, which was addressed to Dawson. The next day, Dawson opened the envelope in Breathitt's presence revealing a note signed "Night Riders." The note promised a beating unless Dawson moved. Dawson testified to having received another threat and to having been questioned by Rob Wood about receiving communications from the Night Riders. Commonwealth's Attorney Denny P. Smith "alleged that the motive which prompted Mr. Wood to write the letter was that he wanted control of the farm" where Dawson resided as tenant for H. D. Wallace. Wood pled innocent, but the jury found him guilty. His first sentence was appealed, and his crime was reduced to a misdemeanor. However, he still served a short jail term and paid a fine.[42]

Rob Wood's actions against a black man came at an inopportune time in a county afflicted by a labor shortage due to blacks leaving to find work elsewhere. Threatening a well-regarded tenant at this time proved unwise. If Wood's threat had been allowed to stand, more black laborers might have fled. Christian County and other areas with large black sharecropper and tenant populations had to perform a careful balancing act to preserve the cheap, docile labor force. Clyde Quisenberry of southern Caldwell, a rich agricultural

41. Scott, interview.
42. *Hopkinsville Daily Kentucky New Era*, March 24, 1908.

section near Christian County, said that the Night Riders did not welcome blacks into the secret order, but at least in that area, they did not do them harm either. In fact, Quisenberry explained, the commander of the Night Riders, physician Dr. David Amoss, performed a tooth extraction for Quisenberry and treated all the blacks well. Where African American labor was essential, paternalism held sway; where black labor threatened whites' economic opportunities, racial violence was employed to eliminate black competition.[43]

Incidents between association members and independents continued throughout the period 1905 to 1909 in all parts of the Black Patch. One case in particular, which occurred in Caldwell County, typifies tobacco Night Rider–inspired violence, Night Rider control of courts, violence resulting from old family animosities, an element of regulator moral enforcement, and Black Patch cultural attitudes toward women. Finally, the lawsuits contributed to the demise of the Night Riders.

Late on a May 1907 night, the Hollowell family—Robert, Mary Lou Eastland, and their young son, Price—slept in their farm house unaware that a Night Rider contingent was converging upon them. Suddenly, gunshots, breaking glass, and cries of the intruders awoke them. The parents and son scrambled to the floor in an effort to dodge the bullets; however, one struck Mary Lou as she tried to protect her child. Members of the gang broke into the home and dragged the adults outside. "Mary Lou . . . was kicked by a well-known young man of the vicinity." Her husband, Bob, bent to the force of lashes on his bare back, which streamed blood. A "highly respected member of the community, a pillar in the Baptist church, applied the stripes. A woman member of the band exclaimed, 'this is sweet revenge to me,'" and the Night Riders shouted that they had nothing to fear from the courts. After the beatings, which young Price watched, the assailants left the Hollowell couple "to writhe the remainder of the night." The next morning, Robert permitted his mother to treat his wounds, then the family fled the Black Patch.[44]

43. Clyde Quisenberry, interview.

44. Miller, *Black Patch War*, 24–26, 29. Miller was the attorney retained by the Hollowells. Bill Cunningham, *On Bended Knees: The Night Rider Story; Clarksville Leaf-Chronicle*, April 23, 1908.

This brutal attack by the tobacco Night Riders ostensibly resulted from the scraping of plant beds on the farm of Robert's brother, John E. Hollowell, and on other neighbors' farms. John Hollowell supported the association and chaired the branch PPA in Caldwell County. His brother, Robert, did not affiliate with the association and continued to raise and sell tobacco independently. Although he kept quiet regarding his views of the association and the Night Riders who had earlier destroyed his tobacco beds, his wife, Mary Lou, boldly spoke out against the Night Riders and their lawless tactics. The ultimate sin for independents, besides remaining independent, was flaunting their success or talking against the Night Riders. Mary Lou even testified before the Caldwell County grand jury concerning suspected Night Riders in the Princeton raid.[45]

Mary Lou violated the rule of silence and drew the wrath of the mob because of her independent stance and for other social and cultural reasons. Mary Lou, in her vocal opposition to the Night Riders, stepped out of her role as a quiet, hard-working, submissive farm wife, an act that did not set well with the community. Her life did not conform to the white farm wife ideal. Instead of staying on the country tobacco farm, she spent much of the school year in Princeton, running a boarding house to enable Price to go the town school. She had been "well-reared . . . dressed well, was tall and well-formed, made a handsome appearance and had associates in town." Her brother, who also remained outside the association, lived near by on a prosperous farm. These things, plus some unknown personal disagreement between Mary Lou and her sister-in-law, Lula, wife of John Hollowell, led to the assault. Mary Lou claimed that her in-laws and others had committed the mob violence that May night. One Princeton official, Ward Headly, told reporters that "this is largely a neighborhood trouble and the tobacco fight has nothing to do with it."[46]

John E. Hollowell and the Night Riders believed that Mary Lou

45. Nall, *Night Riders*, 99; *Paducah Evening Sun*, April 22, 1908; Parker, interview; Samuel Stegar, interview by author, tape recording, Caldwell County, Kentucky, August 24, 1988.

46. Miller, *Black Patch War*, 34–35; *Princeton Twice-a-Week Leader*, August 19, 1976; *Cadiz Record*, March 12, 1908; Hollowell was the daughter of Ernest E. and Lucinda Harris Eastland. She was born near Lamasco in Lyon County.

paid a white man, Steve Choate, and a black man, Ned Pettit, croppers on her husband's place, to scrape their tobacco plant beds. Officers arrested the two croppers in mid-May. Choate paid his bond and
walked free, but Pettit could not raise the cash and stayed in the
Princeton jail. Their cases came to trial at the end of May before
Judge Blalock. "Both waived examination and were held to answer
to the next grand jury in sum of $300 bail."[47]

During the interim, Mary Lou Hollowell received notice to return
to Kentucky from Oklahoma, where the family had taken refuge to
testify against the Night Riders. She appealed to the governor of
Oklahoma, Frank Frantz, to prevent her extradition. Mary Lou cited
fear of the Night Riders as her reason for remaining in Oklahoma.
Black Patch newspapers took a different view. The strongly pro-
association paper, the *Cadiz Record,* claimed that "if reports are
true, and we have them from several reliable sources, there are
other reasons far more serious" for the Hollowells' refusal to return
to the Black Patch. "It is recently reported . . . that the men who have
recently been charged with scraping the plant beds of John Hollowell . . . have implicated others in the crime." Mary Lou, the article
said, paid Steve Choate ten dollars to help Ned Pettit scrape the
beds of association men. Steve Choate implicated Mary Lou, saying
she paid him to do it. The grand jury indicted Mary Lou for her role
in the affair but did not move to bring her to trial.[48]

During the Hollowells' attempts to find an attorney to take their
case against the thirty Night Riders whom they recognized as assailants, Mary Lou continued to deny any involvement in the plant
bed scraping. She appealed to John G. Miller, a lawyer who would
take the case, by dropping to her knees and swearing "I had nothing
to do with the scraping of the plant bed, have no knowledge of who
did it and am as innocent of that charge as an unborn child—so help
me, God."[49]

Miller devised a way to prosecute the case by "causing a diversity
of citizenship that would give the federal court jurisdiction of a civil

---

47. *Cadiz Record,* May 16, 1907, May 23, 1907.
48. Ibid., June 13, 1907; Nall, *Night Riders,* 101; Pettit and Choate pled guilty
to the charge of scraping plant beds and received one-year sentences in the state
penitentiary at Eddyville, according to the *Cadiz Record,* June 27, 1907.
49. Miller, *Black Patch War,* 30.

action" of the Hollowells, now residents of Evansville, Indiana, against the gang who had assaulted them. At this time, at the height of Night Rider power in the county "the Night Riders were in complete control of parts of the county." The federal cases would be held in Paducah, McCracken County, where Miller hoped justice might be done. Night Rider sympathizers showed their antipathy to Mary Lou by publishing statements in the local paper claiming the defendants were "wholly innocent" of all charges. One who signed the statement, a Princeton banker and former client of Miller, had earlier told Miller that he feared a mob would kill Mary Lou Hollowell if she returned to the Black Patch.[50]

The Hollowell cases, *Robert H. Hollowell v. John E. Hollowell* and Mary Lou's and Price's, came to trial beginning in April 1908, in Paducah, Kentucky. John testified that a boyhood friend whipped him and that his brother was in the group, but he had not seen him. Price, however, saw his uncle in the mob. All the defendants swore they were not present, that they had heard the commotion but had not thought to investigate. The defendants saved their sharpest attacks for Mary Lou, whom they castigated as a bad woman. They hoped their efforts would subtly "by innuendo awaken in the minds of the jury the belief that the purpose of the assailants . . . was to run a base woman out of the community." Three women dared to testify on behalf of Mary Lou Hollowell's good character.[51]

One last person spoke in defense of the Hollowells, an ex-Night Rider, Sanford Hall of Lamasco, Lyon County. He claimed that he had been present when the lawyer for the Night Riders met with them before the trial to plan their alibis. Miller believed Hall because "the fact of this meeting could not be denied." Black Patch residents had noticed the "strange visit of distinguished lawyers from another county to a small schoolhouse in a remote corner of Caldwell county." These men had been seen traveling "in horse vehicles over miserable roads in winter." Despite the testimony of Hall, all the defendants produced perfect alibis. Miller also had reason to

50. Ibid., 31, 42–45, 48–49.
51. Ibid., 50–51, 62–63; *Robert H. Hollowell v. John E. Hollowell, et al.*, Case #1877, Civil Docket, United States Circuit Court, Paducah, Kentucky. Vol. H, 1908; *Paducah News-Democrat*, March 5, 1908; *Cadiz Record*, March 12, 1908.

believe a Night Rider sat on the jury. The case resulted in a hung jury because of the suspected Night Rider and another juror. The judge scheduled a retrial for May 1908.[52]

In the interim, Miller received a letter from Governor Augustus E. Willson, which conveyed a copy of a letter sent to the governor by an anonymous writer claiming to be a Night Rider. He stated that no juries could be trusted, that the Night Riders planned the defense and alibis in the Hollowell suit, and that the juror, as Miller already suspected, had been ordered to "hang the jury until hell froze over."[53]

A jury selected from Jefferson and Bullitt Counties retried the case in May 1908, and brought a verdict for $35,000 in damages to be paid to Robert Hollowell. Emboldened by the success of the Hollowells, other victims of the Night Riders, such as Henry Bennett, the black Eddyville teacher, George Groves, and the police chief, C. W. Rucker, filed damage suits against the Night Riders. Miller noticed that following the April trial most "aggressive Night Rider activities as against those outside of the organization" were abandoned. "Old grudges lived, it is true, and secret vengeance was sometimes inflicted, the torch and the bomb covertly applied, here and there, and serious damage done." Nevertheless, he observed, "the vicious influence of the unlawful organization . . . was still active . . . and perhaps has not yet entirely disappeared. It will not die with the generation which saw its birth."[54]

52. Miller, *Black Patch War*, 62–68; *Hollowell v. Hollowell.*
53. Miller, *Black Patch War*, 69–71.
54. Ibid., 72–73, 78–85; *Cadiz Record*, May 14, 1908. Other cases brought afterward were *Cardin v. Neel, Amoss, et al.*, Case #1929, Civil Docket, United States Circuit Court, Paducah, Kentucky, Vol. H, 1908; *Gordon v. Amoss*, Case #1938, Civil Docket, United States Circuit Court, Paducah, Kentucky, Vol. H, 1909; *Rucker v. Amoss*, Case #1933, Records of the District Court of the United States, Federal Archives Center, Atlanta, Georgia.

9

TORN ASUNDER

T he people were soon divided into opposing classes, those condemning such lawlessness and those not condemning it and in some instances justifying it," wrote Charles Meacham after a raid by the Night Riders on Princeton, Kentucky. Meacham, editor of the *Kentuckian* and mayor of Hopkinsville, was a staunch foe of the Night Riders. The December 1, 1906, raid was typical of the violence of the Tobacco Wars, which ripped apart the culture of the Black Patch. Kinfolk took opposite sides in the conflict, old friends became enemies, Night Riders terrorized independents, town people contended with militant farmers, and whites struck out at blacks.[1]

Although the region had a long heritage of violence on grounds of honor, patriotism, Indian fighting, slave oppression and soldiering, the collective Night Rider violence failed to enter the romantic lore of the region. The powerlessness from which it sprang, the condemnation the movement attracted from town leaders, and the devastating effects of terror prevented it from becoming a heroic legend. Even though the Night Riders' violence spurred the success of the Planters' Protective Association's goals of higher tobacco prices, it did not bring unity to the culture. Rather, the violence during the Tobacco Wars brought into the open the factions ever-present in the culture—factions people did not want to dwell upon once the conflict died away. Black Patch residents concealed the fissures the Tobacco Wars unveiled by imposing a folk silence on the happenings of those years, a silence that protected individuals from revenge and allowed them to ignore the implications of social strife. It also allowed the cultural wounds to heal to some extent, but not without leaving ragged scars behind.

The unsettling revelation of tensions in the Black Patch began

1. Meacham, *History*, 46–47; David L. Carlton, *Mill and Town in South Carolina, 1990–1920*, 5–6.

soon after the association formed and people chose sides. Tragic effects of Night Riding occurred frequently. Hugh Jefferies of Stewart County, Tennessee, shot his brother, Totts, in the summer of 1908 over a rent payment. Hugh claimed he tried to collect rent owed him by Totts and some black tenants who had left the county because of Night Rider threats. The brothers argued because Totts refused to pay the black men's shares. Though "bad feelings existed" prior to the slaying, Night Rider intimidation of blacks contributed to the critical situation between these men. High tensions, previous disputes, money problems, and the underlying prejudice against black workers contributed to the killing, but if the Night Riders had not intimidated the black tenants, the murder might have been avoided. Later generations associated the tobacco Night Riders with abuse of blacks, murder, and chaos, even though the tobacco Night Riders tried at the time to distinguish themselves from others who hid behind similar masks in order to wreak racial vengeance. The major impetus of the tobacco vigilantes was to force independent growers to join the association. However, when extralegal violent means became widespread, it opened the way for racist attacks. Those men committed to the association cause could not control the activities of all the masked riders who brutalized the innocent.[2]

Whites and blacks in the Black Patch who had no quarrel with the association or the Night Riders became unwitting victims in the strained, suspicious era. In September 1908, a young newlywed couple who had just moved from Caldwell County to Calloway County became victims of a tragic accident caused by stress and the anxiety created by Night Rider activities. Late one night the husband, John Franklin Dalton, heard a suspicious noise outside and immediately fired into the darkness, hitting and killing his wife. The pair had been warned to watch for intruders by neighbors in the community, and they knew of the Night Rider's practice of interrogating strangers. The local editor theorized that the couple had probably been "investigated, as newcomers usually are in the night rider section," making young Dalton nervous and causing him to fire before assessing the situation.[3]

2. *Cadiz Record*, August 6, 1908.
3. Ibid., September 10, 1908.

Economic hardship, brought on, in part, by the activities of the Night Riders, led to despair. Tom Knight, for example, who was "subject to melancholia," attempted to kill one of his children during a fit of depression. Friends cited several causes for his anguish, one of which included his tobacco crop that "was tied up in the association and that he had been unable to realize on." Often, the Planters' Protective Association could not lend farmers money to cover expenses until the year's crop was sold. Few growers had cash reserves; consequently, they lost confidence in the system of pooling of crops. While they suffered, a neighbor who had remained outside the association might be prospering. Situations like these led to such psychological infirmities as depression, anxiety, anger, and vengeful thoughts. People vented their emotions on others, often family members or neighbors. For instance, police officers arrested J. D. Cossey for breach of peace after he cursed Gary Luton and called him "a liar and a nightrider."[4]

Threats, fear, or hopelessness during these troubled years forced many to flee from the Black Patch during the Tobacco Wars. Henry Bennett, a victim of Night Rider wrath, left the state in February of 1908. "I expect to go to Arizona or Washington State just as soon as I can wind up my business." Another victim, John Heath of Dawson, who had been whipped by the Silent Brigade in January, planned to leave for the West. Several months later, the newspaper reported that Heath had moved to Oklahoma but had not been heard from in over three months. In Montgomery County, Tennessee, W. E. Wall, whose tobacco barn had just been burnt to the ground, and who had previously suffered the loss of his plant beds and the destruction of his general store, gave up and sold his five-hundred-acre farm. Wall's position among the elite did not protect him from terrorism. Previously hidden class antagonisms came to the surface during the social turmoil.[5]

Some of those who left settled in Metropolis, Illinois, just across

4. *Hopkinsville Daily Kentucky New Era*, March 1, 1909; Trigg County, grand jury indictment of J. D. Cossey, January 1910, Trigg County Circuit Court Records, Kentucky Department for Libraries and Archives, Public Records Division, Frankfort, Kentucky.
5. *Cadiz Record*, February 20, 1908, September 17, 1908; Bennett moved to Jeffersonville, Indiana, and filed suit against the Night Riders in federal court in 1908; *Cadiz Record*, February 6, 1908, June 25, 1908, February 6, 1908.

the Ohio River from Kentucky. Former Eddyville city judge C. W. Rucker moved there and filed suit against assailants who had whipped him on his sixty-second birthday for speaking out against the Night Riders. Milton Oliver, a former Night Rider who turned against the Silent Brigade, sold his Lyon County farm and eventually settled in Metropolis. His life had been in danger since he identified Dr. David Amoss as the commanding officer of the tobacco Night Riders before a Christian County grand jury. In fact, on May 25, 1910, he had been shot and wounded in his front yard by men thought to be Night Riders wreaking vengeance for his betrayal. Those who had the resources resettled, not without trouble but at least with the hope of another chance in a new place.[6]

The poor, however, had less choice in deciding their destinations when forced out of the Black Patch. Henry Jackson, his wife, and their five children walked from Christian County to Paducah, a distance of over eighty miles. Intimidated by the Night Riders, penniless and homeless, the family received aid from authorities in the city and eventually resettled in Missouri. A report from Veraz, Indiana, claimed that hundreds of Kentuckians could be seen crossing the Ohio River to Switzerland County. The refugees, the report said, would raise tobacco and become stable residents since "most of them are good, thrifty citizens, and many are buying farms, while others are renting." Some of the Black Patch refugees, though, may have carried the Night Rider spirit with them to their new homes. A report from St. Joseph, Missouri, in 1911 told of the burning of a tobacco barn containing twenty thousand pounds of curing weed. People soon feared Night Riding "in the new tobacco growing country."[7]

The churches of the region also experienced divisive tension, which tended to grow along town-country lines. Country preachers, who lived among the farmers, often grew tobacco themselves and sympathized with the growers' plight, joined, and in some cases, led Night Rider lodges. "There was a preacher [who] was the ring leader. He'd tell the people where to scrape the plant beds." In Lyon County, a

6. *Hopkinsville Daily Kentucky New Era*, January 3, 1909, January 9, 1911; *Cadiz Record*, January 12, 1911, March 2, 1911; Christopher Waldrep, "'Human Wolves': The Night Riders and the Killing of Axiom Cooper," 413–14.

7. *Hopkinsville Daily Kentucky New Era*, April 4, 1908, April 6, 1908, January 13, 1911.

"stalwart man, a prosperous farmer and a part-time Methodist preacher" named Jabe Holloway spoke to many farmers in his neighborhood near Fungo Schoolhouse and Eddy Creek about the benefits of joining the association. Later, he allegedly headed up a Night Rider band in the area. Once the conflict ended, Preacher Holloway never told his son, Robert, about his activities. Not until his nineties did Robert learn from his wife, Macie, that his father had been a Night Rider. Even if rural preachers remained outside the fray physically, they may have purposely ignored their parishioners' nocturnal exploits. Or they too may have been intimidated into silence by threats. One woman recollected that her father, a deacon in the Baptist Church and opponent of the violence of the Night Riders, was "punished for his opposition" by being whipped in the yard of his beloved church.[8]

In the towns, prominent ministers spoke against the lawlessness of the Night Riders. Rev. C. H. H. Branch, of the Hopkinsville Ninth Street Presbyterian Church, drew his sermon one Sunday in March 1908, from the biblical text Acts 18:17: "And Gallio cared for none of these things." Reverend Branch described Gallio as a judge who refused to rule in a case that did not include villainy. Even after the Jews beat up the ruler of the synagogue, Gallio refused to make a ruling. Based on this text, Branch declared that "inevitably it follows that indifference to morality on the part of officials leads to indifference to matters purely civil." Branch and his followers believed the origins of the conflict sprang from officers who refused to enforce the law or morality and "there is a message to us in this present crisis."[9]

8. Vernon E. Ford, interview by Arthur S. Monroe, tape recording, April 29, 1961, Department of Library Special Collections, Folklife Archives, Western Kentucky University, Bowling Green, Kentucky; George Holloway, "Night Rider Days," October 20, 1977, vertical files, George Coon Pennyrile Regional Library, Princeton, Kentucky; Macie McCarty Holloway, interview by author, tape recording, Lyon County, Kentucky, March 10, 1987; Joe Scott, interview; Eunice McCarty, interview; I. B. Hill, interview with author, tape recording, Eddyville, Kentucky, July 21, 1987. Some ministers spoke out against the Night Riders. See *Nashville Tennessean*, January 6, 1908; *Clarksville Leaf-Chronicle*, May 31, 1906, August 29, 1907, March 23, 1908, April 16, 1908; "Are We Any Better?" *Cumberland Presbyterian* (October 29, 1908), 548.

9. *Hopkinsville Daily Kentucky New Era*, March 2, 1908; *Hopkinsville Kentuckian*, March 10, 1908.

For the upper levels of Hopkinsville society who attended Branch's church, loss of morals among the farmers seemed to be the cause of the violence, although they did not question the morals of the tobacco firm owners. Their wealth, town-shaped attitudes, and apparent lack of knowledge about the condition of the poor and middling tobacco growers contributed to their view.[10]

Kentucky governor Augustus Willson shared a similar perception and quickly adopted a law-and-order stance. Willson, elected to office in 1907, came to the governor's seat after the December 1907, raid on Hopkinsville. Shortly thereafter, a telegram alerted Willson that a "Hopkinsville committee of citizens will reach Frankfort tonight desire audience at your office" to discuss the crisis in the Black Patch. Willson decided to send the Earlington, Kentucky, State Guard company to Christian County to protect the town from further attack. Attorney John T. Edmunds wrote enthusiastically about the governor's order. "There is no doubt as to the wisdom of your ordering the Earlington company here for as soon as the news [arrived in Hopkinsville] our local men felt so much encouraged that they formed a splendid posse of about one hundred and twenty-five men and stood guard like veterans."[11]

The previous governor, J. C. W. Beckham, had been criticized for his reticence in enforcing order in the Black Patch, although he had sent troops into the region. The arrival of additional Kentucky guardsmen to Christian County after the attack thrilled the people of Hopkinsville but angered farmers and others who sympathized with the association and Night Riders. Businessmen of Cadiz, Trigg County, a pro-association town, sent the governor a petition opposing the troops. Tobacco growers, most of whom were loyal Democrats, disliked the Republican governor, not only because of his party affiliation, but because he had been an attorney for the American Tobacco Trust. This, combined with his harsh attitude toward the growers' predicament, fueled their hatred. Independents, though, saw in him a man who promised both to enforce the law as they interpreted it and to rid them of the Night Riders. Poignant letters from independents descended upon the new "law-and-order" governor. One woman

10. *Hopkinsville Daily Kentucky New Era*, March 2, 1908.
11. *Louisville Courier-Journal*, December 8, 1908, December 10, 1908.

wrote in desperation, "I feel like this terrible mental strain on account of threats and also actions from . . . night riders, I cannot endure much longer." Her husband had received threat letters, his "old blind mother, 84 years old, had all of her tobacco destroyed. . . . The torture that the poor people are suffering is worse than death. What can you do for us?"[12]

Governor Willson also called a meeting to be held in the state capital, Frankfort, to discuss the tobacco crisis. A letter to Willson from the Department of Justice, Office of U.S. Marshal for the Western District of Kentucky, had urged a forum since the situation was too complex for military force alone. Without the cooperation of state and local authorities, he argued, halting the violence in the Black Patch would be nearly impossible.[13]

Letters supporting Willson's tobacco meeting came from large-scale farmers and businessmen. Some gave full support for the conference while others, such as M. H. Thatcher, chairman of the Legislative Committee, Republican State Campaign Committee, approved the meeting but emphasized the need for strong action. Prince Walker, the secretary of Gardner and Walker Leaf Tobacco Company, Inc., of Mayfield, Kentucky, expressed the buyers' opinion. Although no trouble had started in the Jackson Purchase county of Graves, he feared the trouble would spread to his county. Walker and others in his class agreed that ending the insurgency was of paramount concern.[14]

12. Ibid.; John Stites, Jr., telegram to A. E. Willson, December 12, 1907, Willson Papers; Mott Ayers, telegram to A. E. Willson, December 11, 1907, Willson Papers; John T. Edmunds to A. E. Willson, December 12, 1907, Willson Papers; Christopher Waldrep, "Augustus E. Willson and the Night Riders," 237–39; petition, sent to Willson, April 22, 1908, Willson Papers; F. M. Naive, Hughes and Naive, Dealers in Rough and Dressed Lumber, to A. E. Willson, December 13, 1907, Willson Papers; A. E. Willson, "The People and Their Law," 13 (Annual Address Delivered before the American Bar Association at Detroit, Michigan), August 25, 1909, Willson Papers. The governor's speech includes the quote from a non-association woman.

13. Department of Justice, Office of U.S. Marshal of the Western District of Kentucky to A. E. Willson, December 12, 1907 [signature unclear], Willson Papers.

14. T. S. Coke, dealer in general merchandise, Livia, Kentucky, to A. E. Willson, December 16, 1907; Glave Goddard, Wildwood Stockfarm, Breeder of Short-Horn Cattle, to A. E. Willson, December 16, 1907; I. P. Barnard, director, Louisville Tobacco Warehouse Company, December 16, 1907; M. H. Thatcher to A. E. Willson, December 12, 1907, Willson Papers.

The peace conference failed because the two main antagonists, James B. Duke of American Tobacco and Felix G. Ewing of the Planters' Protective Association, refused to attend. After this attempt at solving the crisis failed, Willson authorized spies to operate in the Black Patch and remained in close contact with the commander of Company H., Maj. George Albrecht, and Maj. E. B. Bassett, sent to the area by former governor Beckham. Another element, state force, was added to the social conflict, arousing new resentments among association sympathizers and providing hope for independents.[15]

Independent tobacco growers did not stand idly awaiting the next Night Rider attack. Disgruntled farmers in Trigg County organized in October 1906, because of their disagreement with the association's method of selling tobacco. Their group, the Trigg Farmers' Independent Organization (FIO), favored loose leaf sales. Rev. J. J. Alexander offered a prayer at the first meeting and talked for nearly half an hour, complimenting the PPA but criticizing its marketing methods. Members then passed a resolution countering the association's resolution of October 2, 1906, which was intended to keep non-association buyers from entering Trigg County. The Farmers' Independent Organization saw the association act as a "threat to resort to lawlessness and force" against Trigg farmers who refused to pledge their crop to the association. However, the Trigg independents believed "as free citizens and free Americans we have the full right of property protection guaranteed to us under the law and may sell to whom we please." They planned to sell at "fair market prices" and "abide by the law." But, they added, if the association agreed to loose leaf sales, then we would join . . . in a body."[16]

Trigg County PPA members disagreed with the Farmers' Independent Organization. Although he had "personal friends" in the FIO, Rev. B. F. Hyde failed to see how a man could be honest with himself and his neighbors and go against the association's goals. He

15. John Stites to A. E. Willson, May 27, 1910; A. E. Willson to John Stites, May 30, 1910; John Stites to A. E. Willson, December 10, 1910, and December 15, 1910; bill of payment to Mr. Z. O. King for his job of spying, May 30, 1911; Report of spy, alias John Smith, Willson Papers.

16. *Cadiz Record*, October 28, 1906. Roscoe Glenn, "The Development and Failure of the Dark Tobacco Growers' Cooperative Association" (master's thesis, Vanderbilt University, 1927), 32.

thought the FIO was "the last kick of the dying calf." The association resolved to continue their efforts and to "denounce . . . the insinuations of our misguided fellow farmers, known as 'hillbillies,' that we are lawless." They denied any connection with the Night Riders and denounced the Duke Trust for swaying "the weak and misguided farmers in fighting against us" and causing divisiveness in the community. Blaming the strife in the Black Patch solely on the Duke Trust proved easier than accepting the real divisions that existed: economic problems, different views on dealing with the tobacco situation, class antagonisms, racial prejudice, and powerlessness.[17]

The two groups met, however, in December 1906, after the Night Rider raid on Princeton. Their joint resolution condemning the violence included a perceptive observation about the cause of tensions: "We can only account for such as the result of intense local feeling peculiar to that locality alone; the outburst of an enraged public, caused by a long series of oppression and the lack of good counsel." Across the Black Patch, farmers victimized by the unseen forces had become angry with their inability to effect change through peaceful means. Collective violence brought attention to their problems and forced hillbillies to cooperate with the association.[18]

In a brief attempt at collective violence, independents showed frustration at being coerced by the Night Riders and PPA men. In September 1908, a small contingent of growers in the Bethany section of Caldwell County retaliated against Night Rider depredations by cutting the tobacco plants of some leading association men in the neighborhood. One man, Burt Calvert, found a bundle of switches and a note warning him to cease attending the association meetings. Other farmers in the county near Farmersville tried to organize in 1907 and 1908 to counter the association. Rumor said they planned a raid on Princeton to punish PPA men, but the attack never came. The terror and power of the Night Riders in the county prevented much opposition.[19]

Men who favored the association had a different perspective on the situation described by tobacco dealer Walker as anarchy. "What started the Tobacco Association was that Duke Tobacco Company

17. *Cadiz Record*, November 1, 1906.
18. Ibid., December 13, 1906.
19. Ibid., September 3, 1908.

bought out most of the other tobacco companies and there was no competition among the buyers," explained Robert Parker, son of a Caldwell County association man. Conditions in the Black Patch got so bad "below where a person could live. Sharecroppers that lived on other people's places in little two-room house[s] didn't have any-thing." They had trouble finding enough work to feed their families, and "it got so the farmers were just as destitute as the croppers were [and] nobody could live." When all the people in the region—rich, middling, and poor alike—began to suffer, something had to be done.[20]

At the critical point, Robert Parker stated, "they organized the association in the Black Patch where dark-fired tobacco" was raised. The pool held the tobacco "for a price and they got it, but the Tobacco Trust didn't like that so they picked out a few people around who thought more of dollars than they did of humans," and paid them a good price for their crops. The hillbillies received better prices than PPA members "and that didn't set very well because they were tear-ing the association up." Jealousy, along with a perceived loss of fair-ness and community cohesion, arose "because when your neighbor sells for twice what you get, it makes you unhappy."[21]

Such feelings led to a decision, Parker continued, "that the best way" to demolish both the trust and the opposition "was to destroy some of the tobacco buyers' warehouses" in Eddyville, Hopkinsville, and Russellville. "And they did," Parker continued, "and most of the whipping and barn burning was done over the country because the people were mouthy or through prejudice."[22]

Parker believed much of the violence against blacks attributed to Night Riders was done by the disreputable elements of society that such movements always attract. But he emphasized that "the burn-ing of the warehouses, they planned that themselves." Parker com-pares the town raids to a story about a little boy that had beaten up another child. The boy's mother commented, "I think the Devil was in you!" And the boy replied, "Might have been, but pulling his hair was my own idea." Similarly, Parker suggested, the "devil might have had something to do with the barn burning and whipping" of

20. Parker, interview.
21. Ibid.
22. Ibid.

hillbillies and blacks, but the burning of trust warehouses was the members' "own idea."[23]

Parker's father avoided active participation in the Night Rider raids, but "he loaned a neighbor boy a mare to ride" in the raid on Hopkinsville. During the chase, after the successful attack, the horse's rider abandoned the mount to escape on foot. The next morning, the animal returned to the Parkers' locked barnyard gate. Parker's father responded to the crisis by giving up tobacco growing for several years "about the time of the Tobacco War." Since he enjoyed "stock raising better than tobacco, and he had his place paid for, he just went to raising hogs and cattle and my mother raised a lot of chickens and sold eggs and hens." Working together, the couple made a fair living without growing tobacco as the cash crop.[24]

After Governor Willson issued a "proclamation that any man would be pardoned in advance if he would kill any man that was accused of being a Night Rider," association and Night Rider sympathizers grew incensed. The Kentucky governor became known as Augustus "Everlasting" Willson because "he had put out this proclamation and there was no end to it." Everyone, Parker claimed, "thought it was utterly ridiculous, vicious and unconstitutional among other things— that was about all you could quote them on!" Association and Night Rider supporters lost all respect for the governor, who seemed to be advocating lawlessness as well as disregard for the interests of tobacco farmers. Willson wrote to Maj. George Albrecht of Company H, stationed in Hopkinsville, that all masked riders should be regarded as outlaws, and he promised that no one who shot or even killed a Night Rider would be prosecuted.[25]

A long anonymous poem conveying prevalent attitudes appeared in the *Cadiz Record* on January 30, 1908, to the interest and glee of many. It accused "Augustus E! Augustus O!" of favoring the Tobacco Trust and of not acting when other vicious acts of violence occurred in the state. Only in the Black Patch did Willson oppose hard-pressed farmers. The poem's author contended, that, although

23. Ibid.
24. Ibid.
25. Ibid.; A. E. Willson to Maj. George Albrecht, February 22, 1908, Willson Papers; Waldrep, "Augustus E. Willson," 247.

Your gutter snipes in soldier's dress,
We look upon with scorn;
Your Gatlin Guns do not impress
Men to the manor born.
Our fathers' blood in us doth flow;
Their memories we revere.
They dealt oppression blow for blow——
With them there was no fear.
Nor was there fear among the Black Patch farmers,
For law and order take your stand,
We'll help you in our way.
While you berate and murder us
The trust will feel our sway.[26]

People who claimed anti-trust sentiment believed, as did former Night Rider Joe Scott, that the people had to act in order to save starving farm children. To Scott and others, morality involved freeing the poor from the trust, even if that involved violent tactics. Although Scott enjoyed the excitement of "racing his slick little pony" while out on the raids, he believed he made things better for farming people by helping to force the price of tobacco up. Nevertheless, town folks thought these issues did not justify the lawless violence that swept across the Black Patch and threatened their comfortable lives.[27]

"I recognize no trust, no association, no independent, only absolute right and wrong, law and lawlessness," Rev. C. H. H. Branch declaimed in his sermon. Those who did not raise a voice for right, as Branch defined it, were cowardly conspirators in the evil. Moreover, he continued, "the man who is indifferent now puts himself on record as in favor of anarchy and as against the laws of his country and the laws of God." Branch declared that the issue involved either right or wrong. By sharply dividing the issues, he could ignore the social and economic complexities that led to the association and to the Night Rider violence. His sermon came after the Night Riders'

26. *Cadiz Record*, January 30, 1908. The paper reported that it received the anonymous poem through the mail with a postmark indicating that it had been sent from a train on the Evansville and Nashville division of the Illinois Central Railroad.

27. Scott, interview; Joe Scott, *The Night Riders*, produced by Bill Cunningham, 90 min., 1985, videocassette.

attack on Hopkinsville, which had caused understandable fears and anger among the citizens. But, his right-or-wrong analysis of the Night Rider movement also derived from the townsmen's business interests. Violently protesting farmers did not help in drawing investors and industry to Hopkinsville.[28]

Soon after the December 1907 raid on Hopkinsville, town citizens founded a Law and Order League to counter the vigilantes and protect the city from future attacks. The league called for prosecution of the mob, asked Governor Willson for more troops to be sent into the region, and even requested a Gatlin gun for their defense. Reverend Branch supported the Law and Order League and spoke on its behalf. Townspeople and association farmers operated at cross-purposes because of different perspectives about the realities of tobacco producing, what constituted law and order, and how morality should be defined during the crisis. Independent growers sought freedom from the PPA and condemned violence but would not welcome town control either.[29]

The Law and Order League also entered the political arena in support of Republican candidates running on a law-and-order platform. For example, in 1909, a race in the Third Judicial District for judge pitted alleged Night Rider sympathizer Judge Thomas P. Cook, of Murray, Calloway County, against John T. Hanberry, the Law and Order League's choice. Incumbent Attorney Denny P. Smith, suspected of having taken the Night Rider oath, ran unopposed for commonwealth's attorney. In the election, Hanberry carried Christian and Calloway Counties by a narrow margin and won. Cook won in Lyon County, a stronghold of the Night Riders and barely lost in Trigg, another Night Rider section. To the consternation of the Law and Order League, Smith returned to his position.[30]

28. *Hopkinsville Daily Kentucky New Era*, March 2, 1908.
29. John Stites to A. E. Willson, December 10, 1907, Willson Papers; E. M. Flack to Willson, December 14, 1907, Willson Papers; Christopher Waldrep, "The Law, the Night Riders, and Community Consensus: The Prosecution of Dr. David Amoss," 241; *Cadiz Record*, December 17, 1908.
30. Waldrep, "Law, Night Riders, and Consensus," 240–42; *Hopkinsville Kentuckian*, June 8, 1909; *Murray Ledger*, November 4, 1909; A. E. Willson to John G. Miller, May 5, 1908, Miller Papers, Department of Library Special Collections, Manuscripts Division, Western Kentucky University, Bowling Green, Kentucky.

Tension among former association members, Night Riders, hill-billies, and townspeople continued after the major conflicts ended. The folk silence concerning the Night Riders and their activities reveals the deep fears and tensions those years produced. Traditionally, the Black Patch people kept quiet, or "closed-mouthed' as they referred to it, about the Night Riders' vigilantism. Members of the Night Rider generation often did not pass stories and tales of the period down to their children or grandchildren. "They didn't talk about it much," recalled Bob Parker. "If you happened to be right quiet when the old folks were talking about it you might hear a little bit." Black Patch "people were afraid to say something about" the Night Riders. Their silence reveals the complex underlying feelings of fear, desire to protect self, family, and former members, and the desire to forget the violence.[31]

Another factor contributed to the folk silence. Increasingly, farmers at the turn of the century faced a larger American society that was turning away from rural values. Political power began to shift from country squires to town politicians. In the South, the newly empowered town business leaders sought to attract industry to their regions. Men with these interests had consistently opposed the Night Riders, formed the Hopkinsville Law and Order League, and espoused the negative effects of agrarian violence. City preachers, like Reverend Branch, assisted the league in decrying the violence and lawlessness of the farmers. A town-country conflict appeared in which town residents looked upon their country neighbors as not only ignorant hayseeds, but worse, as violent lawbreakers. Black Patch farmers perceived that their status in society had declined. Some accepted the arguments of the town leaders and grew embarrassed about the violence. They internalized the condemnation of the town leaders and imposed a ban on discussing the Tobacco Wars. That they had been forced to confront force with force during those years because of a threat to their way of life was not addressed. Later, after emotions died down, businessmen formed the Hopkinsville Businessmen's As-

31. Parker, interview; Elizabeth Coombs, interview by Arthur S. Monroe, May 9, 1961, Tape recording, from D. K. Wilgus; Folklore and Folklife Collection, Department of Library Special Collections, Folklife Archives, Western Kentucky University, Bowling Green, Kentucky.

sociation (HBA) to promote "Hoptown" as a New South city eager for industry and investments. The new organization appealed to farmers to join so everyone could boost the town and county to the benefit of all. Farmers, though, failed to be enthusiastic about the HBA. They had little time for such pursuits and doubtless sensed no genuine welcome or interest in tobacco growers' concerns among the HBA promoters.[32]

Joe Scott, a Night Rider from Lyon County, never talked about the Black Patch War until he reached old age and felt no one else lived to take revenge upon him if he spoke openly. Scott took very seriously the Night Rider oath pledged in his youth, in which secrecy was a cardinal tenet. To violate it might bring death. Stories circulated of men killed by irate Night Riders, but the terrorism of the group inspired most of the fear and obedience to the code of silence. Night Riders whipped victims and ordered them to scream loudly. The screams echoed over the countryside, warning others of their fate if they offended the Silent Brigade. Scott did not talk because he feared the vengeance of the other Night Riders who no longer wanted their role in the notorious band discussed. Revenge by hillbillies who had suffered at the hands of the Night Riders also figured into Scott's decision to preserve the silence. Rumors at the time warned that people who spoke against the Silent Brigade might wind up at the bottom of a sinkhole. Some said missing men had been killed and secretly buried by the Night Riders. Some heard frightening stories about strange, dark, running shadows that sprang from near a schoolhouse frequented by Night Riders. The cautious knew to stay away from haunted places and to keep their mouths shut.[33]

"One reason some of them wouldn't talk was because the brothers would be on opposite sides," suggests Martyne Sivills Parker, a relative of Mary Lou Eastland Hollowell, whose husband and brother-in-law were on opposite sides in the Tobacco Wars. Also, "some of them didn't want to keep it alive" once the disturbances ended. Robert, Martyne's husband, agrees, "They wanted it to die down as much as possible and they didn't tell their children much that their neigh-

32. *Hopkinsville Daily Kentucky New Era*, April 9, 1912; *Hopkinsville Kentuckian*, February 3, 1906.

33. Scott, interview.

bor's had been involved or 'were on opposite sides'" in the conflict. "I've talked to two or three of the old men that I knew were in it and they told me more than my dad did." Former hillbillies kept quiet too. Price Hollowell, the son of Mary Lou, told Martyne that he "just won't go to Princeton very much" because "I don't know who was Night Riders and who wasn't." Animosities toward those on the opposing side ran long and deep.[34]

"Strains and tensions" remained for years, Robert Parker believed. "I happened to be in Cobb the morning after" Milton Oliver, the confessed Night Rider who testified against Dr. David Amoss in his trial, died. "One of the Oliver boys who had been very active in" the Night Riders entered the store and announced that "Milt Oliver, the old confessed Night Rider died last night." All remained silent among the fellows gathered in the general store until "Herman White, an old Night Rider got up and spat at the stove and said, 'confessed damn traitor!'" and stomped out of the building in disgust. Even now, Robert surmised, "a little tension" exists. "Get somebody stirred up a little," warned Eunice McCarty, "and it'd come up, sometimes even among kin folks."[35]

Parker believed the association and the Night Riders were a "good thing because it made the price of tobacco go up and if you look around there's a whole lot of houses built about 1910 and a whole lot of barns built and people lived better." The Night Riders did not achieve success alone. "Some senators that were more or less statesmen then—we don't have any statesmen nowadays, we just have politicians—they worked on the anti-trust law," which broke up the Duke Tobacco trust. "But the association got the praise from the majority of the people who were tobacco growers," because it was local and visible. Parker raised his first dark tobacco crop in 1919 "and I got twenty dollars a pound for it. I had 590 pounds and I got $120, $118 for it. That was good and I thought I had hit the jackpot."[36]

"You might say that the Night Rider trouble was one of the first labor unions and it was considered awful bad to box heads up then," Parker pointed out. But in later years he noticed that "it got per-

34. Parker, interview.
35. Parker, interview; Eunice McCarty, interview.
36. Parker, interview.

fectly all right for the teamsters to bash heads and for the coal miners to bash head, but it was frowned on when the farmers did it." Parker sensed the myth of the backbone of America, the yeomen farmer, who was supposed to be prosperous and content in the American heartland. However, by the turn of the century, when America began to be defined as an industrial, urban, corporate state, the positive image of the farmer fell, and a negative opinion, which portrayed farmers as ignorant, backwoods hayseeds, appeared. Yet, in the transitional period when both myths operated, the farmer as laborer was not accepted either, meaning his right to protest was denied and his protests were even seen as particularly heinous. The romantic tillers of the soil should have no reason to rebel. Furthermore, tobacco producers garnered less sympathy, perhaps, because their plight came when farmers in the Midwest prospered during the "Golden Age of Agriculture" after the demise of the Populist era. Tobacco growers seemed to be a bitter reminder of a chaotic period in America.[37]

Among some former Night Riders, confusion and, perhaps, a sense of shame contributed to their keeping the silence. For many the decision to join had been painful and difficult. Feuding with neighbors and kin did not correspond to the region's professed standards of neighborly behavior in times of distress. Having to participate in the humiliation and violent punishment of a neighbor could not have been easy. Night Rider lodges tried to alleviate this stress by swapping neighborhoods between lodges so that members would not be required to flog a neighbor. Nevertheless, justifying cultural values, standards, and traditions with the vigilante actions proved difficult. Even though the cultural tradition of violent reaction existed and provided cohesion in the Black Patch, the collective violence of the Night Rider era brought division, not unity. The factionalization of the society disturbed the people and their sense of order. They chose to block it out, cover over the rifts, and forget the troubled times by perpetuating the Night Riders' code of silence.[38]

Later generations have tried to rationalize the violence of the Night

37. Ibid.
38. People I interviewed who wished to keep their stories confidential expressed these ideas as well as fear of revenge. See also Kroll, *Riders in the Night*.

Riders, as Robert Parker and Joe Scott did, by pointing to the positive results that the Planters' Protective Association sought and the Night Riders helped to achieve in these years. In their view, when a way of life appeared threatened, liberties jeopardized, and an economy squeezed by outside forces like the Duke Trust, violent response became justified in the tradition of the first American patriots. Concurrently, contemporaries and later commentators sought to distinguish the tobacco Night Riders, who, they asserted, fought for better tobacco prices and the Black Patch community welfare, from the disreputable characters who used the mask to take personal revenge, act out prejudices, and enforce morality. In this way people could come to terms with the violence by separating the good elements from the bad. Most agreed with Todd Countian Robert Penn Warren, who wrote in his novel *Night Rider* about those years that "the good Lord never got any thousand or so men together for any purpose without a liberal assortment of sons-of-bitches thrown in."[39]

After the Tobacco Wars ended, growers, because of the work of the Planters' Protection Association, the violence of the Night Riders, the decline in production of tobacco, and later the breakup of the Duke Trust, began to receive higher prices for their leaf. Prosperity of a sort returned, and they gave up their interest in associating for the common good and turned their attention to rebuilding their farms and their lives. Community action resulted from a dire need—an emergency or other difficulty. Once the group cooperated to alleviate the problem, they returned to their individual lives and goals.[40]

A final display of the association farmers' community sanction of the Night Riders' anti-trust raids on the Black Patch towns and attacks on independents occurred at the trial of Dr. David Amoss, alleged commander of the Silent Brigade. In 1911, the grand jury under the Law and Order League's judge, John T. Hanberry of Christian County, handed down indictment number eighty-eight, charging Amoss with "willfully and feloniously confederating, conspiring and banding together for the purpose of molesting, injuring and

39. Robert Penn Warren, *Night Rider*, 285.
40. *Hopkinsville Daily Kentucky New Era*, October 20, 1913.

destroying property of other persons." Specifically, the indictment referred to the "burning of the warehouse of the late John C. Latham of New York" whose tobacco warehouse first received "the torch at the time of the raid." The indictment cited the old "Ku Klux Law," which forbade two or more people to "unlawfully confederate or band themselves together, and go forth armed or disguised for the purpose of intimidating or alarming" other citizens of the state, as Amoss allegedly did on the December 1907 Hopkinsville raid.[41]

When Dr. Amoss came to trial, the jury chosen to decide his fate did not please the prosecution. Col. E. B. Bassett, officer in charge of the soldiers stationed in the Black Patch, informed Governor Willson that the jury was composed of outlaws and Night Riders. The jury members were not criminals, but they were all farmers, excepting one Hopkinsville carpenter. All claimed to have no affiliation with, or opinion about, the Night Riders, although it is likely that sympathy with the association's cause among these tobacco growers was present. Bassett could not help but suspect that a jury of tobacco men might sympathize with the alleged Night Rider leader on trial in the case.[42]

Bassett feared that any hope of convicting Amoss was lost. His prediction proved accurate. Despite incriminating testimony by former Night Riders, such as Milton Oliver, who had participated in the raid and had seen Amoss give orders; Arthur Cooper, who attended Amoss's raid strategy meetings and saw Amoss get shot during the melee; and Carl Cooper, who witnessed Dr. Amoss's orders to move on Hopkinsville, the jury acquitted him after about forty minutes of deliberation.[43]

The testimony most crucial in saving Amoss was an alibi provided

41. Ibid., March 7, 1911; bill of Indictment, *Commonwealth v. D. A. Amoss, et al.*, Christian County Circuit Court Records, Hopkinsville, Kentucky; Waldrep, "Law, Night Riders, and Consensus," 245–46; John D. Carroll, ed., *The Kentucky Statutes*, 4th ed. (Louisville, 1909), section 1223, a revised version of the April 11, 1873, Ku Klux law; Edward Bullock, et al., comps., *The General Statutes of Kentucky* (Frankfort, 1881), 36–67.

42. E. B. Bassett to A. E. Willson, March 7, 1911, Willson Papers; Waldrep, "Law, Night Riders, and Consensus," 247; *Hopkinsville Daily Kentucky New Era*, March 8, 1911.

43. *Hopkinsville Daily Kentucky New Era*, March 9, 1911; Waldrep, "Law, Night Riders, and Consensus," 248–49.

by William H. White, who stated that Dr. Amoss could not have been leading the Hopkinsville raid because he was visiting White's sick wife that night. Amoss testified to having gone to the White residence around 1:00 A.M. December 7, and tending Ann White for about an hour. His patient ledger showed that he charged the Whites for medical treatment on December 6 and 7, thereby substantiating his claim.[44]

The prosecution had tried to disprove Amoss's alibi by issuing subpoenas for the Whites, as well as for their son-in-law, Wylie Jones, a former Caldwell County deputy. Jones successfully avoided answering the subpoena; he had no desire to testify against his in-laws. Since no one else would dispute Dr. Amoss's alibi, it stood.[45]

However, the diligent prosecutor, Seldon Y. Trimble, carried out a rigorous cross-examination of defense witnesses and successfully exposed them as Night Riders. In Trimble's mind, and in the view of others in Hopkinsville and elsewhere who opposed the Night Riders, the trial's "unmasking" of the gang served the purpose of ending the reign of the Silent Brigade. Even though Amoss received a verdict of "not guilty," the Night Riders had been stripped of their veil of secrecy and, thus, their power to intimidate.[46]

Equally significant was the acquittal of Dr. Amoss by the jury of farmers. The trial captured the attention of Black Patch people, and spectators filled the courtroom during more than a week of testimony and argument. Few doubted that Amoss had led the Night Riders; many knew he had done so. Amoss, though, became a hero among the tobacco growers who supported the association. He had long been a well-respected country doctor and a leading man in his neighborhood of Cobb, Caldwell County. In his rounds as a physician he saw the poor conditions in which the tobacco growers lived. Perhaps this reality, as well as the effect the economy may have had on his income, led him to promote the association and later to commend the Night Riders. Few who knew of the time and dedication Amoss

44. *Hopkinsville Daily Kentucky New Era*, March 10, 1911, March 11, 1911; Waldrep, "Law, Night Riders, and Consensus," 249.

45. Waldrep, "Law, Night Riders, and Consensus," 249–51.

46. Ibid., 252–56; *Hopkinsville Daily Kentucky New Era*, March 17, 1911.

gave to the farmers desired to see him convicted of a crime. The hero and "general" of the Night Riders had to be protected.[47]

A vivid indication that the community, at least the neighborhood of Cobb, would no longer support the Night Rider cause happened not long after the trial ended. William White, a deacon in the Harmony Church, along with "his wife and daughter-in-law went to Hopkinsville and got on the witness stand and swore that he [Dr. Amoss] wasn't out killing," at the time of the 1907 raid. Rather, he "was trying to save lives" that December night and early morning while tending the deacon's wife, who had pneumonia. In essence the church deacon, White, had perjured himself to save David Amoss. White had been an excellent witness because of his standing in the community. According to a black neighbor and observer, Clyde Quisenberry, "William White, they called him Billy White, Square Uncle Billy—he was the leading Deacon of that church and all the white people thought he was an idol god. Whatever Mister Billy said went." In fact, Quisenberry claimed, "that's why they used him. He was the deacon and supposed to tell nothing but the truth. He was a Christian man and that's why they used him" to support Dr. Amoss's alibi.[48]

However, Quisenberry continued, when White "got up in court and swore that lie, they'd knowed he was lying because Doc Amoss was with them" at the Hopkinsville raid and everybody knew it. The Night Rider "boys knowed he was lying and they just lost confidence in him. Knowed he was the biggest liar there was in the county! Couldn't have been no bigger lie told!" According to Quisenberry, the Harmony Church members "done lost confidence in Deacon White" after he perjured himself to save Amoss. That "tore up the white church." White "moved out, he left. People had done lost confidence in him. He moved to Princeton." The whites of Cobb and vicinity needed to see their hero saved, but they could not condone a lie by a leader in the church, even when the lie worked for their benefit.[49]

47. Clyde Quisenberry, interview by author, tape recording, Caldwell County, Kentucky, July 20, 1987; Parker, interview; Scott, interview.
48. Quisenberry, interview.
49. Ibid. Quisenberry knew Amoss. Dr. Amoss had treated his family. Since he was black, Quisenberry says, he was not welcomed into the ranks of the Night Riders, but neither were he and his family bothered.

Dr. Amoss remained in the Black Patch for a time and continued to speak out periodically for the farmers' cause. After a peaceful march of three hundred tobacco growers of the Farmer's Union to Madisonville in Hopkins County in November 1912, Dr. Amoss spoke on the tobacco situation. One year later, the Hopkinsville newspaper reported that Dr. Amoss and his wife were moving to Vicksburg, Mississippi, where he planned to open a new medical practice. However, Amoss became ill and never left. Two years later, the Night Rider commander died in New York City after an operation to remove a tumor. His funeral was well attended by tobacco farmers, former Night Riders, and kinsmen, who followed him to his grave site in Millwood Cemetery.[50]

After the funeral, the mourners left vowing never to reveal the secrets of the Night Rider lodges or their work during the Tobacco War, but they also carried memories of what the collective violence accomplished. The loyal followers of Amoss believed that their violent actions gained the farmers higher prices and made it possible for them to continue living as tobacco growers. The legacy of this belief, that collective violence could effect change, remained. In the coming years, during economic slumps, farmers turned to collective violence to enforce tobacco cooperative efforts and to rid neighborhoods of unwanted black laborers. War on the scale of the 1904–1909 conflict never recurred because those who had opposed the Night Riders struck quickly to halt uprisings. The cultural divisions exposed during the Black Patch War did not disappear, but the people ignored them and returned to the relative safety of familiar customs, traditional violence, and the tobacco patch.[51]

50. *Hopkinsville Daily Kentucky New Era*, November 4, 1912; David A. Moore to Bill Cunningham, April 8, 1983, George Coon Pennyroyal Regional Library, Princeton, Kentucky (photocopy). Moore is the grandson of David Amoss. Cunningham, *On Bended Knees*, 205–6, 209–13.

51. The "normal" violence is evident from surveys of court records of the counties, 1910–1940. Edward Coffman, *The Story of Logan County* (Nashville: Parthenon Press, 1962), 225.

BIBLIOGRAPHY

Primary Sources

Manuscripts

C. E. Boles Farm Journal.

Bowling Green, Ky. Department of Library Special Collections, Western Kentucky University Library. J. H. Bell Tobacco Company, Account Books, November 26, 1898–July 9, 1904.

Center Baptist Church Records.

Dripping Spring Baptist Church Minutes and Lists.

Durham, N.C. Duke University. James B. Duke Papers.

Fort Family Papers.

Frankfort, Ky. Division of Archives and Records. Department of Libraries and Archives. Governor J. C. W. Beckham Papers.

Gasper River Cumberland Presbyterian Church Minutes.

Joseph Buckner Killebrew Papers.

Lewisburg Ladies Literary Society Minutes.

Lewisburg United Methodist Church Records.

Lewisburg United Methodist Church Quarterly Conference Records.

Lexington, Ky. University of Kentucky. Margaret I. King Library. Augustus O. Stanley Papers.

Louisville, Ky. Filson Club Historical Society. Augustus E. Willson Papers.

Louisville, Ky. University of Louisville Photographic Archives.

Lyon-O'Hara Papers.

Murray, Ky. Murray State University. Forrest C. Pogue Library. Special Collections. C. Hall Allen MSS.

Nashville, Tenn. Tennessee State Library and Archives, Manuscript Division. Jeremiah W. Cullom Papers.

Macedonia Church Roll and Record Book.

John G. Miller Papers.

Johanna L. Underwood Nazro Diary.

New Bethel Methodist Church Rolls.

New Salem Baptist Church Minutes.

Pleasant Grove Methodist Episcopal Church South Church Register.

Pleasant Grove [Spring Valley] United Baptist Church Records.

Project Files of Writers' Projects, 1935–1941. American Guide Series.

Red River Presbyterian Church Records.

Shaker *Journal*, 1814–1911.

Slave Narratives: A Folk History of Slavery in the United States from Interviews with Former Slaves. Typewritten records prepared by the Federal Writers' Project, 1936–1938. Washington, D.C.: 1941. MSS 45.

Spring Valley Baptist Church Records.

James W. Street Papers.

Washington Family Papers.

Washington, D.C. Library of Congress Manuscripts Division. Leonard Rapport. ed. "People in Tobacco." Unpublished MSS in Works Progress Administration Papers.

Governor Augustus E. Willson Papers.

James Willis Woods, Business Papers.

Works Progress Administration Papers.

Oral History Collections

Bowling Green, Ky. Western Kentucky University. Department of Library Special Collections. Folklore Archives. Folklore and Folklife Collection.

Frankfort, Ky. Kentucky Oral History Commission.

Lexington, Ky. University of Kentucky. Margaret I. King Library. Oral History Collection.

Murray, Ky. Murray State University. Forrest C. Pogue Oral History Institute. Western Kentucky History and Culture Collection.

Oral Interviews by Author

Tapes and transcripts are now housed at the Oral History Commission, Kentucky State Historical Society, Frankfort, Ky.

Baggett, Henry Eugene
Bell, Floyd
Bennett, H. W. "Son"
Campbell, Dorothy Gregory
Cunningham, Marie Johnston
DePriest, Myrtle Holloway
Flowers, Ruston
Freeman, Louise
Gardner, Lois Henderson
Gill, Alzada
Gingles, Bertie (Mrs. Fred)
Gray, N. C.
Gray, Ruth Glass
Hancock, William Marvin
Hill, I. B.
Hyde, Ben
Holloway, Macie McCarty
Holloway, Martin Guthrie
McGowan, Hercules
McGowan, Mellie
McLin, Charles
McCarty, Eunice Stovall
McCarty, Harry Clifford
McCarty, George H.
Marshall, Fred G.
Marshall, Wilma McCarty
Oatts, Orvil
Oatts, Nell
Parker, Martyne Sivillis
Parker, Robert
Quisenberry, Clyde
Scott, Joe
Scott, Allie
Stegar, Sam
Stovall, Grace Smith Jordan
Stovall, Robert
Walker, Odell

Court Cases

Bennett v. D. A. Amoss, et al. Case #1970, Records of the United States Circuit Court for Sixth Circuit. Western District of Kentucky at Paducah. Federal Archives Record Center. Atlanta, Ga.

Cardin v. Neel, Amoss, et al. Case #1929, Civil Docket United States Circuit Court. Paducah, Ky. Vol. H., 1908.

Commonwealth of Kentucky v. David Amoss. Typewritten transcript of the evidence. Office of the Circuit Court Clerk. Hopkinsville, Ky.

Commonwealth of Kentucky v. C. W. Browning. Lyon County, Kentucky Circuit Court Records. Office of the Circuit Court Clerk. Eddyville, Ky.

Commonwealth of Kentucky v. Herman Richard Crenshaw. Case #3022. Christian County Circuit Court Records. Kentucky Department for Libraries and Archives. Public Records Division. Frankfort, Ky.

Commonwealth of Kentucky v. McKinley Faughn. Lyon County Circuit Court Records. Office of the Circuit Court Clerk. Eddyville, Ky.

Commonwealth of Kentucky v. John W. Kelly. Depositions. Trigg County Circuit Court Records. Kentucky Department for Libraries and Archives. Public Records Division. Frankfort, Ky.

Commonwealth of Kentucky v. D. P. Kennada. Minutes of Examining Court. Trigg County Circuit Court Records. Kentucky Department for Libraries and Archives. Public Records Division. Frankfort, Ky.

Commonwealth of Kentucky v. General McCoy. Indictment. Case #1134. Trigg County Circuit Court Records. Kentucky Department for Libraries and Archives. Public Records Division. Frankfort, Ky.

Commonwealth of Kentucky v. Roy Merrick, et al. Papers filed in Lyon County, Kentucky. Office of the Circuit Court Clerk. Eddyville, Ky.

Commonwealth of Kentucky v. G. B. Powell. Case #2973. Christian County Circuit Court Records. Kentucky Department for Libraries and Archives. Public Records Division. Frankfort, Ky.

Commonwealth of Kentucky v. Hugh Wallace, etc. Trigg Quarterly Court Records. Kentucky Department for Libraries and Archives. Public Records Division. Frankfort, Ky.

Hollowell v. Hollowell, et al. Case #1877, Civil Docket. United States Circuit Court, Paducah, Ky. Vol. H, 1908.

Gordon v. Amoss, et al. Case #1938, Civil Docket. United States Circuit Court, Paducah, Ky. Vol. H, 1908.

Latham v. Amoss, et al. Case #260, Civil Docket. United State Circuit Court, Paducah, Ky. Vol. 2, 1911.

Oliver v. Amoss, et al. Case #2091, Civil Docket. United States Circuit Court. Paducah, Ky. Vol. H, 1911.

C. W. Rucker v. D. A. Amoss, et al. Case #1933. Records of the District Courts of the United States. Federal Archives Center. Atlanta, Ga.

Government Public Documents

Bullock, Edward, et al., comps. *The General Statutes of Kentucky.* Frankfort, Ky., 1881.

Caldwell County, Kentucky. Office of the Circuit Court Clerk. Will Books B, C, D.

———. Grand Jury Indictments, 1890–1940. Office of the Circuit Court Clerk.

Christian County, Kentucky. Grand Jury Indictments, 1900–1940. Circuit Court Records. Department of Libraries and Archives. Public Records Division. Frankfort, Ky.

———. County Court Clerk's Office. Will Books 1 and 2.

Carroll, John D. ed. *The Kentucky Statutes.* 4th ed. Louisville, Ky., 1909.

Lyon County, Kentucky. Grand Jury Indictments, 1890–1940. Office of the Circuit Court Clerk. Eddyville, Ky.

———. *Taxation of Farm Land in Lyon County, Kentucky with a Brief Comparison of the Old and New Tax Laws and a Complete List of Taxpayers.* Compiled for Gordon, Gordon and Moore, 1921.

———. County Court Clerk's Office. Will Books 1 and 2.

Kentucky. Board of Health. "Child Welfare in Kentucky: A Report of a Comprehensive Statewide Study of Conditions Affecting Children in Respect of Health, Schooling, Play, Labor, Dependency, and Delinquency and of Laws and Administration." *Bulletin of the State Board of Health of Kentucky.* Vol. 9, no. 11. Frankfort, Ky.: State Journal Company, 1919.

———. Bureau of Agriculture. *Official Report of the Kentucky State Farmers' Institute at the Third Annual Meeting Held in Frankfort,*

Kentucky, February 18, 19, 20, 1908 Under the Auspices of the State Department of Agriculture. Louisville, Ky.: Globe Printing Company, State Printers, 1908.

———. *Directory: Births and Deaths Registered in Kentucky.* Frankfort: State Register, 1911–1940. Microfilm. Kentucky Department for Libraries and Archives. Public Records Division. Frankfort, Ky.

———. *First Annual Report of the State Fire Marshal Kentucky.* 1907.

———. Geological Survey. *Topography of Kentucky*, by Preston McGrain and James C. Currens. Special Publication 25, Series 10. 1978.

———. *Fourteenth Biennial Report of the Bureau of Agriculture, Labor, and Statistics of the State of Kentucky*, 1900–1901. Frankfort: Kentucky State Journal Publishing Company, 1902.

———. *Nineteenth Biennial Report and the Bureau of Agriculture, Labor, and Statistics for 1910–1911.* Frankfort: Kentucky State Journal Publishing Company, 1912.

Trigg County, Grand Jury Indictments, 1890–1940. Circuit Court Records. Department of Libraries and Archives. Public Records Division. Frankfort, Ky.

United States. Bureau of the Census. *Eleventh Census of the United States (1890): Report on Population Part 1.* Washington, D.C.: United States Government Printing Office, 1892.

———. Bureau of the Census. *Historical Statistics of the United States, Colonial Times to 1970.* 2 vols. Washington, D.C.: United States Government Printing Office, 1972.

———. Congress. House of Representatives. Committee on Ways and Means. Hearings on the Relief of Tobacco Growers before a Subcommittee on Internal Revenue, on H.R. 4482, H.R. 9870, H.R. 10857, H.R. 3574, and H.R. 1971. 60th Congress, 1st session, 1904.

———. Congress. Senate Subcommittee on Finance and Commerce. Relief of Tobacco Growers; Hearings Before the Subcommittee on Finance and Commerce on S. 372. 59th Congress, 2d sess., 1906.

———. Department of Agriculture. Soil Conservation Service. Kentucky Agricultural Experiment Station Co-operating. *Soil Survey, Caldwell County.* September 1966.

———. Department of Commerce, Bureau of the Census. *Fifteenth*

Census of the United States (1930). Washington, D.C.: United States Government Printing Office, 1932.

———. Department of Commerce, Bureau of the Census. *Fourteenth Census of the United States* (1920). Washington, D.C.: United States Government Printing Office, 1922.

———. Department of Commerce, Bureau of the Census. *Sixteenth Census of the United States* (1940). Washington, D.C.: United States Government Printing Office, 1943.

———. Department of Commerce, Bureau of the Census. *Thirteenth Census of the United States* (1910). Washington, D.C.: United States Government Printing Office, 1913.

———. Department of the Interior, *Bureau of the Census. Twelfth Census of the United States* (1900). Washington, D.C.: United States Census Office, 1901.

———. Kentucky Department for Natural Resources and Environmental Protection and Kentucky Agricultural Experiment Station Co-operating. *Soil Survey of Christian County, Kentucky.* July 1980.

———. Kentucky Agricultural Experiment Station and Kentucky Department for Natural Rescources and Environmental Protection Co-operating. *Soil Survey of Lyon and Trigg Counties, Kentucky.* May 1981.

Kentucky Natural Resources and Environmental Protection Cabinet and Kentucky Agricultural Experiment Station Co-operating. *Soil Survey of Todd County, Kentucky.* September 1987.

Washington, D.C., National Archives. Tobacco Investigations Records. Bureau of Corporations. October 13, 1905.

Secondary Sources

Books

Akehurst, B. C. *Tobacco.* 2d ed. London: Longman's Green and Company, 1981.

Angle, Paul M. *Bloody Williamson.* 1952. Reprint. New York: Alfred A. Knopf, 1983.

Arents, George. *Tobacco Bibliography of Manuscripts in Collection of George Arents, Jr.,* Washington, D. C.: Government Printing Office, 1938.

Armentano, D. T. *Antitrust History: The American Tobacco Case of 1911.* Austin: University of Texas Press, 1976.

Arnow, Harriet Simpson. *Flowering of the Cumberland.* Lexington: University Press of Kentucky, 1984.

———. *Seedtime on the Cumberland.* New York: Lexington: University Press of Kentucky, 1983.

Ash, Stephen V. *Middle Tennessee Society Transformed, 1860–1870: War and Peace in the Upper South.* Baton Rouge: Louisiana University Press, 1988.

Axton, W. F. *Tobacco and Kentucky.* Kentucky Bicentennial Bookshelf. Lexington: University Press of Kentucky, 1975.

Ayers, Edward L. *Vengeance and Justice: Crime and Punishment in the Nineteenth-Century American South.* New York: Oxford University Press, 1984.

Badger, Anthony. *Prosperity Road: The New Deal, Tobacco and North Carolina.* Chapel Hill: University of North Carolina Press, 1980.

Bailey, Fred Arthur. *Class and Tennessee's Confederate Generation.* Chapel Hill: University of North Carolina Press, 1987.

Bailey, Kenneth K. *Southern White Protestantism in the Twentieth Century.* New York: Harper and Row, 1964.

Bain, John, Jr. *Tobacco Leaves.* Boston: H. M. Caldwell Company, 1903.

———, comp. *Tobacco in Song and Story.* Boston: H. M. Caldwell Company, 1896.

Baker, Clauscine R. *First History of Caldwell County.* Madisonville, Ky.: Commercial Printers, 1936.

Barefoot, Pamela. *Mules and Memories: A Photo Documentary of the Tobacco Farmer.* Winston-Salem, N.C.: Barefoot Productions, 1978.

Barger, Harold, and Hans H. Landsberg. *American Agriculture, 1899–1939: A Study of Output, Employment and Productivity.* New York: National Bureau of Economic Research, 1942.

Barron, Hal L. *Those Who Stayed Behind: Rural Society in Nineteenth-Century New England.* Cambridge: Cambridge University Press, 1984.

Bartley, Numan V., ed. *The Evolution of Southern Culture.* Athens: University of Georgia Press, 1988.

Bender, Thomas. *Community and Social Change in America*. Baltimore: Johns Hopkins University Press, 1978.

Billings, E. R. *Tobacco: Its History, Varieties, Culture, Manufacture, and Commerce with an Account of Its Various Modes of Use, from Its First Discovery until Now*. Hartford, Conn.: American Publishing Company, 1875.

Blakey, George T. *Hard Times and New Deal in Kentucky, 1929–1939*. Lexington: University Press of Kentucky, 1986.

Boles, John B. *The Great Revival, 1787–1805: The Origins of the Southern Evangelical Mind*. Lexington: University Press of Kentucky. 1972.

———. *Religion in Antebellum Kentucky*. Kentucky Bicentennial Bookshelf. Lexington: University Press of Kentucky, 1976.

Breen, T. H., and Stephen Innes. *"Myne Owne Ground": Race and Freedom on Virginia's Eastern Shore, 1640–1676*. Oxford: Oxford University Press, 1980.

Breen, T. H. *Tobacco Culture: The Mentality of the Great Tidewater Planters of the Eve of Revolution*. Princeton: Princeton University Press, 1985.

Brooks, Jerome Edmund. *The Mighty Leaf: Tobacco through the Centuries*. 1859. Reprint. Boston: Little, Brown, 1952.

Brown, Richard Maxwell. *The South Carolina Regulators*. Cambridge: Harvard University Press, Belknap Press, 1963.

———. *Strain of Violence: Historical Studies of American Violence and Vigilantism*. New York: Oxford University Press, 1975.

Bruce, Dickson D., Jr. *And They All Sang Hallelujah: Plain Folk Camp-Meeting Religion 1800–1845*. Knoxville: University of Tennessee Press, 1974.

———. *Violence and Culture in the Antebellum South*. Austin: University of Texas Press, 1979.

Brundage, W. Fitzhugh. *Lynching in the New South, Georgia and Virginia, 1880–1930*. Urbana: University of Illinois Press, 1993.

Bryant, F. Carlene. *We're All Kin: A Cultural Study of a Mountain Neighborhood*. Knoxville: University of Tennessee Press, 1981.

Burton, Orville Vernon. *In My Father's House Are Many Mansions: Family and Community in Edgefield, South Carolina*. Chapel Hill: University of North Carolina Press, 1985.

Butler, Mann. *A History of the Commonwealth of Kentucky*. Louisville: Wilcox, Dickerman and Company, 1834.

Carr, John. *Early Times in Middle Tennessee*. Philadelphia: Claxton, Remison and Huffelfinger, 1868.

Carter, Dan T. *Scottsboro: A Tragedy of the American South*. Rev. ed. Baton Rouge: Louisiana State University Press, 1979.

Cartwright, Joseph H. *The Triumph of Jim Crow: Tennessee Race Relations in the 1880s*. Knoxville: University of Tennessee Press, 1976.

Cartwright, Peter. *Autobiography of Peter Cartwright*. Edited by Charles L. Wallis. Nashville: Abingdon Press, 1956.

Channing, Steven A. *Kentucky: A Bicentennial History*. New York: W. W. Norton, 1977.

Cherry, Thomas C. *Kentucky*. Boston: n.p., 1923.

Christian County Genealogical Society, Inc. *Christian County, Kentucky*. Paducah, Ky.: Turner Publishing Co., 1986.

Clanton, Gene. *Populism: The Humane Preference in America, 1890–1900*. Boston: Twayne Publishers, 1991.

Clark, Thomas D. *Agrarian Kentucky*. Lexington: University Press of Kentucky, 1977.

———. *Frontier America: The Story of the Westward Movement*. 2d ed. New York: Charles Scribner's Sons, 1969.

———. *The Greening of the South: The Recovery of Land and Forest*. Lexington: University Press of Kentucky, 1984.

———. *Historic Maps of Kentucky*. Lexington: University Press of Kentucky, 1979.

———. *A History of Kentucky*. Rev. ed. Lexington, Ky.: John Bradford Press, 1960.

———. *Kentucky: Land of Contrasts*. New York: Alfred A. Knopf, 1968.

———. *Pills, Petticoats, and Plows: The Southern Country Store*. Indianapolis: Bobbs-Merrill Company, 1944.

———. *The Southern Country Editor*. New York: Bobbs-Merrill, 1948.

Clarke, Kenneth, and Mary Clarke. *The Harvest and the Reapers: Oral Traditions of Kentucky*. Kentucky Bicentennial Bookshelf. Lexington: University Press of Kentucky, 1974.

Clift, G. Glenn. *Governors of Kentucky: 1792–1942*. Cynthiana, Ky.: Hobson Press, 1942.

Coffman, Edward L. *The Story of Logan County*. Nashville: Parthenon Press, 1962.

Coleman, J. Winston, Jr., ed. *A Bibliography of Kentucky History*. Lexington: University Press of Kentucky, 1949.

Collins, Lewis, ed. *Collins' History of Kentucky*. Rev. ed. 2 vols. Covington, Ky.: Collins and Company, 1874.

Connelley, William E., and E. Merton Coulter. *History of Kentucky*. Edited by Judge Charles Kerr. 5 vols. Chicago: American Historical Society, 1922.

Corlew, Robert E. *Tennessee: A Short History*. 2d ed. Knoxville: University of Tennessee Press, 1981.

Cott, Nancy F. *The Bonds of Womanhood: "Women's Sphere" in New England, 1780–1835*. New Haven: Yale University Press, 1977.

Cotterill, R. S. *History of Pioneer Kentucky*. Cincinnati: Johnson and Hardin, 1917.

Couch, W. T., ed. *Culture of the South*. Chapel Hill: University of North Carolina Press, 1934.

Coulter, E. Merton. *The Civil War and Readjustment in Kentucky*. Chapel Hill: University of North Carolina Press, 1926.

Cox, Reavis. *Competition in the American Tobacco Industry 1911–1921: A Study of the Effects of the Partition of the American Tobacco Company by the United States Supreme Court*. New York: Columbia University Press, 1933.

Craven, Avery O. *Soil Exhaustion as a Factor in the Agricultural History of Virginia and Maryland, 1606–1860*. Urbana: University of Illinois Press, 1926.

Cunningham, Bill. *On Bended Knees: The Night Rider Story*. Nashville: McClanahan Publishing House, 1983.

Danbom, David B. *The Resisted Revolution: Urban America and the Industrialization of Agriculture, 1900–1930*. Ames: Iowa State University Press, 1979.

Daniel, Pete. *Breaking the Land: The Transformation of Cotton, Tobacco, and Rice Cultures Since 1880*. Urbana: University of Illinois Press, 1985.

———. *Standing at the Crossroads: Southern Life in the Twentieth Century*. New York: Hill and Wang, 1986.

Davis, D. Trabue. *The Story of Mayfield*. Paducah: Billings Printing Company, Inc., 1923.

Davis, William C. *The Orphan Brigade: The Kentucky Confederates Who Couldn't Go Home*. Baton Rouge: Louisiana University Press, 1980.

Degler, Carl. *At Odds: Women and the Family in America from the Revolution to the Present*. Oxford: Oxford University Press, 1980.

Deetz, James. *In Small Things Forgotten: The Archaeology of Early Life*. Garden City, N.J.: Anchor Press, Doubleday, 1977.

Dorson, Richard M. *American Folklore*. Chicago: University of Chicago Press, 1959.

—————. *Folklore and Folklife: An Introduction*. Chicago: University of Chicago Press, 1972.

—————. *Handbook of Folklore*. Bloomington: Indiana University Press, 1982.

Douglas, Byrd. *Steamboatin' on the Cumberland*. Nashville: Tennessee Book Company, 1961.

Drake, Daniel, M.D. *Pioneer Life in Kentucky, 1785–1800*. Edited by Emmet Field Horine, M.D. New York: Henry Schuman, 1948.

Dunn, Durwood. *Cades Cove: The Life and Death of a Southern Appalachian Community, 1818–1937*. Knoxville: University of Tennessee Press, 1988.

Durden, Robert F. *The Dukes of Durham: 1865–1929*. Durham, N.C.: Duke University Press, 1975.

Egerton, John. *Generations: An American Family*. New York: Simon and Schuster, Inc., 1983.

Eighmy, John L. *Churches in Cultural Captivity: A History of the Social Attitudes of Southern Baptists*. Knoxville: University of Tennessee Press, 1972.

Eldred, Olive, and Nancy Beck, eds. *Pioneers of Caldwell County, Kentucky: Probate Records of the Original Settlers, 1809–1834*. Princeton, Kentucky: Pioneers, 1976.

Erikson, Kai. *Everything in Its Path: Destruction of Community in the Buffalo Creek Flood*. New York: Simon and Schuster, 1976.

Fairholt, Frederick William. *Tobacco: Its History and Associations; Including an Account of the Plant and Its Manufacture; With Its Modes of Use in All Ages and Countries*. 1859. Reprint. Detroit: Singing Tree Press, 1968.

Farish, Hunter D. *The Circuit Rider Dismounts: A Social History of Southern Methodists, 1865–1900*. Richmond, Va.: Deity Press, 1938.

Federal Writer's Project of the Works Progress Administration for the State of Kentucky. *Kentucky: A Guide to the Bluegrass State.* American Guide Series. New York: Harcourt, Brace and Co., 1939.

Fenneman, Nevin M. *Physiography of the Eastern United States.* New York: McGraw-Hill Co., 1938.

Field, Thomas P. *A Guide to Kentucky Place Names.* Kentucky Geological Survey, Series 10. Lexington: University Press of Kentucky, 1961.

Filene, Peter. *Him / Her / Self: Sex Roles in Modern America.* 2d ed. Baltimore: Johns Hopkins Press, 1986.

Fite, Gilbert C. *American Farmers: The New Minority.* Bloomington: Indiana University Press, 1981.

———. *Cotton Fields No More: Southern Agriculture, 1865–1980.* Lexington: University Press of Kentucky, 1984.

———. *The Farmers' Frontier, 1865–1900.* New York: Holt, Rinehart, and Winston, 1966.

Flannagan, Roy C. *Golden Harvest: The Way of Life in the Tobacco Industry.* Evanston, Ill.: Row, Peterson, and Company, 1941.

Flynt, J. Wayne. *Dixie's Forgotten People: The South's Poor Whites.* Bloomington: Indiana University Press, 1979.

Ford, Henry James. *The Scottish-Irish in America.* 1915. Reprint. New York: Arno Press and the *New York Times*, 1969.

Franklin, John Hope. *The Militant South, 1800–1861.* Cambridge: Harvard University Press, 1956.

Franklin, William A. *Regional Atlas of the Jackson Purchase, Kentucky.* Murray, Ky.: Murray State University Press, 1974.

Friedman, Lawrence M., and Robert V. Percival. *The Roots of Justice: Crime and Punishment in Alameda County, California, 1870–1910.* Chapel Hill: University of North Carolina Press, 1981.

Fromm, Erich. *The Anatomy of Human Destructiveness.* New York: Holt, Rinehart, and Winston. 1973.

———. *The Heart of Man: Its Genius for Good and Evil.* New York: Harper and Row, 1964.

Fry, Gladys-Marie. *Night Riders in Black Folk History.* Knoxville: University of Tennessee Press, 1975.

Garner, Wrightman W. *The Production of Tobacco.* Philadelphia: Blakiston Co., 1946.

Gastil, Raymond D. *Cultural Regions of the United States.* Seattle: University of Washington Press, 1975.

Gaventa, John. *Power and Powerlessness: Quiescence and Rebellion in an Appalachian Valley*. Urbana: University of Illinois Press, 1980.

Gelles, Richard J., and Murray A. Straus. *Intimate Violence: The Causes and Consequences of Abuse in American Families*. New York: Simon and Schuster, Inc., 1988.

Generous, William T., Jr., James E. Brittain, and Robert F. Durden. *The Dukes of Durham, 1865–1929*. Durham: Duke University, 1975.

Gingles, Bertie C. *History and Genealogy of William Cunningham and Wife Nancy (Carr) Cunningham*. Murray, Ky.: Murray Democrat Publishing Company, Inc., 1957.

Glassie, Henry. *Folk Housing in Middle Virginia: A Structural Analysis of Historic Artifacts*. Knoxville: University of Tennessee Press, 1975.

———. *Pattern in the Material Folk Culture of the Eastern United States*. Philadelphia: University of Pennsylvania Press, 1968.

Gooch, J. T. *The Pennyrile: History, Stories, Legends*. Madisonville, Ky.: Whipporwill Publications, 1982.

Goodspeed, Thomas. *The Genus Nicotiana: Origins, Relationships and Evolution of Its Species in Light of Their Distribution, Morphology and Cytogenetics*. Waltham, Mass.: Chronica Botanica Co., 1954.

Goodwyn, Lawrence. *The Populist Moment*. Oxford: Oxford University Press, 1978.

Gordon, Linda. *Heroes of Their Own Lives: The Politics and History of Family Violence, Boston, 1880–1960*. New York: Penguin Books, 1988.

Gorn, Elliott, J. *The Manly Art: Bare-Knuckle Prize Fighting in America*. Ithaca: Cornell University Press, 1986.

Graham, Hugh Davis, and Ted Robert Gurr. *Violence in America: Historical and Comparative Perspectives*. (National Commission on the Causes and Prevention of Violence, Vol. 1) Beverly Hills, Calif.: Sage Publications, 1979.

Grantham, Dewey W. *Southern Progressivism: The Reconciliation of Progress and Tradition*. Knoxville: University of Tennessee Press, 1983.

Gray, Lewis C. *History of Agriculture in the Southern United States*. 2 vols., publication 430. Washington, D.C.: Carnegie Institution, 1933.

Green, Archie. *Only a Miner: Studies in Recorded Coal-Mining Songs.* Urbana: University of Illinois Press, 1972.

Greven, Philip. *Spare the Child: The Religious Roots of Punishment and the Pyschological Impact of Physical Abuse.* New York: Alfred A. Knopf, 1991.

Griffith, Anna Laura. *Leach-Leech.* n.p. June 1985.

Hagood, Margaret Jarman. *Mothers of the South: Portraiture of the White Tenant Farm Woman.* 1939. Reprint. New York: W. W. Norton and Company, 1977.

Hahn, Steven, and Jonathan Prude, eds. *The Countryside in the Age of Capitalist Transformation: Essays in the Social History of Rural America.* Chapel Hill: University of North Carolina Press, 1985.

Hambaugh, W. P., and Howard Robinson, eds. *The Tobacco Planter Yearbook.* Guthrie, Ky.: *Tobacco Planter*, 1908.

Hardeman, Nicholas P. *Shucks, Shocks, and Hominy Blocks: Corn as a Way of Life in Pioneer America.* Baton Rouge: Louisiana State University Press, 1981.

Hareven, Tamara K. ed. *Transitions: The Family and the Life Course in Historical Perspective.* New York: Academic Press, 1978.

Harrison, Lowell H. *The Civil War in Kentucky.* Kentucky Bicentennial Bookshelf. Lexington: University Press of Kentucky, 1975.

Harrison, Lowell H., and Nelson L. Dawson, eds. *A Kentucky Sampler: Essays from "The Filson Club Quarterly," 1926–1976.* Lexington: University Press of Kentucky, 1977.

Hayter, Earl W. *The Troubled Farmer, 1850–1900; Rural Adjustment to Industrialism.* Dekalb: Northern Illinois University Press, 1966.

Hicks, John D. *The Populist Revolt: A History of the Farmer's Alliance and the People's Party.* Minneapolis: University of Minnesota Press, 1972.

Hill, Samuel S., Jr. *Southern Churches in Crisis.* New York: Holt, Rinehart, and Winston, 1966.

———, ed. *Religion and the Solid South.* Nashville: Abingdon Press, 1972.

———, ed. *Religion in the Southern States.* Macon, Ga.: Mercer University Press, 1983.

Hilliard, Sam Bowers. *Atlas of Antebellum Southern Agriculture.* Baton Rouge: Louisiana State University Press, 1984.

————. *Hog Meat and Hoecake: Food Supply in the Old South: 1840–1860.* Carbondale, Ill.: Southern Illinois Press, 1972.

Hobsbawm, Eric J. *Bandits.* New York: Delacorte Press, 1969.

————. *Primitive Rebels: Studies in Archaic Forms of Social Movement in the Nineteenth and Twentieth Centuries.* New York: W. W. Norton and Company, 1959.

Hofstadter, Richard. *The Age of Reform: From Bryan to F.D.R.* New York: Alfred A. Knopf, 1955.

Hofstadter, Richard, and Michael Wallace, eds. *American Violence: A Documentary History.* New York: Alfred A. Knopf, 1970.

Howell, Benita J. *A Survey of Folklife along the Big South Fork of the Cumberland River.* Report of Investigations. No. 30. Department of Anthropology. Knoxville: University of Tennessee, 1981.

Ireland, Robert M. *The County Courts in Antebellum Kentucky.* Lexington: University Press of Kentucky, 1972.

————. *The County in Kentucky History.* Kentucky Bicentennial Bookshelf. Lexington: University Press of Kentucky, 1976.

————. *Little Kingdoms: The Counties of Kentucky, 1850–1891.* Lexington: University Press of Kentucky, 1976.

Janssen-Jurriet, Marielouise. *Sexism: The Male Monopoly on History and Thought.* New York: Farrar, Strauss, Giroux, 1982.

Jensen, Joan M. *Loosening the Bonds: Mid-Atlantic Farm Women, 1750–1850.* New Haven: Yale University Press, 1986.

Jillson, Willard Rouse. *Filson's Kentucke: A facsimile reproduction of the original Wilmington edition of 1784.* Louisville, Ky.: John P. Morton Co., 1930.

————. *Pioneer Kentucky: An Outline.* Frankfort, Ky.: State Journal Company, 1934.

John, Raymond. *Tobacco Dictionary.* New York: Philosophical Library, 1954.

Johnson, L. F. *Famous Kentucky Trials and Tragedies.* Lexington: Henry Clay Press, 1972.

Jones, Ann. *Women Who Kill.* New York: Ballantine Books, 1980.

Jones, Jacquelin. *Labor of Love, Labor of Sorrow: Black Women, Work, and the Family from Slavery to the Present,* New York: Basic Books, 1985.

Karan, P. P., and Cotton Mather, eds. *Atlas of Kentucky.* Lexington: University Press of Kentucky, 1977.

Kelsey, Darwin P. *Farming in the New Nation: Interpreting American ɩ griculture*. Washington, D.C.: Agricultural History Society, 1972.

Kenzer, Robert. *Kinship and Neighborhood in a Southern Community: Orange County, North Carolina, 1849–1881*. Knoxville: University of Tennessee Press, 1987.

Killebrew, Joseph Buckner. *Tobacco Leaf; Its Culture and Cure, Marketing, and Manufacture. A Practical Handbook on the Most Approved Methods in Growing, Harvesting, Curing, Packing, and Selling Tobacco*. 1897. Reprint. New York: Orange Judd Company, 1914.

———. *Tobacco; It's Culture in Tennessee, with Statistics of Its Commercial Importance, Etc.* Nashville: n.p., 1876.

Kirby, Jack T. *Darkness at the Dawning: Race and Reform in the Progressive South*. New York: J. B. Lippincott Company, 1972.

———. *Rural Worlds Lost: The American South, 1920–1960*. Baton Rouge: Louisiana State University Press, 1986.

Klotter, James C. *William Goebel: The Politics of Wrath*. Kentucky Bicentennial Bookshelf. Lexington: University Press of Kentucky, 1973.

Kolodny, Joseph. *4000 Years of Service: the Story of the Wholesale Tobacco Industry and its Pioneers*. New York: Farrar, Straus, and Giroux, 1953.

Kroll, Harry H. *Riders in the Night*. Philadelphia: University of Pennsylvania Press, 1965.

Kulikoff, Allan. *Tobacco and Slaves: The Development of Southern Cultures in the Chesapeake, 1680–1800*. Chapel Hill: University of North Carolina Press, 1986.

Lamon, Lester C. *Blacks in Tennessee, 1791–1970*. Knoxville: University of Tennessee Press, 1981.

Lane, Roger. *Roots of Violence in Black Philadelphia, 1860–1900*. Cambridge: Harvard University Press, 1986.

Lee, Lloyd G. *A Brief History of Kentucky and Its Counties*. Berea, Ky.: Kentucky Imprints, 1981.

Lemon, James T. *The Best Poor Man's Country: A Geographical Study of Early Southeastern Pennsylvania*. Baltimore: John Hopkins Press, 1972.

Levine, Lawrence W. *Black Culture and Black Consciousness Afro-*

American Folk Thought from Slavery to Freedom. New York: Oxford University Press, 1977.

Lewinson, Paul. *Race, Class, and Party: A History of Negro Suffrage and White Politics in the South*. 1932. Reprint. New York: Grosset and Dunlap, 1965.

Leyburn, James G. *The Scotch-Irish: A Social History*. Chapel Hill: University of North Carolina Press, 1962.

Link, William A. *A Hard Country and a Lonely Place: Schooling, Society, and Reform in Rural Virginia, 1870–1920*. Chapel Hill: University of North Carolina Press, 1986.

Lyon County High School Seniors. *One Century of Lyon County History*. Eddyville, Ky.: Lyon County Historical Society, 1964.

McFarlan, Arthur C. *Geology of Kentucky*. Lexington: University Press of Kentucky, 1943.

McGaughey, R. H. *Life with Grandfather, 1852–1905: Fifty-three Years with a Country Squire as He Saw Life . . . as He Recorded It*. Hopkinsville, Ky.: R. H. McGaughey, Southern Printer, 1981.

McMath, Robert C. *Populist Vanguard: A History of the Southern Farmers' Alliance*. Chapel Hill: University of North Carolina Press, 1975.

McMath, Roger D. *Gunfighters, Highwaymen, and Vigilantes*. Berkeley: University of California Press, 1984.

McMillen, Neil R. *Dark Journey: Black Mississippians in the Age of Jim Crow*. Urbana: University of Illinois Press, 1990.

Machen, Arthur. *The Anatomy of Tobacco*. 1884. Reprint. New York: Knopf, 1926.

Magdol, Edward, and Jon L. Wakelyn, eds. *The Southern Common People*. Westport, Conn.: Greenwood Press, 1980.

MaGill, John, ed. Thomas E. Clark. *The Pioneer to the Kentucky Emigrant: A Brief Topographical and Historical Description of the State of Kentucky*. Kentucky Reprints No. 2. Lexington: University of Kentucky Publications Committee, 1942.

Martin, Glenn. *History of Martin-Mitchusson Families*. Princeton, Ky.: n.p.

Marshall, Humphrey. *A History of Kentucky . . . .* 2d ed., 2 vols. Frankfort, Ky.: G. S. Robinson, Printer, 1824.

Matthews, Donald G. *Religion in the Old South*. Chicago: University of Chicago Press, 1977.

Matthews, Elmora M. *Neighbor and Kin: Life in a Tennessee Ridge Community*. Nashville: Vanderbilt University Press, 1965.

Maurer, David W. *Kentucky Moonshine*. Kentucky Bicentennial Bookshelf. Lexington: University Press of Kentucky, 1974.

Meacham, Charles Mayfield. *A History of Christian County, Kentucky: From Oxcart to Airplane*. Nashville: Marshall and Bruce Company, 1930.

Miller, Alice. *For Your Own Good: Hidden Cruelty in Child-Rearing and the Roots of Violence*. Translated by Hildegarde Hannum and Hunter Hannum. New York: Farrar, Straus, Giroux, 1983.

Miller, John G. *The Black Patch War*. Chapel Hill: University of North Carolina Press, 1936.

Montell, William L. *Don't Go Up Kettle Creek: Verbal Legacy of the Upper Cumberland*. Knoxville: University of Tennessee Press, 1983.

———. *Killings: Folk Justice in the Upper South*. Lexington: University Press of Kentucky, 1986.

———. *The Saga of Coe Ridge*. Knoxville: University of Tennessee Press, 1970.

Montell, William L., and Michael Lynn Morse. *Kentucky Folk Architecture*. Kentucky Bicentennial Bookshelf. Lexington: University Press of Kentucky, 1976.

Moore, Arthur K. *The Frontier Mind: A Cultural Analysis of the Kentucky Frontiersman*. Lexington: University Press of Kentucky, 1957.

Nall, James O. *The Tobacco Night Riders of Kentucky and Tennessee, 1905–1909*. Louisville: Standard Press, 1939.

Neel, Eurie Pearl Wilford. *The Wilford-Williford Family*. Nashville: Rich Printing Company, 1959.

Odum, Howard W. *Folk, Region, and Society: Selected Papers of Howard W. Odum*. Chapel Hill: University of North Carolina Press, 1964.

———. *The Way of the South: Toward the Regional Balance of America*. New York: Macmillan Company, 1947.

Odum, Howard W., and Harry Estill Moore. *American Regionalism: A Cultural-Historical Approach to National Integration*. New York: Henry Holt and Company, 1938.

Owsley, Frank L. *Plain Folk of the Old South*. Baton Rouge: Louisiana State University Press, 1949.

Peirce, Neal R. *The Border South States: People, Politics, and Power in the Five Border South States.* New York: W. W. Norton and Company, Inc., 1975.

Perrin, William Henry. *Counties of Christian and Trigg, Kentucky, Historical and Biographical.* Chicago: F. A. Battey Publishing Co., 1884.

Pleck, Elizabeth. *Domestic Tyranny: The Making of American Social Policy against Family Violence from Colonial Times to the Present.* New York: Oxford University Press, 1987.

Pope, Liston. *Millhands and Preachers: A Study of Gastonia.* New Haven: Yale University Press. 1942.

Powell, Robert A. *Kentucky Governors.* Frankfort: Kentucky Images, 1976.

Raymond, Jahn, ed. *Tobacco Dictionary.* New York: Philosophical Library, 1954.

Reed, John Shelton. *The Enduring South: Subcultural Persistence in Mass Society.* Lexington, Mass.: D.C. Heath, 1972.

———. *One South: An Ethnic Approach to Regional Culture.* Baton Rouge: Louisiana State University Press, 1982.

———. *Southerners: The Social Psychology of Sectionalism.* Chapel Hill: University of North Carolina Press, 1983.

Reed, John Shelton, and Daniel J. Singal. *Regionalism and the South: Selected Papers of Rupert Vance.* Chapel Hill: University of North Carolina Press, 1982.

Robert, Joseph C. *The Story of Tobacco in America.* New York: Alfred A. Knopf, 1949.

Rone, Wendell, H., Sr. *An Historical Atlas of Kentucky and Her Counties.* Mayfield, Ky.: Mayfield Printing Company, 1965.

Rose, Thomas, ed. *Violence in America: An Historical and Contemporary Reader.* New York: Random House, 1969.

Saloutos, Theodore. *Farmer Movements in the South, 1865–1933.* Berkeley: University of California Press, 1960.

Saloutos, Theodore, and John D. Hicks. *Agricultural Discontent in the Middle West, 1900–1939.* Madison: University of Wisconsin Press, 1951.

Sauer, Carl O. *The Geography of the Pennyroyal.* Series UL. Vol. 25. Frankfort: Kentucky Geological Survey, 1927.

Scott, Anne Firor. *The Southern Lady: From Pedestal to Politics, 1830–1930*. Chicago: University of Chicago Press, 1970.

Shaler, N. S. *Kentucky: A Pioneer Commonwealth*. American Commonwealths Series. Boston: Houghton, Mifflin and Company, 1885.

Shifflett, Crandall A. *Patronage and Poverty in the Tobacco South: Louisa County, Virginia, 1860–1900*. Knoxville: University of Tennessee Press, 1982.

Short, Roy Hunter. *Methodism in Kentucky*. Rutland, Vt.: Academy Books, 1979.

Shover, John L. *First Majority—Last Minority: The Transforming of Rural Life in America*. Dekalb, Ill.: Northern Illinois University Press, 1976.

Singal, David Joseph. *The War Within: From Victorian to Modernist Thought in the South, 1919–1945*. Chapel Hill: University of North Carolina Press, 1982.

Spain, Rufus B. *At Ease in Zion: Social History of Southern Baptists, 1865–1900*. Nashville: Vanderbilt University Press, 1961.

Stegar, Sam W. *Caldwell County History*. Paducah: Turner Publishing Co., 1987.

Steinmetz, Suzanne K. *The Cycle of Violence: Assertive, Aggressive, and Abusive Family Interaction*. New York: Praeger Publishers, 1977.

Stilgoe, John R. *Common Landscape of America: 1580–1845*. New Haven: Yale University Press. 1982.

Straus, Murray A., Richard J. Gelles, Richard J., and Suzanne K. Steinmetz. *Behind Closed Doors: Violence in the American Family*. Garden City, N.Y.: Anchor Press, 1980.

Tapp, Hambleton. *A Sesqui-Centennial History of Kentucky*. 4 vols. Louisville: Historical Record Association, 1942.

Tapp, Hambleton, and James C. Klotter. *Kentucky: Decades of Discord, 1865–1900*. Frankfort: Kentucky Historical Society, 1977.

Terrill, Tom E., and Jerrold Hirsch. *Such as Us: Southern Voices of the Thirties*. Chapel Hill: University of North Carolina Press, 1978.

Thomas, Edison H. *The Thomas and Bridges Story, 1540–1840*. Louisville, Ky.: T & E Publishers, 1972.

Tindall, George B. *The Emergence of the New South, 1913–1945*. Baton Rouge: Louisiana State University Press, 1967.

Trigg County Historical and Preservation Society, Inc. *Trigg County History*. Dallas: Taylor Publishing Co., 1986.

Troutman, Richard, ed. *The Heavens Are Weeping: The Diaries of George B. Browder, 1852–1886*. Grand Rapids, Mich.: Zondervan Publishing House, 1987.

Vance, Rupert B. *Human Factors in Cotton Culture: A Study in the Social Geography of the American South*. Chapel Hill: University of North Carolina Press, 1929.

Vanderwood, Paul J. *Nightriders of Reelfoot Lake*. Memphis: Memphis State University Press, 1969.

Walker, Odell. *A History of the Olive-Walker-Glass Family of Trigg, Graves, and Lyon Counties*. Kuttawa, Ky.: Odell Walker, 1982.

Wallace, Anthony F. C. *Culture and Personality*. New York: Random House, 1961.

———. *Religion: An Anthropological View*. New York: Random House, 1966.

Watkins, Floyd C., John T. Hiers, and Mary Louise Weaks, eds. *Talking with Robert Penn Warren*. Athens: University of Georgia Press, 1990.

Watkins, Floyd C. *Then and Now: The Personal Past in the Poetry of Robert Penn Warren*. Lexington: University Press of Kentucky, 1982.

Webb, Ross A. *Kentucky in the Reconstruction Era*. Kentucky Bicentennial Bookshelf. Lexington: University Press of Kentucky, 1979.

Werner, Carl Avery. *A Textbook on Tobacco*. New York: Tobacco Leaf Publishing Company [1909].

Williams, Marion. *The Story of Todd County, Kentucky, 1820–1970*. Nashville: Parthenon Press, 1972.

———. *Todd County: A History and a Heritage in Brier*. Cadiz, Ky.: Barkley Lake Print Shop, 1971.

Williams, Raymond. *The Country and the City*. New York: Oxford University Press, 1973.

———. *Marxism and Literature*. Oxford: Oxford University Press, 1977.

Wilson, Charles Reagan, ed. *Religion in the South*. Jackson: University of Mississippi Press, 1985.

Wolf, Eric. *Peasants*. Englewood Cliffs, N.J.: Prentice-Hall, 1966.

Wolfgang, Marvin E., and Franco Ferracutti. *The Subculture of Violence: *Toward an Integrated Theory in Criminology*. London: Tavistock Publications, 1967.

Woodward, C. Vann. *The Origins of the New South, 1877–1913*. Baton Rouge: Louisiana State University Press, 1951.

Wright, George C. *Racial Violence in Kentucky, 1865–1940: Lynchings, Mob Rule, and "Legal Lynchings."* Baton Rouge: Louisiana State University Press, 1990.

Wyatt-Brown, Bertram. *Southern Honor: Ethics and Behavior in the Old South*. New York: Oxford University Press, 1982.

Young, Chester Raymond. ed. *Westward into Kentucky: The Narrative of Daniel Trabue*. Lexington: University Press of Kentucky, 1980.

Dissertations, Theses, and Papers

Applewhite, Joseph Davis. "Early Trade and Navigation on the Cumberland River." Master's thesis, Vanderbilt University, 1940.

Bleidt, Helen M. "A History of the Development of Growers' Organizations." Master's thesis, University of Kentucky, 1952.

Broadbent, Smith Dudley, Jr. "Curing Fired Tobacco." Master's thesis, University of Kentucky, 1935.

Clark, Harold B. "The Role of Farmers' Cooperative in the Marketing of Dark Tobacco in Kentucky and Tennessee, 1931–1950. Ph.D. diss., University of Kentucky, 1950.

Culver, Gregory K. "The Impact of the 1918 Influenza Epidemic in the Jackson Purchase." Master's thesis, Murray State University, 1978.

Erwin, Carlos C. "Economic Analysis of the Dark Tobacco Association of Western Kentucky and Tennessee." Master's thesis, University of Kentucky, 1948.

Fridy, Wilford Eugene. "Robert Penn Warren's Use of Kentucky Materials in His Fiction as a Basis for His New Mythos." Ph.D. diss., University of Kentucky, 1968.

Glass, James R. "Autobiography of James R. Glass." Unpublished paper. Original owned by Odell Walker, Kuttawa, Kentucky [1912].

Glenn, Roscoe E. "The Development and Failure of the Dark Tobacco Grower's Cooperative Association." Master's thesis, Vanderbilt University, 1927.

Gregory, Rick. "The Crop and the Physical Setting." 1986. [photocopy] in author's possession.

———. "Desperate Farmers: The Planters' Protective Association of Kentucky and Tennessee, 1904–1914." Ph.D. diss., Vanderbilt University, 1989.

———. "Human Factors in Tobacco Culture." 1986. [photocopy] in author's possession.

———. "Origins of Black Patch Violence," 1986. [photocopy] in author's possession.

Hansen, Karen V. "The Power of Talk in Antebellum New England," paper presented at the Symposium on Rural Farm Women in Historical Perspective, University of California, Davis, June 1992.

Harris, Paul S. "The Place of Tobacco in the Development of Cooperative Marketing Legislature with Special Reference to the Period 1900 through 1922 in Kentucky." Master's thesis, University of Kentucky, 1952.

Henderson, Wallace W. "The Hollowell Case." *Christian County, Kentucky Sketches*. (Typewritten.) Manuscripts Section. Kentucky Building. Western Kentucky University.

———. "A Hot Time in the Old Town." (Typewritten) Department of Library Special Collections. Manuscripts Division. Western Kentucky University, Bowling Green, Ky., n.d.

Kline, John B. "A Tool Collector's Guide: Tobacco Farming and Cigar Making Tools." (Mimeograph.) Museum of Tobacco Art and History. Nashville, Tenn., 1975.

Koons, Kenneth E. "Families and Farms in the Lower Cumberland Valley of South Central Pennsylvania, 1850–1880." Ph.D. diss., Carnegie-Mellon University, 1986.

Miller, Jim Wayne. "Words and Ways: Raising Burley Tobacco in Western North Carolina." [typewritten] Western Kentucky University Folklore, Folklife and Oral History Archives, 1969.

Prichard, Edward F., Jr. "Popular Political Movements in Kentucky." Senior thesis, Princeton University, 1935.

Ramage, Thomas W. "The House Career of Augustus Owsley Stanley, Kentucky Congressman, 1903–1905." Master's thesis, University of Kentucky, 1961.

Taylor, Marie. "Night Riders in the Black Patch." Master's thesis, University of Kentucky, 1934.

Tipton, Jeff Todd. "Powerhouse for God: Speech, Chant, and Song in an Appalachian Baptist Church." MSS, Coon Library, Princeton, Ky., 1986.

Tullos, Allen. "The Habits of Industry: A Study of White Culture, Protestant Temperament, and the Emergence of the Carolina Piedmont." Ph.D. diss., Yale University, 1985.

Articles

Anthony, Allen. "The Linton Mailboat on the Cumberland River: A Link with the Outside World." *Filson Club History Quarterly* 59 (January 1985): 5–39.

Ashby, Rickie Zayne. "The Possum Hunters in the Oral Tradition." *Kentucky Folkore Record* (April-June 1975): 56–61.

Bennett, John. "Food and Social Status in a Rural Society." *American Sociological Review* 8 (1943): 561–69.

Bland, Gayle K. "Populism in the First Congressional District of Kentucky." *Filson Club History Quarterly* 51 (1977): 31–43.

Bode, Frederick A. "Religion and Class Hegemony: A Populist Critique in North Carolina." *Journal of Southern History* 37 (August 1971): 417–38.

Bowen, Don R. "Guerilla War in Western Missouri, 1862–1865: Historical Extensions of the Relative Deprivation Theory." *Comparative Studies in Society and History* 19 (January 1977): 30–51.

Brearly, H. C. "The Pattern of Violence." In *Culture of the South*, edited by W. T. Couch. Chapel Hill: University of North Carolina Press, 1934.

Brown, James S. "Social Class, Intermarriage, and Church Membership in a Kentucky Community." *American Journal of Sociology* 57 (1951): 237–42.

Brown, Richard Maxwell. "Legal and Behavioral Perspectives on American Vigilantism." *Perspectives in American History* 5 (1971): 95–144.

Brown, Thomas J. "The Roots of Bluegrass Insurgency: An Analysis of the Populist Movement in Kentucky." *Register of the Kentucky Historical Society* 78 (summer 1980): 219–45.

Burckel, Nicholas C. "A. O. Stanley and Progressive Reform, 1902–

1919." *Register of the Kentucky Historical Society* 79 (spring 1981): 136–61.

Cohen, Yehudi A. "Social Boundary Systems." *Current Anthropology* 10 (February 1969): 103–26.

Coleman, J. Winston, Jr. "The Code Duello in Antebellum Kentucky." In *A Kentucky Sampler: Essays from the Filson Club History Quarterly, 1926–1976,* edited by Lowell Harrison and Nelson L. Dawson, 54–62. Lexington: University Press of Kentucky, 1977.

Dorson, Richard M. "A Theory for American Folklore." *Journal of American Folklore* 72 (1959): 197–216.

Dykstra, Robert R. "Town-Country Conflict: A Hidden Dimension in American Social History." *Agricultural History* 37 (October 1964): 195–204.

Friedberger, Mark W. "Handing Down the Homeplace: Farm Inheritance Strategies in Iowa, 1870–1945." *Annals of Iowa* 3rd ser., 47 (fall 1984): 518–36.

Flemming E. McClung. "Early American Decorative Arts as Social Documents." *Mississippi Valley Historical Review* (September 1958): 276–84.

Gastil, Raymond D. "Homicide and a Regional Culture of Violence." *American Sociological Review* 36 (1971): 412–27.

Glassie, Henry. "Eighteenth-Century Cultural Process in Delaware Valley Folk Building." *Winterthur Portfolio* 7. Charlottesville: University of Virginia Press for the Henry Francis DuPont Winterthur Museum (1972): 29–57.

Gorn, Elliott J. "Gouge, Bite, Pull Hair and Scratch: The Social Significance of Fighting in the Southern Backcountry." *American Historical Review* 90 (February 1985): 18–43.

Grantham, Dewey W., Jr. "'Black Patch War': The Story of the Kentucky and Tennessee Night Riders, 1905–1909." *Southern Atlantic Quarterly* 59 (1960): 215–25.

Green, Archie. "Hillbilly Music: Source and Symbol." *Journal of American Folklore* 78, issue 309 (July-September 1965): 204–27.

Gregory, Rick. "Robertson County and the Black Patch War, 1904–1909." *Tennessee Historical Quarterly* 39 (1980): 341–58.

Guthrie, Charles S. "Tobacco: Cash Crop of the Cumberland Valley." *Kentucky Folklore Record* 14 (April-June 1968): 38–42.

Hackney, Sheldon. "Southern Violence." *American Historical Reivew* 74 (1969): 909–10.

———. "The South as a Counterculture." *American Scholar* 42 (spring 1973): 283–93.

Hagler, D. Harland. "The Ideal Woman in the Antebellum South: Lady or Farmwife?" *Journal of Southern History* 46 (August 1980): 405–18.

Halpert, Herbert. "American Regional Folklore." *Journal of American Folklore* 60–61 (1947–48): 355–66.

Henderson, William W. "'The Night Riders' Raid on Hopkinsville." *Filson Club History Quarterly* 24 (1950): 346–48.

Henretta, James A. "Families and Farms: *Mentalite* in Pre-Industrial America." *William and Mary Quarterly* 3d ser., 35 (January 1978): 3–32.

Holmes, William T. "Whitecapping: Agrarian Violence in Mississippi." *Journal of Southern History* 36 (May 1969): 165–85.

Horton, Mellie Scot. "A History of the Scotch-Irish and Their Influence in Kentucky." *Filson Club History Quarterly* 34 (July 1960): 248–55.

Ireland, Robert M. "Acquitted Yet Scorned: The War Trial and the Traditions of Antebellum Kentucky Criminal Justice." *Register of the Kentucky Historical Society* 84 (spring 1986): 107–45.

———. "Homicide in Nineteenth-Century Kentucky." *Register of the Kentucky Historical Society* 81 (spring 1983): 134–53.

Jonas, Edward A. "The Night Riders: A Trust of the Farmers." *Worlds Work* 17 (February 1909): 11213–18.

Joyner, Charles. "Reconsidering a Relationship: Folklore and History." *Kentucky Folklore Record* 32 (fall 1986): 17–33.

Klotter, James C. "Clio in the Commonwealth: The Status of Kentucky History." *Register of the Kentucky Historical Society* 80 (winter 1982): 65–88.

———. "Feuds in Appalachia: An Overview." *Filson Club History Quarterly* 56 (1982): 290–317.

Kniffen, Fred, and Henry Glassie. "Building in Wood in the Eastern United States: A Time-Place Perspective." *Geographical Review* 51 (January 1966): 40–66.

———. "Folk Housing: Key to Diffusion." *Annals of the Association of American Geographers* 55, issue 4 (December 1965): 549–77.

Kulikoff, Allen. "Historical Geographers and Social History: A Review Essay." *Historical Methods Newsletter* 6:3 (June 1973): 122–31.

Lawson, Hughie G. "Geographical Origins of White Migrants to Trigg and Calloway Counties in the Ante-Bellum Period." *Filson Club History Quarterly* 57 (July 1983): 286–304.

Loftin, Colin, and Robert H. Hill. "Regional Subculture and Homicide: An Examination of the Gastil-Hackney Thesis." *American Sociological Review* 39 (1974): 714–24.

Maclachlan, John. "Distinctive Cultures in the Southeast: Their Possibilities for Regional Research." *Social Forces* 18 (December 1939): 210–15.

McCulloch-Williams, Martha. "The Tobacco War in Kentucky." *American Review of Reviews* 37 (February 1908): 168–70.

McDonald, Forrest, and Grady McWhiney. "The Antebellum Southern Herdsman: A Reinterpretation." *Journal of Southern History* 41 (May 1975): 147–66.

Malone, Ann Patton. "Piney Woods Farmers of South Georgia, 1850–1900: Jeffersonian Yeomen in an Age of Expanding Commercialism." *Agricultural History* 60:4 (fall 1986): 51–84.

Mann, Ralph, "Mountains, Land and Kin Networks: Burkes Garden Virginia, in the 1840s and 1850s." *Journal of Southern History* 58 (August 1992): 411–34.

Margolis, Eric. "Mining Photographs: Unearthing the Meanings of Historical Photos." *Radical History Review* 40 (winter 1988): 33–50.

Matthews, John L. "The Farmer's Union and the Tobacco Pool." *Atlantic Monthly* 102 (October 1908): 482–91.

Maupin, Judy. "History of Pleasant Hill (Missionary Baptist Church)." *Murray Ledger and Times* 2 (December 1978): 4.

Otto, J. S., and G. D. Gilbert. "Excavation of a 'Plain Folk' Log Cabin Site, Meade County, Kentucky." *Filson Club History Quarterly* 18 (1984): 40–53.

Owsley, Frank L. "The Patterns of Migration and Settlement on the Southern Frontier." *Journal of Southern History* 11 (May 1945): 147–76.

Porter, Patrick G. "Origins of the American Tobacco Company." *Business History Review* 43 (1969): 59–76.

Purvis, Thomas L. "The Ethnic Descent of Kentucky's Early Population: A Statistical Investigation of European and American Sources of Emigration, 1790–1820." *Register of the Kentucky Historical Society* 80 (summer 1982): 1–28.

Ransom, Robert, and Richard Sutch. "The Impact of the Civil War and of Emancipation on Southern Agriculture." *Explorations in Economic History* 12 (January 1975): 1–28.

Reed, John Shelton. "To Live—and Die—in Dixie: A Contribution to the Study of Southern Violence." *Political Science Quarterly* 86 (1971): 429–43.

Reynolds, Albin L. "War in the Black Patch." *Register of the Kentucky Historical Society* 56 (1959): 1–10.

Rosenbaum, H. Jon, and Peter C. Sederberg. "Vigilantism: An Analysis of Establishment Violence." In *Vigilante Politics*, edited by H. Jon Rosenbaum and Peter C. Sederberg. Philadelphia: University of Pennsylvania Press, 1976.

Siegal, Bernard J., and Alan R. Beals. "Pervasive Factionalism." *American Anthropologist* 62 (1960): 394–417.

Vandiver, Frank. "The Southerner as Extremist." In *The Idea of the South*, edited by Frank Vandiver, 43–56. Chicago: University of Chicago Press, 1964.

Waldrep, Christopher R. "A 'Trust Lawyer' Tries to Help Kentucky Farmers: Augustus E. Willson's 1907 Letter to George B. Cortylou." *Register of the Kentucky Society* 83 (autumn 1985): 347–55.

———. "Augustus E. Willson and the Night Riders." *Filson Club History Quarterly* 58 (1984): 237–52.

———. "'Human Wolves': The Night Riders and the Killing of Axion Cooper." *Register of the Kentucky Historical Society* 81 (1983): 407–24.

———. "Immigration and Opportunity along the Cumberland River in Western Kentucky." *Register of the Kentucky Historical Society* 80 (1982): 392–407.

———. "The Law, the Night Riders, and Community Consensus: The Prosecution of Dr. David Amoss." *Register of the Kentucky Historical Society* 82 (1984): 235–56.

———. "Migration of Some South Carolinians into What Is Now Lyon County, Kentucky." *Kentucky Ancestors* (April 1980): 219–21.

———. "Planters and the Planters' Protective Association in Kentucky and Tennessee." *Journal of Southern History* 52 (November 1986): 565–88.

——. "Tobacco Farmers, the Tobacco 'Trust,' and the Federal Government." *Journal of Kentucky Studies* 1 (July 1984): 187–201.

Wilson, M. L. "Cultural Patterns in Agricultural History." *Agricultural History* 12:1 (January 1938): 3–10.

Wish, Harvey. "The Slave Insurrection Panic of 1856." *Journal of Southern History* 5 (May 1939): 206–22.

Wissler, Clark. "The Culture-Area Concept in Social Anthropology." *American Journal of Sociology*, 32 (May 1927): 881–91.

Witt, Robert W. "Robert Penn Warren and the 'Black Patch War.'" *Register of the Kentucky Historical Society* 67 (1969): 301–16.

Wyatt-Brown, Bertram. "Religion and the Formation of Folk Culture." In *The Americanization of the Gulf Coast*. Vol. 3. Edited by Lucien Ellsworth. Pensacola, Fl.: Historic Pensacola Preservation Board, 1972.

——. "The Antimission Movement in the Jacksonian South: A Study of Regional Folk Culture." *Journal of Southern History* 36 (November 1970): 501–29.

Youngman, Anna. "The Tobacco Pools of Kentucky and Tennessee." *Journal of Political Economy* 18 (January 1910): 34–49.

Zelinsky, Wilbur. "Changes in Geographical Patterns of Rural Population in the United States, 1790–1960." *Geographical Review* 52:4 (October 1962): 492–524.

INDEX

African Americans. *See* Blacks
Aingell, Joe, 53
Albrecht, George, 148, 151
Alexander, J. J., 148
Allen, Ethan, 27
Allen, Newton, 22
Allen, William B., 2
Allensworth, James L., 129
American Snuff Company, 109
American Tobacco Company, 108;
  Night Rider raid on, 123
Amoss, David, 125, 144; death of,
  162; trial of, 158–62
Anderson, Joseph F., 48
Anderson, W. P. "Old Shanks," 116
Askew, Thomas Lee: and memories
  of Black Patch life, 65

Baggett, Henry: and memories of
  Black Patch life, 42–43, 85
Barker, Charles E., 108, 109, 111
Bassett, E. B., 148, 159
Bell, Floyd: and memories of Black
  Patch life, 77–78
Bell, Mary Walker Meriwether,
  52
Bennett, H. W. "Son," 126, 127
Bennett, Mrs. Henry: and Night
  Riders, 125
Bennett, Henry: and Night Riders,
  123–25, 126–27, 143
Berry, Eulace, 92, 93
Berry, Mrs. "Wint," 92–93
Berry, Winchester "Wint," 92, 93
"Between the Rivers," 66; as par-
  ticularly violent area, 102–3
Bingham, G. B., 116, 121

Black Patch Journal, 111, 116
Black Patch, the: class structure
  in, 106–7; the elite in, 105, 106;
  factions in, 141, 157; formation
  of, 4; insularity of, 47; maps of,
  xviii; settlement of, 1–8
Black Patch War, 89, 141–54,
  155, 158
Blacks: in Civil War census, 51;
  and emancipation, 57; emigration
  from Black Patch, 107, 129–30;
  immigration to Kentucky, 7, 8;
  as labor source, 129; and Night
  Riders, 122, 127–28, 131–32, 133,
  134–35, 142, 150; and the PPA,
  113, 119, 131, 132; and right to
  vote, 99, 129; status of, 8, 86–87,
  106, 107, 129, 130; violence
  against, 99, 122, 127–29, 132,
  133, 134–35, 142; violence among,
  92. *See also* Slaves
Bleidt, Mary Emma: and memories
  of Black Patch life, 64, 65
Blout, Dick, 8
Boren, P. C., 115
Bouyer, John, 88
Boyle, Jerry T., 56
Branch, C. H. H.: on Night Riders,
  145–46, 152, 153, 154
Breathitt, Gus, 135
Breathitt, John W., 48
Breckinridge, John C., 48
British Imperial, the, 109
Browder, George: and memories of
  Black Patch life, 46, 52, 53, 54,
  55–56
Browder, Rufus, 88, 89